VICTORIAN LITERATURE AND THE ANOREXIC BODY

Anna Krugovoy Silver examines the ways nineteenth-century British writers used physical states of the female body – hunger, appetite, fat, and slenderness – in the creation of female characters. Silver argues that anorexia nervosa, first diagnosed in 1873, serves as a paradigm for the cultural ideal of middle-class womanhood in Victorian Britain. In addition, Silver relates these literary expressions to the representation of women's bodies in the conduct books, beauty manuals, and other non-fiction prose of the period, contending that women "performed" their gender and class alliances through the slender body. Silver discusses a wide range of writers including Charlotte Brontë, Christina Rossetti, Charles Dickens, Bram Stoker, and Lewis Carroll to show that mainstream models of middle-class Victorian womanhood share important qualities with the beliefs or behaviors of the anorexic girl or woman.

ANNA KRUGOVOY SILVER is Assistant Professor of English and Director of Women's and Gender Studies at Mercer University. She has published essays on Victorian literature, children's literature, and film in *Studies in English Literature, Arizona Quarterly, Children's Literature Association Quarterly*, and *Victorians Institute Journal*.

CAMBRIDGE STUDIES IN NINETEENTH-CENTURY
LITERATURE AND CULTURE

General editor
Gillian Beer, *University of Cambridge*

Editorial board
Isobel Armstrong, *Birkbeck College, London*
Leonore Davidoff, *University of Essex*
Terry Eagleton, *University of Manchester*
Catherine Gallagher, *University of California, Berkeley*
D. A. Miller, *Columbia University*
J. Hillis Miller, *University of California, Irvine*
Mary Poovey, *New York University*
Elaine Showalter, *Princeton University*

Nineteenth-century British literature and culture have been rich fields for interdisciplinary studies. Since the turn of the twentieth century, scholars and critics have tracked the intersections and tensions between Victorian literature and the visual arts, politics, social organisation, economic life, technical innovations, scientific thought – in short, culture in its broadest sense. In recent years, theoretical challenges and historiographical shifts have unsettled the assumptions of previous scholarly synthesis and called into question the terms of older debates. Whereas the tendency in much past literary critical interpretation was to use the metaphor of culture as 'background', feminist, Foucauldian, and other analyses have employed more dynamic models that raise questions of power and of circulation. Such developments have reanimated the field.

This series aims to accommodate and promote the most interesting work being undertaken on the frontiers of the field of nineteenth-century literary studies: work which intersects fruitfully with other fields of study such as history, or literary theory, or the history of science. Comparative as well as interdisciplinary approaches are welcomed.

A complete list of titles published will be found at the end of the book.

VICTORIAN LITERATURE
AND THE ANOREXIC BODY

ANNA KRUGOVOY SILVER

PUBLISHED BY THE PRESS SYNDICATE OF THE UNIVERSITY OF CAMBRIDGE
The Pitt Building, Trumpington Street, Cambridge, United Kingdom

CAMBRIDGE UNIVERSITY PRESS
The Edinburgh Building, Cambridge CB2 2RU, UK
40 West 20th Street, New York, NY 10011-4211, USA
477 Williamstown Road, Port Melbourne, VIC 3207, Australia
Ruiz de Alarcón 13, 28014 Madrid, Spain
Dock House, The Waterfront, Cape Town 8001, South Africa

http://www.cambridge.org

First published 2002

Printed in the United Kingdom at the University Press, Cambridge

Typeface Baskerville Monotype 11/12.5 pt   *System* LaTeX 2ε [TB]

A catalogue record for this book is available from the British Library

ISBN 0 521 81602 5 hardback

For George and Christel Krugovoy
and
Andrew Brian Silver

Contents

Acknowledgments   *page* x

   Introduction   1

1 Waisted women: reading Victorian slenderness   25

2 Appetite in Victorian children's literature   51

3 Hunger and repression in *Shirley* and *Villette*   81

4 Vampirism and the anorexic paradigm   116

5 Christina Rossetti's sacred hunger   136

   Conclusion: the politics of thinness   171

Notes   179
Bibliography   203
Index   217

Acknowledgments

I take pleasure in acknowledging the many people who made this book possible. I was fortunate to be guided in my research by Walter Reed and Martin Danahay, whose helpful and honest criticisms helped shape my project. Alan Rauch has been a model to me both intellectually and professionally, and I would particularly like to thank him for the many meetings in which we discussed my work and the profession.

Mercer University has been a stimulating and collegial place to teach in part because of my friendships with colleagues too numerous to name. I am grateful to Dean Douglas Steeples for an Improvement of Teaching grant that enabled me to complete the research for this project. Thank you also to my two department chairs, Charlotte Thomas and Chester Fontenot, for their support both financial and intellectual. I would be remiss if I did not acknowledge Mary Alice Morgan's and Gary Richardson's generous mentoring and their friendship. The librarians at Mercer University tracked down many difficult to find sources that were essential to my work. In particular, thank you to Russell Palmer, Valerie Edmonds, Arlette Copeland, and David Greenebaum. I would also like to thank my editor at Cambridge, Linda Bree, and my copyeditor, Gillian Maule, for their guidance and criticism.

My graduate school experience was made immeasurably more enjoyable and humane because of my friendships with Kathryn McPherson, Karen Brown-Wheeler, and Rae Colley, who supported me through both my qualifying exam and my dissertation, from which this book developed.

Very special thanks to my parents, George and Christel Krugovoy, for their unfailing faith in me and my work. They were my first, and still are my most important, teachers.

My deepest thanks go to my husband Andrew Silver, who patiently read many drafts of this book and provided invaluable advice and assistance, as well as much needed time away from my computer and books.

It is with great love that I dedicate this book to my parents and my husband.

Introduction

It was the close of the fall term, and to thank a class of exceptionally bright and enthusiastic students for a wonderful semester, I passed out some homemade cream cheese brownies. The plate went around the room and not a single female student took a brownie. When I commented on their apparent lack of appetite, two students informed me that they were unwilling to eat such a fattening snack the week of a formal dance. Although disappointed at their extreme self-discipline in the face of culinary temptation, I forgot about the incident until a summer afternoon in the British Museum Library, when I read Samuel Ashwell's 1844 case study of a fifteen-year-old patient: "Her appetite," writes Ashwell, "was capricious . . . She was sedulously watched; and her exercise, diet, and clothing were carefully regulated . . . The appetite was, at times, morbidly great; while at other times scarcely anything was eaten."[1] This anonymous young woman, who eventually died, reminded me of the young women in my classroom and in high-school and college classrooms across the country who are not only extremely thin, but who are obsessively concerned with the amount and kinds of food that they eat and who resort to both fasting and vomiting in order to control their weight.

Could "Miss ----" have suffered from anorexia nervosa or bulimia, as an estimated one million American teenage girls and two million American women between the ages of nineteen and thirty-nine do today?[2] Even before anorexia nervosa was independently diagnosed by two physicians, Charles Lasègue and Sir William Withey Gull, in 1873, doctors had described diseases very much like it. For example, the American William Stout Chipley discussed sitomania, a fear of eating, in 1859, while the Frenchman Pierre Briquet described women who consistently vomited whatever they ate in *Traité Clinique et Thérapeutique de l'Hystérie*.[3] Ashwell diagnosed Miss ----'s problems as symptomatic of chlorosis, a disease prevalent among middle-class girls in

I

nineteenth-century Britain. Like anorexia nervosa, chlorosis affected a girl's eating patterns: sometimes she craved strange substances such as chalk, dirt, ashes, or vinegar, and in other instances she lost her appetite altogether, sometimes refusing to eat; Ashwell notes that "Patients in this condition eat scarcely any thing."[4] In other cases, a girl ate enormous amounts of food and then vomited. "Bulimia, pica, and strange longings are morbid modifications of the appetite," Thomas Laycock wrote in 1840, "and belong to the same class of phenomena as . . . anorexia . . . and, like it, are characteristic of the pregnant, chlorotic, and hysterical female."[5] Like anorexia nervosa and bulimia, chlorosis usually affected girls at puberty and was most common among the middle and upper classes.[6] It is possible, therefore, that many of the fasting and bingeing girls once diagnosed by physicians as chlorotic, including "Miss ____," may have suffered from what we today would call anorexia nervosa.[7]

Because of the impossibility of diagnosing diseases such as anorexia nervosa a century after someone's death, we will never know for certain how many Victorian girls may have succumbed to a disease that has become such a prominent part of today's medical and cultural landscape. Although historical statistics on the number of anorexic women are imprecise, William Parry-Jones's archival research suggests that anorexia nervosa existed as early as the 1820s. Between 1826 and 1899, for instance, the Warneford Asylum admitted 975 patients, of whom five have case histories that suggest anorexia nervosa; one patient, for example, entered the asylum in 1831 with "a history of refusing food and drink, constipation and menstrual irregularity," all symptoms of anorexia nervosa.[8] In addition, the Warneford archives show: "Numerous cases of food refusal and emaciation in melancholia, mania, dementia" which may or may not have been related to anorexia nervosa.[9] Throughout the nineteenth century, one finds numerous case histories of prolonged food abstinence published in medical journals that may or may not describe anorexia nervosa. For example, in 1882, a physician named D. McNeill describes an "extraordinary fasting case" in which a fourteen-year-old girl: "For twenty-one months . . . continued eating little or nothing except a little jelly, 'sweeties,' and sherry"; McNeill does not offer a diagnosis or use the term "anorexia nervosa," merely presenting the patient as an example of remarkable fasting.[10] While we can never know whether Maggie Sutherland, the girl in question, suffered from anorexia nervosa, her food refusal was already, in 1882, being treated by McNeill as an independent medical problem rather than as a byproduct or symptom of another disease, or as a religious affliction. As an institutionally

recognized disease, then, anorexia stems from the Victorian era, discovered and diagnosed almost simultaneously in the mid-nineteenth
century by doctors in Britain, France, and America.

This book does not seek simply to apply today's medical diagnoses
to women of the last century. Rather, my study investigates the shared
characteristics between anorexia nervosa and some key aspects of
Victorian gender ideologies. Susan Bordo, one of the foremost authorities
on anorexia nervosa and its place in contemporary culture, writes that
"the psychopathologies that develop within a culture, far from being
anomalies or aberrations, [are] characteristic expressions of that culture . . . the crystallization, indeed, of much that is wrong with it."[11]
Anorexia nervosa, I argue, is deeply rooted in Victorian values, ideologies, and aesthetics, which together helped define femininity in the
nineteenth century. Given the clear parallels which exist between the
symptoms of the disease and Victorian gender ideology, I argue that
the normative model of middle-class Victorian womanhood shares
several qualities with the beliefs or behaviors of the anorexic girl or
woman. One can thus "read" Victorian gender ideology through an
anorexic lens. Briefly, the qualities that many (though, of course, not
all) Victorians used to define the ideal woman – spiritual, non-sexual,
self-disciplined – share what Leslie Heywood has called an "anorexic
logic."[12] The anorexic woman's slender form attests to her discipline
over her body and its hunger, despite the persistence of that hunger,
and indicates her discomfort with or even hatred of her body and its
appetites, which may or may not include her sexuality. If one reads
the disease *metaphorically*, then, it becomes evident that the pathology of
anorexia nervosa and predominant Victorian constructions of gender
subscribe to many of the same characteristics.[13]

I am not, however, retroactively diagnosing particular nineteenth-
century women as anorexic. This book is not an examination of the
institutional history of anorexia nervosa or even a social history of the
disease, although it draws on much important work, to which I am
indebted, that has been done in those fields. Instead, I explore the ways in
which ideologies of food and fasting, and anorexia in particular, function
figuratively in narratives, particularly in literary narratives. My project is
twofold: first, I analyze how images of hunger and appetite work within
particular texts and what they signify within those texts; second, I relate
those texts to popular culture at large, not merely as a reflection of
other discourses but as part of an ongoing cultural dialogue.[14] Authors
responded to their culture in various ways, so that signs such as hunger,

appetite, fat, and the body generated many different and often competing meanings between and within texts, both transgressing and underscoring the cultural validation of the slender female form. Sometimes hunger is at the very core of a text, while at other times it is fairly incidental; in some texts, fasting serves the ideal of the slim body, while in others it becomes a largely religious undertaking. Images of eating, like any other images or representations in a text, must be understood within the shifting and competing ideologies that determine their environment. Eating does not have any one "meaning," even in any one given text.[15] It is just as important, in other words, to examine when a text's representation of eating *does not* conform to an anorexic aesthetic as when it does.

Before examining anorexia nervosa's development, however, one must be familiar with theories about the disease. According to the American Psychiatric Association's guidelines in the *Diagnostic and Statistical Manual of Mental Disorders* (1994), anorexia nervosa is clinically defined by the following four criteria: (a) an individual's "refusal to maintain body weight at or above a normal weight for age and height," (b) a fear of "gaining weight or becoming fat, even though underweight," (c) a "disturbance in the way in which one's body weight or shape is experienced, undue influence of body weight or shape on self-evaluation, or denial of the seriousness of the current low body weight" and (d) in women, at least three consecutively missed menstrual cycles.[16] These twentieth-century criteria are a helpful framework with which to turn toward the nineteenth century, although Victorian physicians, who were just beginning to examine anorexia nervosa, did not devise such clear delineations of the disease. Lasègue's and Gull's descriptions of anorexia nervosa, for example, do not explicitly address the fear of fat, though that fear already existed in the nineteenth century, as I will discuss at length in the next chapter. Lasègue's and Gull's main contribution to medical history is that they introduce the medical community and public to the fact that some women consciously refuse to eat, and that their loss of appetite is not the result of another disease, such as tuberculosis. Thus, Gull, in 1874, admits that he is incapable of "determining any positive cause from which [anorexia] springs"; however, both Gull and Lasègue recognize a psychological component to the disease.[17] Gull writes that: "The want of appetite is, I believe, due to a morbid mental state . . . That mental states may destroy appetite is notorious, and it will be admitted that young women at the ages named are specially obnoxious to mental perversity" (25). Similarly, Lasègue, in 1873, suggests that the anorexic: "A young girl, between fifteen and twenty years of age, suffers from some emotion which she avows or conceals."[18] What is important about the work of these two physicians, then, is that they establish that anorexia nervosa is a disease that manifests itself most often in young, adolescent women, and that the disease has "nervous" origins which can be located in a girl's life, family situation, etc.[19] Moreover, both doctors mention the amenorrhea (cessation of menstrual periods) that is one of the *DSM*'s key signs of anorexia nervosa, indicating that they examined cases of extreme anorexia.

Though the symptoms of anorexia nervosa are recognizable, psychiatrists agree that anorexia is a multidimensional and frustratingly protean illness, which unfortunately makes the disease very difficult to treat. According to many therapists, the disease is, at least in part, a power strategem in which a girl refuses to eat in order to gain influence and attention in her family. The anorexic family is often – but not always – controlling and non-confrontational, while the anorexic girl herself is generally academically and socially successful, a goal-oriented perfectionist, who is perceived as a "good" child. However, she often has a problematic, conflicted relationship with her mother. According to family systems therapy, anorexia grows out of suppressed emotions like guilt, fear, and anger that a girl experiences because of her passive position in the home.[20] Consequently, because of harmful family dynamics, the anorexic develops a weak sense of self that collapses at puberty. "The anorexic's ego simply cannot cope with the demands of adolescence," Morag Macsween explains, "and she withdraws into her own body as the only place she feels she can control."[21] As a result, a girl seeks control over her appetite, perceiving other areas of her life as out of control; disciplining her body becomes her particular arena of mastery, and she considers her capacities for self-denial and self-discipline virtuous.[22] However, these family dynamics do not occur in all cases of anorexia nervosa, and one should not generalize about *all* of the families of anorexic girls. In addition, establishing cause and effect is often very difficult in family systems therapy, so that a girl and her mother's power struggles may be the *result* of the girl's refusal to eat, rather than the root cause of it.

Since anorexia most often appears in adolescent girls, and because many anorexics try to avoid intercourse and even non-sexual touch, some psychiatrists have posited that the anorexic turns to food refusal because of her fear of sexual maturation, as symbolized by the development of secondary sexual characteristics like breasts and hips. By fasting, a girl not only achieves a certain measure of control over her life, but she also stops the sexual maturation that she finds so disturbing. Fasting essentially slows down sexual maturation by halting menstruation and preventing the buildup of "womanly" fat, so that the anorexic girl gains a feeling of self-control over her own biological processes by refusing to eat. Of course, this sense of control is chimerical, since the victim of anorexia eventually loses the ability to control her own behavior; in advanced stages of the disease, eating become physiologically difficult or even impossible.

Although plausible and widely accepted, none of these theories applies to every case of anorexia nervosa, suggesting that pinpointing a single "anorexic family" or "anorexic personality type" is ultimately a fruitless endeavor. Nor do the theories explain why anorexia developed when it did, or why anorexia is an overwhelmingly female, middle-class disease. Why, in other words, are 90 percent of the victims of anorexia nervosa women if the root cause of anorexia is something as universal as an overbearing mother or a non-communicative family? Why, also, does the disease primarily affect white middle- and upper-class women rather than poor women or women of African descent, who might have similar family dynamics? Questions such as these have led therapists to analyze contemporary culture by identifying some contemporary belief systems that may have shaped and contributed to women's fasting behavior. Cultural explanations of anorexia vary, but they all posit that the disease is in some sense a distillation of specific ideologies about femininity and its relation to appetite. In particular, many critics, researchers, and therapists have focused on constructions of beauty within contemporary culture, arguing that, because women are bombarded with images that teach them that female beauty consists of thinness, girls are trained to associate weight with ugliness and "badness." Such an explanation of anorexia nervosa has become axiomatic today, and evidence in support of it is impressive. April Fallon, for instance, contends that: "All cultures that have reported numbers of eating disorders have a thin ideal. Cultures that do not have the thin ideal have few reported cases of anorexia and bulimia. Thus, these disorders are, in part, an overcommitment or 'overadaptation' to the cultural ideal that is in vogue."[23]

Of course, media images alone are not responsible for individual cases of anorexia nervosa, and women do not become anorexic "on purpose" merely because they want to conform to specific standards of beauty. The disease is much more complicated than that. Recent studies, for instance, suggest that many anorexic girls develop the disease after starting a diet in order to lose weight and that they then become "addicted" to the attention, envy, and feeling of control that weight loss confers upon them. Dieting thus provides many girls with an entrance, a gateway, to anorexia nervosa and bulimia. The continuum, or normative, model of anorexia nervosa stresses that eating disorders are on a continuum with dieting in general, since both dieting women and anorexic/bulimic women share a similar concern with weight and a desire to shape their bodies. L. K. George Hsu argues that:

The evidence suggests an individual who embarks on a diet is more likely to develop an eating disorder if she is experiencing significant adolescent turmoil, has a low self-concept and body concept, and is having difficulty with identity formation . . . Once the pathological eating disturbances are established, they may then be perpetuated by both positive and negative reinforcers, the former including the exhilaration and triumph associated with weight loss and the approval and attention of others, and the latter including the fear of fatness and its attendant meanings, such as psychosexual maturity.[24]

Though the blame for eating disorders does not fall directly or solely at the door of fashion magazines and fashion designers, the sociocultural emphasis on slimness does play a crucial, central role in the prevalence of eating disorders, particularly when the slender body is linked to feelings of self-esteem and self-worth.[25] Just as important, the behavioral continuum between "casual dieting" and obsessive dieting or fasting implies that eating disorders are often instances of dieting gone out of control. Countless more women than those who actually succumb to anorexia nervosa or bulimia qualify as disturbed eaters, and the distinction between the two groups is a blurry one. Rather then focusing solely on women diagnosed with the full-blown disease of anorexia, it is thus more helpful and more accurate to look at women's behavior and relationship with food in general. Even the word "pathological," which Hsu uses in his work, obscures the normative nature of women's dieting and concern with weight loss, conferring illness and abnormality on a behavior that, in its less extreme form, is viewed as perfectly normal. Janet Polivy and C. Peter Herman write, in fact, that: "The meaning of a phrase such as normal eating is no longer obvious [because] 'normal' eating for North American women is now characterized by dieting."[26] On the contrary, a woman in contemporary culture who shows no concern with her body size would, statistically speaking, be much less "normal" than the woman who methodically counts the fat grams or calories of each meal.[27] Dividing women into anorexics and "normal women" obscures the many ways in which our culture encourages a majority of women to worry about the shapes of their bodies, to monitor the firmness of their thighs, to enter weight-loss programs, or merely to see their bodies, and fat, in particular ways.

Moreover, when examining the etiology of eating disorders, it is artificial to separate "culture" from a woman's psychological makeup, since individual psychological development occurs *within* culture, not in a genetic or familial vacuum. Culture, in the way that I use it in this book, is not outside of an intact, separated, essential Platonic "self." Susan Bordo writes that research about anorexia nervosa "point[s] to culture – working not only through ideology and images but through the organization of the family, the construction of personality, the training of perception – as not simply contributory but *productive* of eating disorders."[28] A cultural explanation of anorexia nervosa, then, goes beyond a simple and reductive understanding of culture as equivalent to fashion magazines or movies. Nor does the word "culture" refer to a monolithic set of institutions, practices, and beliefs. Not all women develop eating disorders because no two women grow up in the exact same culture. Social class, race, religion, family dynamics, ethnicity, access to schooling and technology, education, and genetic makeup, to name only a few factors, work together to create an individual woman's life and environment. Finally, when I refer to women, I do not mean *all* women; I focus rather on particular gender ideologies, each of which affects individual women in very different ways.

The roots of any culture run centuries deep. In the case of anorexia nervosa, important feminist critics including Susan Bordo, Kim Chernin, Allie Glenny, Leslie Heywood, Mara Selvini-Palazzoli, and others have pointed to Western culture's split between the body and soul, a split that is often gendered, as a philosophical underpinning to the disease. The argument is convincing. Historically, the body has been designated (as in the work of Aristotle, for example) as female, while the mind, spirit, and culture have been designated as male. Simultaneously, the body has been denigrated and reviled as inferior and needing to be disciplined, punished, and ultimately transcended. In one classic, foundational statement of such a body/mind split, Socrates argues, in Plato's "Phaedo," that, "as long as we have a body and our soul is fused with such an evil we shall never adequately attain . . . the truth. The body . . . fills us with wants, desires, fears, all sorts of illusions and much nonsense, so that . . . if we are ever to have pure knowledge, we must escape from the body and observe matters in themselves with the soul by itself."[29] Socrates' language associates the body with corruption, infection, "contamination," and "folly" that keep a human being from the knowledge that can come only through the reasonings of the soul.[30] The woman who suffers from anorexia, also, relentlessly tries to escape her body, which she views as heavy, slow, and repulsive, through fasting and obsessive exercise. Metaphorically, then, the anorexic girl enacts the philosophy and theology that teach her that the body is somehow not her essential "self" – that she is in fact imprisoned within her body – and that this fundamentally evil body must be controlled and subjected. One woman who suffered from an eating disorder, for instance, laments, "When can I get out of this box? I drag my body around as if it's some gross foreign object ... Ugly, filthy, fat slob."[31] The language that the woman uses to describe her "gross" body is startlingly similar to the language about the body found in the work of such philosophers as Plato, Aristotle, and Augustine. Leslie Heywood writes: "In their relentless process of designating the soul, the mind, subjectivity, and civilization as masculine, these figures have formed a tradition that some women, to whom the tradition is newly accessible, internalize in an attempt to enter the magic inner circle of culture and become something other than the bodies, sexualities, loves, and flesh with which this tradition equates them."[32] The anorexic girl, in other words, wants to be less "flesh," and all that the word "flesh" implies. Paradoxically, then, although many anorexic girls are extremely concerned about appearing "feminine" (which often explains why they diet in the first place), they live out a hatred and resentment of their soft, "loose," "jiggly," fat-storing female bodies.[33]

Accepting a cultural component to the disease, however, one turns next to the question of why anorexia nervosa developed in the nineteenth century. I have already suggested that certain ways of conceptualizing the Victorian woman – though, of course, not all – were ideologically akin to the etiology of anorexia nervosa. It has become axiomatic that the middle-class Victorian woman was represented as highly spiritual, a creature of disinterested love and nurture, the moral center of the home and of society as a whole. To conform to that ideal, women were urged to downplay every aspect of their physicality, including (but not limited to) their sexuality. Meal times, in particular, were seen as opportunities for women to demonstrate their incorporeality through the small appetite and correspondingly slender body. Emotional self-restraint became an extraordinarily important aspect of a nineteenth-century woman's life. "The portrait of the appropriately sexed woman," writes Helena Michie, "emerges as one who eats little and delicately."[34] A woman's materiality – her body – threatened the ideal of a woman's heightened spirituality and purity. Michie's claim that the woman with a delicate appetite appeared uninterested in and unaware of the needs and desires of her body is borne out by the prototypical heroine of nineteenth-century fiction, who almost inevitably displays a tiny appetite: Dickens's Little Dorrit, Eliot's Dorothea Brooke, and Brontë's Jane Eyre are only three of the most well-known heroines defined in part by their slight, pale bodies. In *Ruth*, Elizabeth Gaskell establishes her fallen heroine's fundamental innocence and passionlessness with repeated allusions to her slimness, her "little figure," and "beautiful lithe figure."[35] This is particularly interesting in the case of Ruth. By bestowing her heroine with a slender figure, Gaskell writes against stereotypical depictions of fallen women as large, fleshly and aggressively sexual, demonstrating Ruth's essential innocence and goodness through her body. The slim body, in general, emblematizes the sexually pure and ethereal woman in Victorian discourse. It is unclear, of course, how such representations affected the behavior of actual women. The appearance of a slim body in a particular narrative does not have a clear one-to-one causative correlation with a "real" woman's slim body. However, narrative is important on its own terms, not only because discourses directly or indirectly influence women's behavior, but because the ideologies of the slender body help us understand what the Victorians thought about the relationships of eating to femininity and to class.

At the same time as medical books, conduct books, and literature extolled the pure woman, they also represented a more dangerous female. The dark side of Agnes Wickfield is the kept woman who flits in and out of Dickens's novels, pressing money into Nell's palm and furtively following little Em'ly; for every Dorothea Brooke there exists a murderous Lady Audley stuffing her neglectful husband down the water well. Feminist critics have done essential work dispelling the myth of the angelic Victorian woman, arguing that, although women were idealized as ethereal beings, they were simultaneously viewed as potential demons – aggressive, angry, and sexually voracious – ruled by their physiology, particularly their menstrual cycles. For that reason, self-control became an integral part of the Victorian woman's life: she was expected to control her behavior, her speech, and her appetite as signs of her dominion over her desires. The slender body became a sign not simply of the pure body, but of the *regulated* body. As Susan Bordo writes, the fear of flesh is "a metaphor for anxiety about internal processes out of control – uncontained desire, unrestrained hunger, uncontrolled impulse."[36] Because fat did in fact symbolize desire, hunger, and impulse for the Victorians, slenderness signified the containment of those same qualities.

In her 1837 book *The Young Lady's Friend*, Eliza Farrar describes the manner in which a woman should, and should not, hold her body:

Some girls have a trick of *jiggling* their bodies (I am obliged to coin a word in order to describe it); they shake all over, as if they were hung on spiral wires, like the geese in a Dutch toy; than which, nothing can be more ungraceful, or unmeaning... When not intentionally in motion, your body and limbs should be in perfect rest... Your whole deportment should give the idea that your person, your voice, and your mind are entirely under your own control. Self-possession is the first requisite to good manners.[37]

Farrar makes explicit what is implicit in other conduct books, namely that femininity depends upon the moral, and even aesthetic, imperative of self-control. The problem with the "jiggling" body is that it indicates a more general lack of discipline. If the body moves loosely and unnecessarily, then a woman's "voice" and "mind" might also be unpredictable and unrestrained. A woman's carriage and deportment speak for her and about her.

A central premise of this book is that control over the body, a fundamental component of Victorian female gender ideology and anorexia nervosa, theoretically links the model of the passionless or self-regulated Victorian woman with the anorexic woman. Using a continuum model of eating disorders, those women in both the nineteenth and twentieth centuries who restrict their food intake in order to conform to feminine standards of slimness and to demonstrate their spiritual rather than carnal natures, thereby exhibit a milder form of the repression of appetite that constitutes anorexia nervosa. James Rosen argues that: "Besides clinical eating disorders, which fall at the endpoint of a continuum of disordered eating and negative body image, there are milder but distressing forms of the disorders which fall at intermediate points along the continuum and are widespread among women."[38] One must therefore look beyond case histories of anorexia nervosa to examine the evidence that many "normal" Victorian women (like women today) fell along an anorexic continuum. If anorexia nervosa is thus the "paradigm of our age," in Roberta Seid's phrase, it can also be viewed as a paradigm for the Victorian age, because cultural ideologies of the nineteenth century encouraged women to adopt, to a lesser degree, anorexic behavior.[39] Perhaps most importantly, the cultural narrative that emphasizes discipline over the body as an essential aspect of femininity can be situated on a continuum of anorexic thought. And though this was only one model of womanhood among others theorized in the Victorian period, it was nonetheless an important and widespread one, and one connected to the etiology of anorexia nervosa.

Victorian conduct books indicate that downplaying their bodilessness was an important aspect of many Victorian women's lives and that they engaged in food refusal to do so. In *The Daughters of England* (*c.* 1841), for instance, Sarah Stickney Ellis complains that: "Fanciful and ill-disciplined young women . . . indulge the most absurd capriciousness with respect to their diet, sometimes refusing altogether to eat at proper times, and eating most improperly . . . all these they appear to consider as most engaging features in the female character."[40] Ellis does not go into detail about women's fasting behavior, but, by assuming that women who abstain from food do so in the service of the "female character," she indicates that fasting was interpreted as a specifically "feminine" behavior, almost certainly connected with the nineteenth-century Romantic cult of invalidism. At any rate, not eating must have been widespread enough among women in the early nineteenth century for Ellis to have interpreted it as peculiarly "female." Ironically, Ellis criticizes fasting women as "ill-disciplined," thereby linking control and discipline over the body with femininity, when in fact women who *refuse* to eat are extremely self-disciplined. Although Ellis only mentions finicky eating and abstinence from food, other conduct books disclose that women resorted to potentially harmful diets in order to lose undesirable fat. While defending the corset, for instance, an author writing under the pseudonym Madame de la Santé (1865) reveals that women ate dirt and drank "large quantities of vinegar" (as Flaubert's Emma Bovary does) in order to keep their figures slim; references to drinking vinegar, in particular, occur quite frequently in beauty literature and fashion magazines of the nineteenth century.[41] Another pamphlet on beauty, *The Art of Beautifying the Face and Figure*, advises women that "Vinegar and lemon-juice will reduce corpulency, but their excessive use injures digestion" and additionally recommends "castile soap dissolved in water."[42] Comments such as these are fairly common in the literature of beauty, and, since such books reached a broad public (as opposed to medical textbooks, which had a more limited audience), one can reach two conclusions. One, dieting was a fairly commonplace occurrence among Victorian women. And two, women controlled their food intake in order to conform to Victorian proscriptions about feminine behavior and the feminine "character."

In his series of lectures *On Visceral Neuroses* (1884), published a decade after Lasègue's and Gull's findings, physician T. Clifford Allbutt writes that, in cases of anorexia nervosa, girls display "an invincible distaste for food. To yield to such a distaste may seem at first to many high-spirited girls a merit than otherwise; it may seem but a distaste for indulgence, a denial of the animal propensities."[43] Like Ellis, Allbutt connects fasting not to a physical, gastrointestinal ailment, but to a cultural linkage between not eating and femininity; food refusal is considered a "merit" because it demonstrates a girl's rejection of her "animal propensities," bespeaking her spirituality and her control over the carnal aspects of her nature. Allbutt's use of the word "denial" indicates that these "propensities" actually *do* exist in girls, but that they refuse them. Food restriction is thus implicitly connected to the larger cultural validation for self-control. Elsewhere, Allbutt hypothesizes that anorexia nervosa may grow out of the "*nobler* avoidance of self-indulgence," thereby validating the very motivation that he views as productive of the disease.[44]

In addition to demonstrating a woman's laudable control over her corporeality, the slim body functioned as an important and visible class marker. In 1899, Thorstein Veblen noted that the slender body, particularly small hands and feet and a slim waist, "go to show that the person so affected is incapable of useful effort and must therefore be supported in idleness by her owner. She is useless and expensive, and she is consequently valuable as evidence of pecuniary strength."[45] The middle-class woman who did not need to work outside the home used her pale, corseted physique to differentiate herself from the "robust, large-limbed" working-class woman, to assert her decorative, rather than laboring, social role.[46] Victorian conduct books occasionally chastise women for associating a ruddy complexion and plump body with the "coarseness" of the working classes, and the relative frequency of such admonitions suggests that such a viewpoint was widely held among middle-class women and men. In Trollope's *Can You Forgive Her?* (1864–1865), for example, the unctuous Mr. Bott insults Alice Vavasor after her long nocturnal ramble with Lady Glencora by suggesting that her healthiness demonstrates her lack of physical delicacy. "Alice knew that she was being accused of being robust herself," the narrator reveals. "Ploughboys and milkmaids are robust, and the accusation was a heavy one."[47] In this context, the word "robust" signifies the working-class body and, as class and sexuality are so often intertwined in Victorian discourse, suggests Alice's promiscuous sexuality (because she has been out at night, unchaperoned). Mr. Bott thus hints not only at Alice's unfeminine healthiness, but, by comparing her body to that of a milkmaid, also impugns her moral purity. As Joan Jacob Brumberg writes: "By eating only tiny amounts of food, young women could disassociate themselves from sexuality and fecundity and they could achieve an unambiguous class identity."[48] Victorian gender ideology was thus built upon an anorexic logic that validated the slim body as a symbol of woman's lack of corporeality, her sexual purity, and her respectable middle-class social status. These symbolic meanings were, furthermore, interlocking and reinforcing.

Elizabeth Gaskell satirizes the linkage between delicate eating and social class in both *Cranford* (1851–1853) and *Wives and Daughters* (1866). The ladies of Cranford downplay their poverty and demonstrate their "elegant economy" by serving only the sparest buffets at their gatherings; Betty Barker, a former ladies' maid not part of the inner circle of the novel, violates decorum with her sagging trays of cake, oysters, and brandied macaroons.[49] "Oh, gentility," comments Mary Smith wryly, "Can you endure this last shock?"[50] As though she were emulating the Amazons of Cranford, Mrs. Gibson, eager to demonstrate her improved position in society, scorns her new husband's diet, informing her stepdaughter that "I shouldn't like to think of your father eating cheese; it's such a strong-smelling, coarse kind of thing . . . Cheese is only fit for the kitchen."[51] Mrs. Gibson's protest against cheese, rests, first, on its smell, which evokes the physicality of nourishment and digestion, and, second on its lower-class status as the kind of food eaten by servants and laborers. She obsessively differentiates between commonplace, working-class foods such as "rounds of beef, legs of mutton, great dishes of potatoes, and large batter-puddings" with elegant upper-class food, "the tiny meal of exquisitely cooked delicacies, sent up on old Chelsea china, that was served every day to the earl and countess and herself at the Towers."[52] Mrs. Gibson's affected manners collapse sexual purity and gentility: she dislikes cheese because she considers it "coarse," a word that connotes both the common and obscene, and especially scorns meat, a food believed by many nineteenth-century physicians to inflame lust. In contrast, the smallness and presentation of a meal make it a marker of affluence. One's relationship to food is clearly a barometer of one's social status, though poor Betty Barker misreads the rules.

Anorexia nervosa developed in, and still overwhelmingly affects, women from affluent families rather than women of the working classes. In her groundbreaking *Fasting Girls: The History of Anorexia Nervosa*, Brumberg theorizes why anorexia nervosa developed as a middle-class disease. First, she argues that food refusal in the nineteenth century was played out in a European–American culture in which family meals were considered extraordinarily important in part because they symbolized the prestige of the bourgeois family. Refusing to eat, Brumberg writes, "was antithetical to the very ideal of bourgeois eating."[53] Mealtimes, when the family came together around the table, stood for morality, affluence, love, and the health of the family, which was, in turn, the cornerstone of a healthy society. Isabella Beeton, for instance, notes in her *Book of Household Management* (1861) that: "The nation which knows how to dine has learnt the leading lesson of progress," linking the dinner table with the evolution of civilization.[54] Within the nineteenth-century bourgeois family (as today), food functioned as a means of discipline and punishment (particularly through the withholding of food), as an affectional bond between members of a family, and as a symbol of worldly success and security. An adolescent daughter's refusal to eat was perceived then as now as a baffling and hurtful rejection of the family and its values.

Of course, food refusal necessitates there being food to reject. Brumberg explains that:

The efficacy of food refusal as an emotional tactic within the family depended on food's being plentiful, pleasing, and connected to love. Anorexia nervosa required a certain standard of family provisioning and a regularity of fare for the girl's rejection of food to have any meaning. Where food was eaten simply to assuage hunger, where it had only minimal aesthetic and symbolic messages... refusal of food was not particularly noteworthy or troublesome.[55]

Though, as I have argued, it was not socially acceptable for Victorian women to eat large amounts of food at the table, and though a small appetite connoted the appropriately "bodiless" woman, not to eat *at all* was extremely disruptive of social norms, specifically middle-class norms. A woman who did not eat disobeyed her family's directives and did not conform to rules of passive and obedient female behavior. Moreover, she called into question the entire stability of the middle-class home, in which wife and children thankfully accepted the bounty put before them by the hard-working man. Not to eat was, essentially, to be ungrateful and antisocial. It is worth noting, by the way, that not eating as a class phenomenon has remained intact: today, anorexia nervosa and bulimia still overwhelmingly affect women from affluent homes.

Eating is, of course, a gendered activity. Men and women in the nineteenth century were expected to eat differently: meat consumption, for example, was perceived as particularly "male," so that a woman slicing into several servings of roast beef would have been viewed very differently than a man doing the same thing. The preparation and serving of food was, also, a specifically female concern. Nineteenth-century domestic handbooks focus upon the preparation of meals as one of women's most important roles, whether she did the cooking herself or, more likely considering the audience of such handbooks, employed a cook or maid-of-all work to do much or all of the work for her. Both of these circumstances – the different expectations for men's and women's consumption, and women's key role in food preparation – meant that a woman refusing to eat would have had different social implications than a man refusing to eat. In part, the woman's behavior could be interpreted as a rejection of the womanly activity of presiding over the table, and thus her domestic role in general. Moreover, in a culture that values obedience, docility, and order in its women, the refusal to eat is none of these things and therefore transgresses gender norms.

Gull, for instance, quotes a report from a fellow doctor, Dr. Anderson, about a patient named "Miss C." Dr. Andersen writes Gull that Miss. C "used to be a nice, plump, good-natured little girl." Here, the adjectives used to describe Miss C. before her illness conflate her "plumpness" (in 1873, the ideal female form was slender-waisted but with soft arms and bust, as I will explain later) with being "nice" and "good-natured." The doctor clearly connects her fasting with obstinate and, I would argue, *unfeminine* behavior, as the label "little girl" implies. Similarly, the physician John Ogle, who recounted a case of prolonged food abstinence in 1870, describes a girl who refuses to eat and vomits whatever she does eat as "sly," "saucy," and "obstinate."[56] These traits are the same ones that doctors today might use to describe anorexic girls, who stubbornly refuse treatment, but within the Victorian context they are particularly resonant, since they run counter to the construction of open, guileless, obedient femininity to which girls were expected to conform. These traits, in other words, would have been particularly unattractive in a girl.

In an extended discussion, Lasègue describes the torments of a family trying to induce their daughter to eat:

The delicacies of the table are multiplied in the hope of stimulating the appetite; but the more the solicitude increases, the more the appetite diminishes. The patient disdainfully tastes the new viands, and after having thus shown her willingness, holds herself absolved from any obligation to do more. She is besought, as a favour, and as a sovereign proof of affection, to consent to add even an additional mouthful to what she has taken; but this excess of insistence begets an excess of resistance. ("On Hysterical Anorexia" 266)

Lasègues's description of the dinner power play might well have been written in this century. The concerned family interprets eating as a "sovereign proof of affection," and the daughter's food refusal as a rejection of her kin. She is "disdainful" about their concern, and the more her family pressures her to eat, the less she agrees to do so. The girl's starvation, thus, is explicitly linked to rebellion against her parents and her familial role. Hers is both a personal and a social, cultural rejection.

Florence Nightingale's *Cassandra* (1852) offers a glimpse into the centrality of dining in a Victorian woman's life from an early feminist perspective. For Nightingale, women's ubiquitous presence in the kitchen and in the dining room was a major obstacle to intellectual achievement and meaningful work because of the tremendous amount of time that dinner planning, overseeing, and eating took. "If she has a knife and fork in her hands during three hours of the day," Nightingale protests, "she cannot have a pencil or brush. Dinner is the great sacred ceremony of this day, the great sacrament. To be absent from dinner is equivalent to being ill. Nothing else will excuse us from it. Bodily incapacity is the only apology valid."[57] Dinner is not only an obligation, but a "sacred ceremony," the "great sacrament" of family life in which women are forced to take part. Set against Nightingale's rhetoric, one can understand the familial confusion that would have resulted from a woman's fasting behavior. In the nineteenth-century cult of the home, the dinner table served as the altar. Against this oppressive feeding of the body, Nightingale posits the simultaneous starvation of women's minds, setting the body and soul against each other much as the anorexic girl might interpret herself as trapped within a hungry, demanding body from which the mind/soul seeks to free itself. Women, who "fast mentally" (27) by denying their dreams and intellectual needs, end up "withered, paralysed, extinguished" (36): their souls, if not their bodies, are self-starved. Women, Nightingale suggests, suffer from a symbolic, emotional, and spiritual anorexia. However, by basing her arguments within a dualistic hierarchy of body and soul, in which the body's needs (albeit the socially proscribed needs of the body) interfere with and are less important than the workings of the mind, Nightingale herself employs an anorexic logic that indicates a desire to free herself of the troublesome gendered body.

One of Nightingale's most fascinating metaphors is her use of force-feeding as symbolic of being read to by a family member: "And what is it to be read aloud to? The most miserable exercise of the human intellect. Or rather, is it any exercise at all? It is like lying on one's back, with one's hands tied and having liquid poured down one's throat" (34). *Cassandra* was written in 1852, before doctors began discussing the force-feeding of anorexic women; nevertheless, her trope is eerily prescient.

She figures the mentally starved woman as brutally force-fed, "liquid poured down [her] throat" by the same family that starves her or, more accurately, forces her to starve herself by denying her the time and support for meaningful work. The bourgeois family is represented as the *locus* of oppression, that literally pushes the domestic role down women's throats.

Within this context, it is an easy step toward viewing anorexia nervosa as rebellion against the family, even as proto-feminist rebellion. The historians Walter Vandereycken and Ron Van Deth, for instance, write that sickness "offered many women a chance to express their dissatisfaction with their lives in a covert (passive–aggressive) way and to temporarily escape from the family duties, imposed by the cult of true womanhood."[58] As feminist critics have long noted, women such as Elizabeth Barrett Browning and Nightingale herself, who worked from her sick bed, certainly received "benefits" from their illnesses in terms of being freed from certain domestic duties. At a time when women had few outlets for their desires for autonomy and freedom, food was one aspect of their lives that they could control. However, while anorexia nervosa can be interpreted as a response to, and perhaps even rebellion against, the roles allotted middle-class women in Victorian Britain, one should be careful about romanticizing the disease or about linking it to any coherent feminist ideology or theory. Some critics have, directly or indirectly, equated the refusal of nourishment with feminist protest. Kim Chernin, for instance, writes that anorexia nervosa "can be understood as part of women's struggle for liberation during the last decades . . . elective starvation may come to express cultural conflict or even social protest," while Susie Orbach argues that: "Like a hunger striker, [the anorexic] is in protest against her conditions. Like the hunger striker she has taken as her weapon a refusal to eat."[59] Such a model of anorexia nervosa is, as Leslie Heywood writes, "problematic in that it gives artistic status to a 'strategy of resistance' that is only self-destructive."[60] Equating the victims of a disease with feminist hunger-strikers at the turn of the century or with feminist activists today is both misleading and irresponsible. As Heywood as pointed out, assuming that anorexia is in many ways a "crystallization" of culture does not mean either that its victims are heroines or that the disease itself is merely a medical and psychiatric construct. On the other hand, there is no doubt that not eating can be interpreted as a kind of, ultimately self-annihilating, rebellion.

I have divided this book into five main chapters, each of which explores a different aspect of representations of eating, fasting, and the body in Victorian literature and culture.

I begin, in chapter 1, by examining the Victorian culture of anorexia through conduct books, beauty manuals, and medical texts. In this chapter, which lays the cultural groundwork for the following chapters, I continue the work begun by scholars such as Joan Jacobs Brumberg who have sought to understand the historical context in which anorexia nervosa developed. I open by arguing that a Victorian "beauty myth" existed which validated female slenderness and which was a primary cause of the development of anorexia nervosa.[61] My one argument with Brumberg's invaluable study of Victorian culture is that she downplays the cultural work of such a myth in the nineteenth century, claiming that "the disease itself preceded the familiar body-image imperatives usually associated with it."[62] The general image that many people have of the fashionable Victorian woman is that of a red-cheeked, plump woman who cultivated her feminine fat.[63] However, although Victorian ladies were ideally supposed to have plump arms and a round bosom, the focal point of erotic beauty after the Regency period was the small "wasp" waist. To achieve the tiny waist that was considered so lovely, women laced themselves into corsets and limited their food intake, sometimes to the detriment of their health. Standards of beauty were undeviating in part because the pursuit of beauty was considered such an important aspect of woman's feminine role; very different writers, from the anonymous authors of beauty pamphlets to physical anthropologists, agreed that women's role was in part ornamental and aesthetic. Moreover, the slender waist that characterized the beautiful woman signified her larger femininity, her passivity, and her incorporeality. I then move from the Victorian beauty myth to examine the control over female desire that informed women's lives and that constitutes the second major aspect of Victorian anorexic culture. Other scholars have established that women were subjected to constant management in the form of specific dictates about which foods they should eat, how they should behave, and what they should or should not be permitted to do. I posit, in addition, that these systems of etiquette are a manifestation of an anorexic logic that overwhelmingly emphasizes self-control, sexual purity, and the denial of the body.

The book then turns, in chapter 2, to analyses of Victorian literature. I begin with an examination of the depictions of appetite and fat in Victorian literature for children. Because of the didactic nature of much children's literature, it is the ideal genre with which to begin an investigation into a culture's attitude toward female appetite. Continuing my study of beauty manuals and fashion magazines, the chapter opens with an examination of the extraordinarily popular girls' magazine *The Girl's Own Paper*, which reveals patterns of disorderly eating among girls. I then analyze the work of three of the Victorian era's most popular authors, John Ruskin, Lewis Carroll, and Kate Greenaway, examining the ways that all three authors validate the body of the pre-pubescent girl over that of the adult woman. By symbolically arresting the development of their heroines, these authors parallel the behavior of the anorexic woman, who starves her body in order to forestall sexual maturation.

My third chapter resumes chapter 2's analysis of the control and denial of female appetite, and the representation of female body size, through readings of Charlotte Brontë. After briefly examining the work of Charles Dickens, chapter 3 explores two of Brontë's novels in which hunger plays a major role. The overt denigration of hunger found in much children's literature continues in Brontë's work, albeit more implicitly and with more complexity. In *Shirley*, Brontë links hunger and starvation to the suffering that her protagonists experience when they are forced to repress voicing their desires and their ambitions: while women stop consuming food, they are metaphorically consumed within romantic relationships. In *Villette*, Brontë depicts varying degrees of feminine abnegation by using images of starvation and the renunciation of appetite. Though she portrays the suffering of denied appetite in Lucy Snowe's depression and mental breakdown, Brontë also consistently links fat to promiscuous sexuality, stupidity, and the lower classes, finally validating hunger over gluttony. Brontë's novels, rather than the radical texts of protest that some critics consider them, are complicated and ambiguous novels that express the anorexic logic of Brontë's culture at the same time as they depict the suffering of the hungry woman.

Chapter 4 examines one of the most grotesque and deadly forms of eating: vampirism. Vampire literature takes the negative representation of eating already found in the work of Brontë and others to its hyperbolic end, transforming eating into a grotesque and monstrous act. Women's hunger, in particular, with its symbolic associations with lust, aggression, and lack of self-control, finds its apogee in vampirism, which exaggerates cultural anxieties about consumption, especially female consumption, in the figure of the bloodthirsty vampire. I focus on the act of eating and on body size in two of the nineteenth-centuries greatest vampire tales, Bram Stoker's *Dracula* and Sheridan Le Fanu's "Carmilla," and in George Du Maurier's *Trilby*, with its vampiric villain, Svengali.

Chapter 5 examines Rossetti's poetry, devotional prose, and children's story *Speaking Likenesses*. I end with Rossetti because her work moves the analysis of representations of hunger in Victorian literature from the secular to the sacred sphere. Rossetti's work has already been termed anorexic by some scholars, which, while at first glance convincing, ignores her deeply held theological beliefs. Though the denial of appetite is a major theme of her work, I contend that it must be read within the tradition of medieval saints and mystics, for whom both fasting and feasting were integral parts of worship. Like the Oxford movement's reconstruction of medieval ritual, Rossetti's work offers a historical reconstruction of medieval conceptions of fasting and eating. Rossetti does not simply deny her appetite; rather, she denies secular appetite while simultaneously reveling in a sacred fulfillment of hunger through union with Christ. Her work should thus be situated within her involvement with the Tractarian movement. Rossetti's work problematizes ahistorical assessments of a wide variety of fasting behaviors as anorexic.

Because the literature that I analyze in this book is British, the cultural sources, such as conduct books and beauty manuals, to which I refer are also largely British, although I have often used American editions of those texts because they are more readily available in the United States. Other texts that I use were written and published in America, but were also available and read in Britain (as evidenced from the fact that they are housed in British research libraries or are referred to in the works of English writers). Those American texts that I cite are also representative of widespread transcontinental ideologies and beliefs. Patricia Vertinsky contends that, in the case of medical literature: "The discourse of a recognized group of establishment male physicians had a powerful and wide-reaching effect. Their writing in professional medical journals in America and Britain was remarkably similar and very widely diffused, and a good case has been made for regarding such writings as typical of mainstream Victorian medical thought."[64] Vertinsky's argument applies to most etiquette manuals as well. In those cases where I have used American texts, they have been texts that could well have been written in Britain, despite minor cultural and historical differences.

Of course, the mediation between the culture of anorexia and the authors whom I discuss is rarely direct. Both Christina Rossetti and Charlotte Brontë fasted, but for very different reasons, and, in any case, the representations of fasting in their work do not simply reflect their own experiences. Rather, both authors use hunger and the refusal of food for specific purposes within their texts, purposes that I explore in chapters 2 and 3. There is no proof that either Rossetti or Brontë read the conduct books and beauty manuals that I discuss in chapter 1, and it is particularly unlikely that Rossetti, with her fear of worldliness, would have done so. I cannot claim, therefore, that fashion magazines extolling the slender female figure directly influenced these authors' preference for pale and slender heroines. On the other hand, Brontë does equate the slim body with the educated middle class, and the heavy body with the lower classes, thus echoing widely held Victorian beliefs. In this study, I look for conversations between literary texts and other manifestations of culture, but resist "proving" that one text was directly influenced by another. I am also not concerned with diagnosing authors such as Brontë and Rossetti as anorexics; rather, I am interested in the systems of signs that these authors elaborate and enunciate, sign systems informed by the logic of anorexia.[65]

Although I do not directly engage the work of Michel Foucault or Judith Butler, it is worth mentioning that, like so many other feminist critics who have done work on the body, I draw implicitly upon both of their theories, most generally the well-discussed argument that bodies and illness are constructed differently in various cultural contexts, a theory supported by the fact that ideals of beauty have shifted innumerable times in different cultures and through the centuries. I take as a starting point that, while the female body is a material entity, the *feminine* or *woman's* body is a symbolic construct: namely, what size, shape, color, the ideal feminine body is, how much hair it has, in what it is clothed, and how it walks and takes up space are all socially constructed. In fact, it is through the adoption of these behaviors and ornaments that a woman signifies herself as a woman, and her body as a woman's body. In Butler's classic formulation, one enacts, or performs, one's gender through the body, although "gender is not written on the body" naturally or inherently, but rather through cultural formulations of masculinity and femininity: "Gender is an identity tenuously constituted in time, instituted in an exterior space through a stylized repetition of acts. The effect of gender is produced through the stylization of the body and, hence, must be understood as the mundane way in which bodily gestures, movements, and styles of various kinds constitute the illusion of an abiding gendered self."[66] The clothes one wears and the way one sits in those clothes, for instance, is a "stylization" of the body that indicates one's gender. More centrally to my own project, body size and shape mark one's gender. In the nineteenth century, as today, women performed gender and class through slenderness, though slenderness does not "naturally," and has not, transculturally or historically, consistently symbolized either femininity or affluence. Understanding the particular

constructions of femininity in a given culture is thus essential for understanding anorexia nervosa, which is, in large part, a product of culture.

Foucault's analysis of discourse as power also helps explicate the ways
that Victorian ideologies about the body affected individual women and
came to be represented in narrative. Foucault argues that:

> Power is everywhere; not because it embraces everything, but because it comes
> from everywhere. And "Power," insofar as it is permanent, repetitious, inert,
> and self-reproducing, is simply the over-all effect that emerges from all these
> mobilities... power is not an institution, and not a structure; neither is it a
> certain strength we are endowed with; it is the name that one attributes to a
> complex strategical situation in a particular society.[67]

Foucault's understanding of power as a multiplicity of forces rather than
something wielded by the ruler of a state or by certain institutions (like the
fashion industry) is indispensable for an understanding of how anorexic
logic works both in culture and in literary texts. There is obviously no one
institution "responsible" for the normalizing pressures that women and
men in a given culture feel about their bodies. Different levels of power
exist in any society: the school headmistress who forced her students to
tighten their corsets every week in order to attain a small waist manifested
a more direct form of power than the angelic representation of a woman
in a piece of parlor poetry; nevertheless, both these and other "innumerable points" of power pervaded the atmosphere in which the Victorian
girl grew up, and they tended toward the control of a girl's appetite in
the service of femininity.[68] Sandra Lee Bartky writes that: "Feminine
bodily discipline has this dual character: on the one hand, no one is
marched off for electrolysis at gunpoint, nor can we fail to appreciate the
initiative and ingenuity displayed by countless women in an attempt to
master the rituals of beauty. Nevertheless . . . the disciplinary practices of
femininity . . . must be understood as aspects of a far larger discipline, an
oppressive and inegalitarian system of sexual subordination."[69] Bartky's
point that women themselves seek out disciplinary practices (whether
cosmetics or liposuction) is particularly important to acknowledge, since
any effective workings of power must be diffused throughout a society
and depend upon women's compliance, as survival strategy or source of
validation, for success. Bartky, like Butler, draws attention to the fact that
the woman who refuses to accept "appropriate bodily discipline . . . faces
a very severe sanction indeed in a world dominated by men: the refusal
of male patronage. For the heterosexual woman, this may mean the loss
of badly needed intimacy; for both heterosexual women and lesbians it

may well mean the refusal of a decent livelihood," in addition to sanctions such as shame, lack of sense of herself as a "woman," and lack of general assimilation into her family and community.[70] It is my hope that critics, by acknowledging this more complex view of the workings of power, will eventually put to rest the tiresome criticism that there exists no conspiracy to make women thin: of course there does not. Power is far too dispersed and anonymous for there to be any such organized plan; nevertheless, power relations as they stand in the twentieth century *do* make women suffer.

Finally, in my conclusion, I draw similarities between Victorian and contemporary cultures, arguing that our own attitudes toward the body have changed remarkably little in the past century, and speculating about the kind of political work that literary and cultural criticism can accomplish in the effort to curtain anorexia nervosa as a pathology and as a paradigm of femininity. Although this book examines nineteenth-century texts, I hope that the reader will draw parallels between the Victorian period and the early twenty-first century in which we live. The differences between the two cultures is not, finally, as great as we tend to believe, particularly when it comes to our attitudes toward the body. The ideal female body has changed from the hourglass figure to the lean and muscular physique sported by today's supermodels, but women's responses to these varying ideals have changed depressingly little: the majority of middle-class American women today are obsessed with their figures, and even those women who are not defined as anorexic often suffer from an anorexic mind-set, in which control over the body becomes a virtue to be pursued through dieting and exercise. Victorian culture may thus have helped generate both contemporary standards of beauty and their centrality to the lives of today's middle-class women.

I have written this book as a literary critic; however, as a woman in twenty-first-century America, I have watched some of my dearest friends struggle with a disease that takes over their lives, stealing the attention that they could have given to intellectual, creative, and political pursuits and giving it to a relentless concern with their bodies. Female beauty is a cultural construction that has led – but does not need to lead – to the suffering and death of many of America's young women; I hope that an understanding of the poetics of anorexia in fictional works of the past will participate in the abatement of a terrible disease in the real world of the present.

CHAPTER I

Waisted women: reading Victorian slenderness

The extraordinary variety that is woman's body is systematically ignored in our culture. The richness of our different shapes is reduced to the overriding image of slimness.

Susie Orbach, *Fat is a Feminist Issue*

It has always appeared to me to be one of the greatest existing absurdities, that a whole community of people, differing in complexion, form, and feature, as widely as the same species can differ, should . . . desire to wear precisely the same kind of dress.

Sarah Stickney Ellis, *Daughters of England*[1]

The remarkable similarity between Orbach's and Ellis's observations indicates that the wish to adapt to one predominant standard of beauty bridges nineteenth- and twentieth-century women's experiences, and that contemporary complaints about the tyranny of slenderness have antecedents in the Victorian era. Nineteenth-century writers were well aware of the importance of beauty, including slenderness, in women's lives, so discussions of the existence of a Victorian "beauty myth" do not merely impose a twenty-first-century concept upon the nineteenth century. Beauty has, of course, concerned both men and women throughout history, but Ellis's statement alludes to a specific body type that many women cultivated in order to conform to a fashionable Victorian silhouette, "to wear *precisely* the same kind of dress" as their neighbors. Ellis's interpretation of women's behavior, therefore, requires an investigation into the body types that most appealed to fashionable Victorian women. Taking its cue from Ellis's quotation, this chapter will examine what Joan Jacobs Brumberg has referred to as the "powerful cultural imperative that makes slimness the chief attribute of beauty."[2] Brumberg denies the existence of such an imperative during the mid-nineteenth century, and it is certainly true that the obsessive and ubiquitous pursuit of thinness that one sees in contemporary Anglo-American culture did

not exist to the same degree then as it does now. The look of overall thinness, including the fashion for boniness, did not claim its predominant
place in fashion until after the turn of the century. Nevertheless, archival
evidence reveals that body image concerns, and specifically a fear of fat,
existed a century ago in incipient form. One can safely argue that the
Victorians were already beginning to be preoccupied with slimness on
a broad cultural scale by the 1840s, a concern that was almost wholly
focused upon the slender waist. This turn toward slimness as a beauty
ideal was in turn intensified and underscored by the widespread belief
that one of women's main duties in life was to be beautiful.

Keeping in mind Gull's and Lasègue's clinical work on anorexia nervosa (or hysterical anorexia, in Lasègue's phraseology), my aim in this
chapter is to demonstrate that body size concerns appear in a wide
range of Victorian discourses, including beauty manuals, medical texts,
and conduct books. Taken individually, these disparate texts take part
in very different debates; for example, an educational treatise that uses
the physiology of the female reproductive system to argue against education for girls undertakes a different project than an advertisement for a
corset. However, seemingly dissimilar works may, albeit unintentionally,
reinforce cultural ideas central to the etiology of eating disorders. At
no point in the century did there exist a consensus about the meaning
of fasting, slimness, or women's beauty among the Victorian public, as
these ideas were constantly being contested and revised. Even within
their particular classes and professions, Victorians did not think as a
unified front about any single aspect of women's bodies and behavior.
Commentators during the century proposed many different theories
about individual women's fasting behavior, including religious, medical,
and cultural hypotheses. Moreover, most of these authors do not use the
term "anorexia nervosa," even after Gull's invention of the term. What
I want to demonstrate, however, is that a concern with slenderness (and
with women's desire to appear slender) appears again and again in a
variety of texts, and that these texts reveal a nascent anorexic culture.
Much of this work is of necessity speculative, because there is no real
way to *prove* the existence of the disease among Victorian women except
perhaps for those cases detailed in medical texts that explicitly describe
fasting behaviors. Nevertheless, the texts that are available to us today
offer compelling testimony to a nascent cultural obsession with thinness.

I am proceeding, as do most feminist scholars of eating disorders, from
the hypothesis that anorexia nervosa is in part a culturally determined
disease. Like its sister disease hysteria, anorexia nervosa arose in the

nineteenth century because certain ideologies were in place that made
its existence possible. When I refer to the Victorian culture of anorexia,
I am not arguing that a certain percentage of women actually suffered
from the disease (though many women, like those described by Gull
and Lasègue, certainly did), but rather that the culture *itself* manifested
an anorexic logic; in other words, that several of its gender ideologies
meshed closely with the etiology of anorexia nervosa. The five basic
characteristics of the Victorian culture of anorexia, as I employ the term,
are as follows:

1 an aesthetic validation of the slender female form as the physical ideal
   of beauty and a concomitant fear of fat as ugly and/or unfeminine;
2 an understanding of the body as an entity that must be subordinated
   to the will and disciplined as an emblem of one's self control;
3 the related, gendered, belief that the perfect woman is the one who
   submits her physical appetites (including, but not limited to, her hunger
   for food and, relatedly, her sexuality) to her will, and that the "good"
   woman is either by nature or by training more spiritual and less carnal
   than men;
4 the belief that the slender body corporealizes this self-mastery and/or
   spirituality;
5 the belief that slenderness carries particular class connotations, and
   most often is a sign of a woman's affluence. This last point, of course,
   draws an important distinction between the woman who chooses not
   to eat, and the woman who cannot eat because of sickness of poverty.

Because any culture shifts in innumerable ways during the course of a
century, these ideas never comprised a static set of unquestioned ideologies. Women and men would have responded in varying ways to the
presence or lack of such beliefs in their lives. However, these ideas were
commonplace enough, and conform closely enough to anorexia nervosa as an illness, that Victorian Britain represents a developing, if still
inchoate, anorexic culture. If anorexia was first diagnosed in 1873, in
other words, and if culture is productive of eating disorders, then there
must have been aspects of Victorian ideology, specifically gender ideology, that made the development of the disease possible. It is these aspects
of Victorian culture that this book will explore.

After a brief overview of the fashionable Victorian figure, and the
means by which women approximated that figure, I will do what contemporary critics have done for twentieth-century Anglo-American culture, namely to begin to "read" the meaning of Victorian slenderness.
What matters is not just whether or not slenderness was considered an

aesthetic ideal for Victorian women, but what that slenderness signified and why it was valued. Though noting that thin women "were not in vogue," Patricia McEachern writes that "there were ample social forces encouraging women to believe that restricting their food intake was both a moral imperative and a sign of their femininity."[3] Specifically, conduct books and beauty manuals from the mid-Victorian period indicate that slenderness was enmeshed in larger constructions of femininity that emphasized the need for women's self-regulation and the regulation of appetite and that, further, linked the small waist to affluence and high social standing.

THE SYLPH IN THE DRAWING ROOM

The assumption that the pursuit of a slender body matters to women undergirds theories that connect anorexia nervosa with the "beauty myth." It is important, therefore, to consider whether or not this was the case in the nineteenth century. In fact, costume historians have long established, based on sartorial evidence, that looking beautiful was an important concern, across class lines, for Victorian women.[4] Whereas men's clothing became plainer and more somber during the course of the nineteenth century than it had been during the Regency period, women's clothing remained elaborate and highly decorative. According to critics like Helene Roberts, who has analyzed the gender politics of Victorian clothing, women's and men's dress differed markedly because their clothing signified their respective spheres. She argues that:

Men were serious (they wore dark colors and little ornamentation) women were frivolous (they wore light pastel colors, ribbons, laces, and bows); men were active (their clothes allowed them movement), women inactive (their clothes inhibited movement); men were strong (their clothes emphasized broad chests and shoulders), women delicate (their clothing accentuated small waists, sloping shoulders, and a softly rounded silhouette).[5]

Roberts overstates the case somewhat, apparently basing her conclusions on the extravagant, highly feminine "Romantic" styles of the 1820s and 1830s while ignoring the menswear and military style dresses that appeared intermittently throughout the century. Nor were Victorian women limited to pastel colors, as Roberts claims. The 1850s, for instance, witnessed the invention of new aniline (chemical) dyes that inspired a trend for very bright, garish colors, whereas softer, earthier vegetable dyes were favored in the 1870s and 1880s by proponents of "Aesthetic dress." Nevertheless, since any culture's clothing interprets and expresses its notions of the beautiful, female clothing in the Victorian era clearly attests to affluent women's decorative role. The fact that men's and women's clothing styles were more diametrically opposed during Victoria's reign than they had been in the eighteenth and early nineteenth centuries (when men, for instance, wore very tight pants, lace, and lavish embroidery) suggests that beauty had become a predominately female concern, while men's beauty had become sublimated to their work. Costume historian Penelope Byrde believes that the plainness of men's clothing was a response to the need among professional men for "hard-wearing, comfortable" clothes, so that the shift in men's costume represents the gradual ascendancy of middle-class values of professionalism and sobriety over aristocratic leisure.[6] Women's highly decorative clothing, on the other hand, differentiated the affluent woman's world from the world of work, identifying her with leisure and prosperity and allowing her visibly to perform both her gender and class identities.

Victorian conduct literature consistently reinforces the idea of beauty as woman's special duty and domain, typically positing female beauty as the correlative of "masculine" qualities such as strength and intellect. "It is the duty of the fair sex to cultivate their personal attractions," one author writes in 1856, "as these are the chief ornaments of a household, and stand in the same important relation to woman as mental endowments do to man."[7] An "education" in beauty thus became essential if women were to fulfill their responsibilities to their families and to a larger society constantly in need of beautification – a need that the burgeoning market of beauty manuals was eager to fill. The rhetoric of beauty manuals deflected attention from women's lack of educational and professional opportunities, positing the cultivation of beauty as an essential, rather than incidental, part of women's true and natural mission. Some writers went so far as to propose the incompatibility of intellectual development with female beauty. Mrs. Alexander Walker (1837) claimed, for instance, that "immoderate development of the intellectual faculties, cannot exist without, in some respect, encroaching upon beauty and the graces."[8] Walker identifies traditional "masculine" forms of knowledge such as research and philosophy as particularly risky for the female sex. Certainly the Victorian emphasis on beauty education went hand in hand with an equal and concurrent emphasis on the dangers of women's intellectual education, especially the ever-present risk of hysteria and amenorrhea that many physicians argued that female students faced. The medical psychologist Henry Maudsley, for instance, in his famous 1874 *Fortnightly*

Review essay "Sex in Mind and in Education," warns that the energy a girl expends on her education drains essential energy from the needs of her developing reproductive system, imperiling her future childbearing and child rearing capacities. Quoting Milton's *Paradise Lost*, Maudsley concludes that: "Whether it be only the statement of a partial truth, that 'for valour he' is formed, and she 'for beauty and sweet attractive grace,' or not, it cannot be denied that they are formed for different functions . . . There is sex in mind and there should be sex in education."[9] In fairness to Maudsley, he explicitly notes later that women should not be educated merely as "ornaments of the drawing-room," but his overall argument, that girls are too physically weak to endure a traditional masculine education, and that girls' educations should take into account their inherent nature and future roles in life (including, for instance, training in child care), complements the notion advanced in beauty manuals that beauty is the appropriate vocation for women, as intelligence is for men.[10] Moreover, Maudsley chooses to employ a Milton passage that specifically praises Eve and all women for "beauty" and "attractive grace," focusing on a woman's physical appearance rather than character. Despite opposition from other physicians like Elizabeth Garrett Anderson and Mary Putnam Jacobi to the idea that an education for girls inevitably produced physical and mental ills, Maudsley's hypotheses continued to be widely accepted.[11] Simultaneously, the focus on female beauty remained undiminished as the century progressed. In her 1878 book *The Art of Beauty*, Mrs. H. R. Haweis confidently asserts that "the old-fashioned notion that a woman's first duty is to be beautiful, is one that is justified by the utter impossibility of stamping it out."[12] The ever-increasing popularity of beauty manuals, such as Haweis's, and fashion magazines in the late nineteenth and early twentieth centuries, attests to the tenacity of this "old-fashioned notion."

If beauty was a pivotal concern for Victorian women, the costume of the nineteenth century reveals the central place of slenderness within that beauty imperative. The ideal female figure from the 1830s through the 1860s replicates two cones touching point to point, with the center of sartorial interest at the "wasp" waist. To offset a small waist and to distinguish her female body from the muscular male body, a woman's face, arms, shoulders, bosom, and hips were to look round and curvaceous, and a certain amount of fat was highly valued. As Valerie Steele has already noted, this body type is, of course, self-contradictory, since "emphasis on a desirable plumpness was almost antithetical to the ideal of a slender waist."[13] Nevertheless, this paradoxical look, like that of

the big breasted, slender-hipped woman today, was the norm throughout the century. Reading the nineteenth-century woman's body, Patricia
McEachern argues that the Victorian woman "must simultaneously appear angelic and alluring: She was encouraged to retain a certain degree
of 'embonpoint,' (or plumpness) yet remain fashionably svelte, a task
more easily accomplished today with the availability of breast implants
than it was in the nineteenth century."[14] While the plumpness of some
body parts was admired, this was combined with an almost fetishistic focus on the small waist, which, as I will discuss below, carried tremendous
symbolic importance. Even a cursory glance at the fashion plates of the
nineteenth century reveals that, while the nineteenth-century fashionable figure was not gaunt, or even thin, as fashionable bodies are today,
women in fashion magazines and beauty manuals are consistently and
almost invariably portrayed as slender-waisted. And, though it would be
reductive to argue that particular fashions "make" a woman anorexic,
fashion was and is one node in a "chain or a system" of power relations that determined and still determines women's (and men's) lives.[15]
Throughout history, clothing has functioned as a signifying system that
reveals a person's gender, class, social standing, and even, depending on
whether one does or does not conform, one's acceptance of dominant
social and moral mores. This continued to be the case throughout the
nineteenth century, as today.

In the 1840s, the popular Gothic style dress was characterized by a
long waist and boned bodice, which both created and accentuated an
hourglass figure. Writing about the 1840s, costume historian C. Willett Cunnington notes that: "It was the fashion to be willowy, and young
ladies assiduously practiced slimming so that they might be able to display
an eighteen inch waist."[16] Although the waist remained the focal point
during the next decade, increasingly wide skirts after the invention of
the wire (cage) crinoline in 1856 (illustration 1) made the waist look proportionately smaller, so that the practice of tight lacing probably de-
creased until the 1860s, when it again revived in popularity as a result
of shrinking crinolines. One fashion magazine from 1864, for instance,
announces that "all efforts tend to make the figure appear as slim as possible below the waist."[17] When the crinoline became smaller and looped
up behind, eventually turning into the bustle by 1869, lacing or bows on
the back of tight dresses continued to call attention to the wasp waist.
Fashionable clothing was tight and form-fighting through the 1870s and
1880s, with slim skirts, bustles, and drapery accentuating the buttocks
(illustration 2). Meanwhile, the corsets which moulded women's figures

VELVET CASAQUE.

1. After the invention of the wire (cage) crinoline in 1856, increasingly wide skirts made women's waists look proportionately smaller (Peterson's Magazine, 1857).

NEWEST STYLES FOR HOUSE-DRESSES.

2. In the 1870s and 1880s, tight bodices and skirts continued to call attention to the wasp waist (Peterson's Magazine, 1883).

into the desirable shape became increasingly decorative and luxurious, attesting to their increased importance in a woman's *toilette*. A writer in the influential fashion journal *La Mode Illustrée* wrote, in 1876, that: "Fashion is inflexible on one point, ladies must be slender," and the engravings in fashion magazines of the 1870s consistently portray more slender women than those of the previous decade.[18] By the 1890s, the bustle had disappeared and the fashionable figure became more voluptuous than it had been at any previous point in the century, with a very full bosom and hips and a minuscule waist. The new "S" curve corset, which modified the hourglass silhouette, pushed the bust (often enhanced by layers of ruffles) forward and the hips back. Although the new beauty was substantially larger than she had been in the 1840s – picture the Gibson Girl and Lily Langtry rather than Little Dorrit and the young Queen Victoria – the fashion ideal was by no means more "natural" or easy to achieve than it had been earlier. On the contrary, because the new look required that most women wear very rigid corsets, tight lacing was a commonplace practice.

Even those writers at the end of the century who wrote against tight lacing, or corseting in general, in favor of a more "natural" appearance took care to differentiate a fashionable fullness from "downright vulgar" fatness.[19] In *Beauty of Form and Grace of Vesture* (1892), for instance, authors Frances Mary Steele and Elizabeth Livingston Steele Adams emphasize the ugliness of fat, writing that: "Corpulence destroys the beauty of form and grace of motion ... Beauty of form is destroyed when fat accumulates."[20] The alternative, for Steele and Adams, is either to eliminate fat through exercise or to disguise it through means *other* than the corset, which merely displaces fat into other parts of the body. Fat itself, however, is figured throughout the text as something that should be carefully controlled and kept within proper bounds. Even Mrs. Haweis, who castigates tight lacing as ugly, unnatural, and dangerous to one's health, concedes that: "We are not denying the necessity for some close fitting garment as a support to the body, and an improvement to the figure; people who refuse to wear any corset at all look very slovenly."[21] An emphasis on the discipline of the body was thus maintained throughout the century, a discipline that theoretically links Victorian beauty culture to the intense self-control of anorexia nervosa. As the historian Casey Finch argues, by the late Victorian period, "what has come to be called the anorectic body was placed more or less permanently at the very center of the sexual imagination."[22]

Although the slim-waisted hourglass figure occupied fashion's spotlight throughout the nineteenth century, this was not always the case. It is important to keep in mind that erotic and fashionable conceptions of beauty have changed tremendously through the centuries. In fact, the fashionable Victorian silhouette constitutes a fairly radical change from previous ideals of European beauty, which until the late seventeenth century had been belly-centered. Anne Hollander writes that in Renaissance art, for example, "there seems to have been no impulse to constrict what we call the waist . . . In the erotic imagination of Europe, it was apparently impossible . . . for a woman to have too big a belly."[23] While the hourglass shape was not new to the nineteenth century, it was, first, exaggerated, and, second, presented in discourse as an inflexible fashion ideal.[24] As the matter-of-fact author of *The Science of Dress* (1856) proclaims: "in present society we all have agreed to conform to one particular standard."[25] The attempt to change that standard with a revival of empire fashions, which are characterized by high, undefined waists, did not catch hold of the public imagination until about 1910.

In order to achieve a small waist and still be desirably plump in other areas of the body, women of all economic classes turned to the corset. European women had worn corsets since the sixteenth century, but the nineteenth-century corset was a very different garment from its predecessors: instead of the eighteenth-century undergarment's straight lines, the new "stays" molded the waist into a small circumference and thereby exaggerated the curve of breasts and hips. Finch writes that: "Especially after the innovation of the metal eyelet in 1828 – which allowed the corset to be violently tightened for the first time – what might be characterized as an assault on the midriff and a concomitant emphasis on the breast and the extremities began in earnest."[26] Women had tight laced before 1828, but new technologies and mass production made tight lacing increasingly easy and more affordable. This "assault" on the waist thus occurred across the social spectrum, from the working classes through the upper classes, because of the easy availability of cheap corsets side by side with the custom-made corsets that wealthier women wore. For instance, the author of the 1873 manual *How to Dress on £15 a Year As a Lady* assumes that all women, even those with little money set aside for clothing expenditures, wear corsets, and builds the corset into her very detailed yearly clothing budgets. While it is unclear, then, exactly how many women wore corsets, the majority of middle-class women and large numbers of working-class women wore them on a regular basis.

Nineteenth century commentators describe the corset as a standard article of women's clothing. Madame de la Santé, in 1865, claimed that about 2,000,000 corsets were imported to England from France and the Continent annually, while Arnold J. Cooley estimated, in 1866, that "most women do not permit themselves to exceed twenty-four inches round the waist," and therefore rely on corsets.[27]

In any case, the specific numbers, though significant, are less important than the sartorial symbolism of the corset, which is a visible marker of the culture of anorexia. The corset both demonstrates the cultural imperative to be slim and constitutes the method by which women approximated that imperative: throughout the century, women re-shaped their bodies, particularly their waists, to conform to normative standards of beauty. Although food refusal did not stem solely from corset-wearing, tight lacing, like the fasting of anorexia nervosa, epitomizes control over the body in the service of beauty and, as I will discuss later, wider gender ideologies, particularly the need for female self-regulation.[28] Proponents of tight lacing frequently employ the word "discipline" to discuss the practice, viewing the body as something that must be disciplined, literally bent, into the desirable shape to produce what Foucault calls "subjected and practiced bodies, 'docile' bodies."[29] For example, one nineteenth-century advertisement for a corset suggests that a girl "lie face down on the floor in order that [her mother] might then place a foot in the small of the back to obtain the necessary purchase on the laces."[30] In this instance, admiration for the small waist leads directly to an extreme instance of bodily self-discipline. Relatedly, the anorexic girl attempts to control her physical appetite and her body, to subject her body to her will. Although tight lacers did not necessarily fast, a tight corset prevented women from consuming much food. One writer to the *Englishwoman's Domestic Magazine*, for instance, writes in 1867 that: "I suffered sometimes perfect torture from my stays, especially after dinner, not that I ate heartily, for that I found impossible," while William Barry Lord, the author of the anonymously published *The Corset and the Crinoline* (1868), writes that: "A very sparing diet has . . . been one great aid to the operation of the corset."[31] Although the members of most cultures have disciplined the body in one form or another, Victorian Britain represents the first *cross-class* attempt to deny fat (especially the fat stomach) in the service of beauty, as corsets were no longer worn primarily by the aristocracy and the affluent, but by middle- and working-class women as well.

In their general addresses to readers, beauty manuals imply that a large group of women not only corseted themselves, but tight laced as well, with most manuals aiming to dissuade women from a practice widely considered harmful. In the 1834 *Art of Dress, or Guide to the Toilette*, the author writes that: "Perhaps, one of the greatest evils in a figure, in the eyes of a lady of the present day, is that of a thick waist. It is out of our province here to insist on the mischievous effects to which this noxious opinion has given rise, by means of tight-lacing, &c. This defect may, however, be readily got over . . . by a judicious arrangement of the dress."[32] The ambivalent author of *Art of Dress* first calls the fear of "a thick waist" a "noxious opinion," but then concurs that the large waist is a "defect" and offers suggestions to make it appear smaller. By 1860, the rhetoric against tight lacing had grown much stronger, with authors frequently comparing tight lacing to foot-binding and other forms of female mutilation. The tone of the following quotation from a domestic medical handbook (1858) is typical of its time: "We can at once distinguish among thousands, from their stiff, starched awkwardness, the forms that have been pinioned and tortured by wicked inventions to turn beauty into deformity."[33] In 1859, another author writes, "did [tight lacers] not appear, like moths flickering round a candle, to become infatuated and enraptured with the thing the nearer they approach to the altar of their destruction."[34] The writer, who equates tight lacing with self-immolation and pagan sacrificial rites, implies that the practice of tight lacing is not only dangerous but immoral, perhaps because tight lacing drew attention to a woman's erotic beauty. From being merely "mischievous," tight lacing had become portrayed as downright evil, vilified with such vocabulary as "destruction," "pinioned," "tortured," and "wicked." This intensification of anti-lacing rhetoric at first suggests an escalation of the practice, but the fashion for enormous skirts during the 1850s actually renders such a hypothesis unlikely. The sensationalizing of critics' language suggests, instead, that opponents may have been writing against an increasing acceptance of tight lacing.

The fashionable waist from the 1840s through the 1860s ranged from 17 to 23 inches wide, with most women – though not the tight lacers – falling somewhere at the larger end of the scale.[35] Tight lacers claimed to have waists as small as fifteen and sixteen inches in circumference, but they were not the norm and may well have exaggerated their smallness. One young woman who wrote to *The Queen* in 1863, for instance, reports that her waist "is sixteen and a-half inches, and, I have heard, is considered small"; as she implies, a sixteen-inch waist would have been considered something of an oddity.[36] Just as the "super models" of the 1980s and 90s do not accurately represent most women's bodies, so the fashionable Victorian waist should not be conflated with the average woman's waist size, which was larger. In any case, the ideal waist against which women measured themselves was very small. Although most Victorian women did not habitually tight lace, the majority did wear corsets to reduce their waists. Helene Roberts concludes that "[most women] did not reduce their waists by four inches or more. But most did lace sufficiently to reduce their waists by two or three inches, causing themselves discomfort, fatigue, and perhaps physical debility."[37] In addition, women altered their corset-wearing practices depending upon the time of day and their social environment, tight lacing on formal occasions, but loosening their corsets at home. Tight lacers carried normative corset wearing to an extreme, but standards of beauty influenced most women's behavior: whether or not they acted on it, the majority of middle-class Victorian women felt the cultural enthrallment of the waist.

The waist was a highly unstable and contested site that both sexualized *and* desexualized the body. On the one hand, the waist, more than any other part of the clothed female body from 1840 until 1900, distinguished the erotic female from the male body. Madame de la Santé writes that the waist "suggests the reverse of masculine muscularity, and stamps an essentially feminine characteristic on its possessor."[38] The waist was perceived as feminine but not, like the bosom and hips, simultaneously maternal. Men who wrote into the *Englishwoman's Domestic Magazine* (*EDM*) during that journal's infamous exchange about the virtues and vices of tight lacing in 1867 identify the waist as the main characteristic of the beautiful woman. One correspondent, for instance, writes that: "there is no more deplorable sight than a large and clumsy waist."[39] A man claiming to be a baronet concurs, asserting that: "there is not one man in a thousand who does not admire a graceful slenderness of the waist. What young man cares to dance with girls who resemble casks in form. I have invariably noticed that the girls with the smallest waists are the queens of the ballroom."[40] Even while acknowledging that the *EDM*'s tight-lacing correspondence (which was perceived by readers as risqué) undoubtedly drew from that segment of the population particularly enamoured of the practice, the disdain that these letter-writers voice for women who are not slender-waisted suggests the tremendous social pressure that women must have felt to adapt their figures to the accepted erotic standard. For many women, who relied on marriage for financial security, being "the queen of the ballroom" was more than pleasant flattery: the letters to the *EDM* spotlight women's economic and social vulnerability and their need to fit the standards of beauty of their day. And although, as

Steele has recently discussed, the fevered sentiments in favor of tight lacing in the *EDM* are "a particularly notorious example of a more specialized 'fetishist' interest," the adulation of the small waist is on a continuum with the idealized representations of small-waisted women in fashion magazines and in other Victorian discourses of femininity.[41] The "fetishists," like the tight-lacers themselves, merely put into practice exaggerated versions of mainstream conceptions of female beauty. Moreover, letter-writers to other magazines, including *The Queen, Girl's Own Paper* and *Ladies' Treasury*, express similar sentiments as the correspondents in the *EDM*. As the nineteenth-century writer Eliza Farrar notes, echoing many other writers: "So long as gentlemen admire small waists, and praise those figures the most, which approach nearest to the shape of a wasp, or an hour-glass, it is vain to tell young ladies, that the practice is destructive of health, and that there is no real beauty in the small dimensions at which they are aiming."[42]

David Kunzle has argued, controversially, that tight lacing was actually a progressive expression of sexual attractiveness, pointing out that many attacks on tight lacing are predicated upon the idea that women ought to focus on their domestic roles rather than be worrying about sexual attractiveness. Women who laced too tightly, Kunzle argues, were often targeted with insinuations about their moral purity: "Tight-lacers were, as a matter of definition, self-conscious women, and this kind of self-consciousness, which imprinted itself upon body carriage, movement, and a woman's aura, was considered quite improper."[43] Kunzle cites, for example, an 1869 editorial from the *Times* that claims that "tight-lacing creates more domestic unhappiness than any other domestic circumstance in life."[44] However, he overstates his generally persuasive case when he claims that tight lacing was simply "a personal and inner compulsion" and "largely voluntary."[45] The body is too much of a social construction for tight lacing merely to have been simply a "personal" choice, especially considering that most women wore corsets. Did the vast majority of middle-class women really feel a purely personal, individual "compulsion" to lace? Why did so many women and men connect the small waist to femininity? Kunzle ignores the cultural evidence that a large appetite, symbolized by the large waist, was widely perceived as unfeminine and that, for many women, the small waist was part of the complex performance of femininity in the nineteenth century. Rejecting dominant ideas of beauty, refusing to properly "perform" one's gender, always risks incurring sanctions ranging from social rejection and hostility to loss of employment or marriage. However, Kunzle's argument is valuable in that it demonstrates what an unstable signifier the small waist was during the nineteenth century. On the one hand, as I have argued, the small waist signified a woman's lack of appetite and her self-control. On the other hand, this physical discipline clearly carried an erotic edge for many people, emphasizing a part of the body that marked a woman as sexually attractive. Hollander contends, likewise, that tight lacing was "entrenched in erotic ambiguity, an emblem of female narcissism and submission."[46] The small waist, then, can be "read" as *both* sexual and non-sexual, physical and non-physical.

It is important to note, also, that, although the small waist sexualized the body, those women who did not lace at all, such as the proponents of Aesthetic dress reform, were also viewed as sexually provocative. Going in public entirely without a corset was generally considered lewd or slatternly. Arguing in favor of the corset, Madame de la Santé writes that the Regency period, during which less structured empire-waist dresses were in vogue, was "characterized by a loose state of society as well as of costume."[47] As Santé indicates, the corset, which imposes external control on the body, symbolized a woman's more important self-control. To refuse to wear a corset thus suggested a simultaneous refusal to control one's sexual behavior and desire. The "kept" woman of William Holman Hunt's *The Awakening Conscience*, for example, signals her licentiousness with her loose gown. Because of the association of the large waist with lack of control of the appetites, Victorian erotic photographs often depict what we today might refer to as heavy or even overweight women (though even their fat is more often located in the buttocks and thighs than in the waist). Victorian standards of beauty were not more monolithic than standards of beauty are today in terms of personal preference, and so both the small and large-waisted woman could be perceived as erotic. However, because the large waist carried connotations of lack of self-control not carried by the small waist, the large, fleshy woman was more likely to be viewed as overtly sexual than the sylph-like woman, whose smallness spoke, through her body, of her lack of carnality.

The small waist also embodied important class connotations. The *EDM*, which hosted the tight-lacing debate, was a lower middle-class magazine, so its correspondence indicates that tight lacing and corset wearing in general were not confined to the middle and upper classes. Large numbers of working-class women, including both factory workers and domestic servants, did in fact wear both corsets and crinolines. However, evidence from the letters suggests that the small waist was a class marker that, during a time of increased social mobility, represented one way to "fix" a woman's social standing and differentiate the middle-class woman from her working-class counterpart. It is unlikely, for instance, that the letter writer quoted above really was a baronet; however, by adopting that moniker, he associates the small waist with aristocracy. The lower middle-class readers of the *EDM* may have laced in part to distinguish themselves from the working poor when such a distance in terms of income, education, and financial security was relatively small and because they *perceived* small waists as aristocratic (whether or not aristocratic women were actually more likely to tight lace). Letters to the journal frequently refer to fashionable boarding schools, resorts, and assemblies, thereby echoing the rhetoric of novels of fashion and magazines such as *The Queen*, whose readers were generally wealthier. In a letter to *The Queen*, for instance, one author contrasts her childhood "at a small provincial school" where she was "suffered to run as nearly wild as could well be" with her later education at a Paris boarding school.[48] The author implies that the small waist is a visible, outward sign of improved fortunes and that only unsophisticated rural women are content with natural waists.

The letter is similar to an article entitled "Torture in the Nineteenth Century: Fashion in Tight Lacing" in the 1859 *Ladies' Treasury*, in which a physician refers to "a fashionable school in the most aristocratic neighborhood in London" in which "young ladies are compelled to wear stays night and day, and . . . no pupils are received whose parents object to this custom"; the author notes that "the establishment is always full, with others awaiting a vacancy."[49] Here, too, the author assumes that the small waist's association with wealth and femininity is widespread.[50] At least one reader of the magazine apparently responded to the story with doubts about its veracity, because a few months later, the editors included a remarkable note that reads: "A Lover of True Beauty is informed that the details of tight lacing, given in the May number of the Ladies' Treasury, are quite true."[51] Although it is impossible to verify the truthfulness of this particular article, or whether it repeats a kind of Victorian urban legend, the article reinforces the conjunction of the small waist and the upper classes that runs through diverse texts of the period.

Victorian fashion magazines, such as the *EDM*, and conduct books consistently support Elizabeth Langland's conclusion that the split between the pure and sexual woman was often perceived as occurring along class lines, so that "women of the working class became vested with a dangerous sexuality, and middle-class women, seemingly sexless, became the guardians of spirituality."[52] The slender body was one site on which these class distinctions played themselves out. The author of *Etiquette for Ladies* (1857) expresses concerns that women were harming their health in the attempt to perform class and gender identities through their bodies:

It is not too much to say that women in general, from a dread of falling into coarseness, neglect a good deal the care of their health, and in particular, all such exercises as tend to robustness. This is a great mistake. It would not be easy to convince any delicately-nurtured lady that a Newhaven Fisherwoman came nearer to the type of the female constitution than the pale, slim-waisted, tiny-footed sylph of the ballroom, so familiar to the Physician's black-book.[53]

Here, "robustness" marks a female body as working class, whereas the incorporeal body, "pale, slim-waisted, tiny-footed," indicates a woman's middle class-ness. According to Patricia Vertinsky: "Society doctors viewed affluent women as being in special need of protection because of their delicate nature and refined life-style, and saw working women as naturally robust and less susceptible to difficulties brought on by bodily exertion. Lower-class women were believed to be physically stronger and to feel little pain in comparison to middle-class women."[54] The anonymous author of *Etiquette for Ladies* translates this idea from medical to non-medical discourse, suggesting that "ladies," to whom the book is addressed, are physically different than working-class women (although the author also critiques this idea by arguing that affluent women should not be afraid of some fat and muscle). The word "coarseness," with its contemporary connotation of obscenity, further associates the strong female body with sexuality, thereby linking the sexual body with a working-class, "Fisherwoman's," body, whose labor outside the home already excludes her from the lady's domestic realm, with its attendant qualities of purity and delicacy. Slenderness is thus closely enmeshed with conventional class ideologies. The author's claim that these slender women were "familiar to the physician's black-book" touches upon the pervasiveness of the desire to be slim, suggesting that this desire may well have had real repercussions in terms of women's health.

The consensus, according to beauty and conduct manuals, is that women were unhealthy at least in part because of their "infatuated regard to fashion" [1858].[55] In Gaskell's *Ruth* (1853), an older woman explicitly connects the desire for a fashionable figure with her need to lose weight, telling Ruth that: "I'd be quite thankful for a fit of anxiety as would make me feel easy in my clothes, which them manty-makers will make so tight that I'm fairly throttled."[56] Although the woman cheerfully concludes that dieting "is no use, it's against my nature; so I laugh and grow fat again," many Victorian women reached different conclusions.[57] Concurring with the author of *Health for the Million*, Henry Clarke, in *The English Maiden: Her Moral and Domestic Duties* (1841), blames men for women's "[slavery] to every new mode of dress," writing that: "There may be men who encourage women in a culture of a false delicacy in reference to their health . . . Else had we never witnessed that affected fastidiousness of appetite, and that affected sickliness, so fashionable in some circles."[58] At least according to Clarke, women's disorderly eating is directly linked to the quest for the fashionable figure and to the cultural validation of female invalidism. Clarke's argument eliminates female agency and to some degree infantilizes women, painting them as helpless votaries before the altar of fashion. Considering the centrality of beauty to the construct of femininity, however, his argument is compelling. Furthermore, there is no real evidence that women merely "affected fastidiousness of appetite"; one might just as easily assume that women actually *did* starve themselves in order to conform to "every new mode of dress." Later nineteenth-century physicians, writing several decades after Clarke, certainly assumed that they did. In 1884, T. Clifford Allbutt, for instance, blamed anorexia nervosa on "the fear of growing stout," a fear that generally does not appear in cultures which consider fatness beautiful.[59] More explicitly, in 1871, the physician George Beard claimed that "Fashion has joined hands with superstition, and through fear of looking gross or healthy . . . our young ladies live all their growing girlhood in semi-starvation, they become thin and poor."[60] Both Allbutt and Beard, arguing from their case work, indicate that a fear of fatness existed among women by the late nineteenth century and conjecture that this fear leads to fasting behavior. We will never really know why the adolescent girls to whom the two physicians refer chose not to eat. Food refusal does not stem simply from the desire to conform to fashion, and slenderness, of course, carried important symbolic connotations in the nineteenth century above and beyond simply indicating personal stylishness. However, the frequent descriptions of sickly women across the discourses and through the decades, when read alongside Gull's and Lasègue's "discoveries" of anorexia nervosa in 1873, do provide anecdotal, though speculative, evidence that women were, in fact, harming themselves in an attempt to be beautiful, and that predominant notions of the beautiful valued slenderness.

Assuming that the small waist was not simply fashionable because of an inherent, essential beauty, the larger question remains as to why the waist signified femininity and gentility for the Victorians. In part, as allusions to "delicacy" and "sickliness" indicate, the small waist draws resonance from the larger nineteenth-century fashion for invalidism. Bram Dijkstra writes that: "More and more the mythology of the day began to associate even normal health – let alone 'unusual' physical vigor in women – with dangerous, masculinizing attitudes. A healthy woman, it was often thought, was likely to be an 'unnatural' woman. Proper human angels were weak, helpless, ill."[61] The waist, in particular, could signify a woman's light weight and demonstrate her literal and metaphorical bodilessness. The physiognomist Alexander Walker (1840) describes a woman's body as "precise, striking, and often brilliant. – From its proportions, it sometimes seems almost aerial; and we would imagine, that, if our hands were placed under the lateral parts of the tapering waist of a woman thus characterized, the slightest pressure would suffice to throw her into the air."[62] Walker's violent image of masculine prowess suggests that the erotic appeal of a woman's small waist derives from her physical weakness and vulnerability, especially when juxtaposed with man's strength. Symbolically, the waist signifies woman's ethereal nature, the "aerial" qualities that separate her from man; a woman's light weight suggests her spiritual, rather than carnal, nature.[63] Her "angelic" nature is thus reflected in her weak, slight body.

One brief anecdote will illustrate this cultural linkage of femininity and invalidism. Sarah Jacob, a Welsh "fasting girl," claimed to live without food from 1867 until her eventual death from starvation in December 1869, when an autopsy revealed that Jacob, who still had the remnants of food in her stomach and a healthy amount of body fat, must somehow have been secretly eating before being sedulously monitored by nurses from a London hospital. During the time of her fasting, Jacob became a minor celebrity who was visited by hundreds of people. After meeting Jacob, a doctor named John Thomas wrote, in 1869, that: "She was decked with ribbons and brooches, and her hair nicely put up; in fact, it gave me the idea that they were aping an angelic appearance."[64] According to Thomas's testimony, Jacob and her family drew a clear relation between the girl's fasting behavior and her heightened spirituality, as the phrase "angelic appearance" suggests. Not eating became, for her family and for the fascinated public, a sign that Sarah had wholly rejected her physical needs and appetites. Moreover, the great attention that Jacob's family gave to dressing their daughter in ribbons, lace, jewelry, and even a white bridal wreath indicates that they understood her weakness and invalidism, demonstrated by her lack of appetite, as closely connected to a hyperbolic femininity. Thomas, however, hints that her family is creating a false image of Jacob as a publicity stunt, using the verb "aping" to bring Jacob squarely back into the realm of the physical, even "sub" human.

Since one of the barometers of woman's sensuality was her appetite, the waist assumed importance as a visible and conspicuous measure of how much a woman ate. Mrs. Alexander Walker correlates the waist and the stomach when she admonishes women to wear corsets "to conceal the size of the abdomen when it becomes disproportionately large."[65] A large stomach/waist was unattractive because a woman's appetite for food illustrated her sensual appetites: small gustatory appetites and a slim waist, on the other hand, signified small carnal appetites. The waist is also near the site of the uterus, so the small waist distinguished the virgin who was sexually inexperienced from the woman who had given birth. Mrs. Alexander Walker suggests such an interpretation of the fashion for slim waists when she writes: "Every young woman knows that one of the most conspicuous differences between the maiden and the matron consists in the same less or greater distension of the waist. Is it unnatural, then, that she should prefer seeming maidenly to seeming matronly?"[66] Walker, assuming that women desire small waists because such waists are a sign of the "maiden," encourages women to bind their bellies after birth to preserve the "beauty of the shape."[67] Maternity may have been woman's function and purpose in life, but erotic beauty depended upon a woman's sexual purity.[68]

In *Fasting Girls*, Joan Jacobs Brumberg examines the conflation of food and sexuality in the nineteenth-century, arguing that:

The woman who put soul over body was the ideal of Victorian femininity. The genteel woman responded not to the lower senses of taste and smell but to the highest senses – sight and hearing – which were used for moral and aesthetic purposes. One of the most convincing demonstrations of a spiritual orientation was a thin body – that is, a physique that symbolized rejection of all carnal appetites. To be hungry, in any sense, was a social faux pas.[69]

Foods were popularly classified as "male" or "female" depending on the effects that they were thought to have on mood and sexual propensity. Since sexual passion was unseemly in women, and even dangerous to their health, women were to eat only those foods that calmed their desires. Meats, as well as salty, spicy, and rich foods, were often considered off-limits, while bland foods were thought the safest, though some physicians did prescribe meat in cases of invalidism and chronic weakness.

Mrs. Alexander Walker, for instance, recommends milk because "it appears even to calm the passions and to impart a gentleness to the character," but warns women against meat because: "Immoderate indulgence in this food often becomes pernicious."[70] Similarly, the French physician Colombat de l'Isère, in 1840, cites "acrid and spicy dishes . . . fat meats, pastry" as one cause of chlorosis, while the physician Thomas Trotter singles out rich food as one cause of hysteria.[71]

Even when the food consumed was appropriate for women, the very act of eating was potentially awkward because of its associations with physical processes like mastication, digestion, and defecation. *The Etiquette of Courtship and Marriage* (1859), for instance, advises men that "oranges should be peeled and then cut in slices extremely thin . . . It is impossible for a lady to eat an orange in any other way without stretching her mouth."[72] Cherries, asparagus, and peas are frequently singled out in etiquette manuals and women's magazines as difficult to eat; one article advises, of cherry tarts: "Once in, [the stones] must come out; and therefore, I should advise a lady not to eat of dishes that entail this inconvenience in company. There is always a choice."[73] The focus on food "coming out," which suggests the less seemly bodily process of waste evacuation, leads to the reminder that women can always control whether or not they eat something, as though the very idea of having to go to the bathroom should remind women not to eat. However, the article acknowledges, in a non-judgmental manner, that: "Old bonvivants, who care for nothing and nobody but the dainty before them, make no difficulties, and eat all things in the way most convenient to them."[74] The author suggests that older women are not subjected to the same behavioral scrutiny, perhaps because their age already relegates them to asexuality. In general, however, because appetite was a key emblem of sexual desire, even something as seemingly simple and innocent as biting into fruit indicated the physical act of consumption and so became the focus of behavioral management. Conduct books thus provide detailed directions on how to eat, what to eat, how much to eat, and how slowly to eat.

The prescriptions about women's diets complicate the view that the Victorians considered women naturally and inevitably more spiritual than men, instinctive but not rational, emotional rather than intellectual. The separate spheres argument did claim these things about women, and the thin body, as I have argued, underscored such a distinction between men and women. However, contrary to the theory that middle-class women were merely regarded as angelic beings and domestic fairies, historians have established that women were just as often viewed as potentially sexually voracious and emotionally unstable, and that their sexuality and emotions had to be constantly controlled and kept within proper bounds.[75] Moreover, these dual conceptions of women as both angelic and monstrous might be used to describe the same woman. Menstruation, for instance, was regularly supplied as proof that women were ruled by their reproductive organs rather than their reason, and that women themselves had little self-control, an idea that, of course, has an ancient history dating back to Aristotle, Pliny, and Aquinas. On the other hand, a heightened self-control was expected of these same women. As Sally Shuttleworth argues, women "were expected to be more controlled than men, but were also presumed to be physiologically incapable of imposing control . . . They were helpless prisoners of their own bodies."[76] The fact that women were warned away from certain foods – meat, for instance – supports Shuttleworth's contention by illustrating the belief that it required constant vigilance to repress woman's sensual nature. A woman constantly risked revealing her appetitive and insatiable nature, for carnality always remained just under a woman's angelic crust. Farrar, for example, advises that: "By dining on one dish, and that the plainest on the table, you will preserve your habitual temperance, and have time to be sociable with your neighbors . . . In the manner of eating the good things provided, the characters of individuals are shown, and very greedy propensities will occasionally appear, under very fair forms."[77] Farrar counsels women to exhibit their "habitual temperance" through restrained eating at dinner parties, where their private eating habits become public. By noting that the "fair forms" of women sometimes disguise unladylike "greedy propensities," Farrar implies that women are not naturally abstemious, but must learn to behave so. Self-control, again, becomes crucial to femininity.

In her exploration of illness in Victorian culture, Athena Vrettos writes that: "Narratives of illness, whether in medical case histories, advice manuals, or literary texts, could shape individual experiences of suffering. They could also shape how people perceived relationships between mind and body, self and other, private and public spheres."[78] The same can be said for the representations of the female body in Victorian literature, beauty manuals, fashion magazines, and conduct books. Although one cannot prove a direct line of mediation between Victorian culture and the rise of eating disorders in the late nineteenth century, it is surely not coincidental that the disease was first diagnosed at a time when fashionable women were often tight laced and subject to strict restrictions in their eating habits. Theoretically, the focus on self-control closely links the Victorian woman with the disorderly eater. The ideal Victorian woman was expected to regulate her food intake and monitor her appetite in order to conform to a slim ideal of beauty and, on a deeper and more important level, to normative, incorporeal conceptions of femininity that posited the body as in constant conflict with the soul. Like the woman who achieves an exultant sense of control over her body by obsessively fasting and exercising, many nineteenth-century women pursued discipline over the body through their eating habits and through the use of the corset. In addition, the Victorian woman's attempt to indicate her sexual purity through a slim figure recalls the anorexic girl's refusal of her own physical needs and desires (including the sexual) through starvation, which puts a stop to menstruation and the accumulation of body fat. Ultimately, such a rejection of appetite can be interpreted as the transcendence of the true self, whether conceptualized as soul or mind, over the corrupt and temporal body. Rather than merely looking for clinical victims of anorexia nervosa in the nineteenth century, then, one can rather conceive of many "normal" Victorian women as acting within the logic of anorexia. A slender waist mattered to Victorian women.

Writing about trends in feminine beauty in the United States, Allan Mazur argues that "there is little doubt that the overall trend in self-starvation has been produced by our culture's increasing idealization of the slenderness as the model for feminine beauty," and relates today's trends in beauty to the hysterical woman of the nineteenth century: "Classical hysteria is the extreme of overadaptation for the fragile woman, for with it she carries the ideal of beauty to the point of incapacitation, just as some women today starve (and die) to epitomize their modern sense of beauty."[79] Actually, the hysterical or neurasthenic woman has much in common with the anorexic woman, one of which is a propensity to restrict her eating. In *Lectures on Diseases of the Nervous System*, the American physician S. Weir Mitchell discusses a letter that he received from one of his patients, who writes: "I carried on a sort of starvation process, physical and mental. Why that process should have brought me into such a condition, I must leave with someone wiser to unriddle."[80] Although we will never know why this anonymous woman began to starve herself, it is likely that there is some overlap between fasting hysterics and women who would later be diagnosed as anorexic. As Mazur suggests, both diseases can be theoretically linked to the cultures in which they appear and which initially diagnosed them.

Codes of etiquette in the nineteenth century provided men and women with behavioral guidelines that delineated gender differences and defined the values of the middle class.[81] Rules of etiquette ranged from the general, such as, "a spirit of obedience and submission . . . are required of [women]" (1859), to the specific: "No lady can make advances of a character bold and obvious to a gentleman" (1841).[82] Authors frequently describe manners as a form of protection for women; what may seem like trivial rules theoretically kept women safe from men's lascivious advances. However, the rules depended as well on the fear that, as one marriage manual from 1856 claimed: "there is nothing so delicate as a woman's purity."[83] Woman's weakness needed control in the form of understandable and unyielding rules and maxims that kept men and women from too great an intimacy.

The irony of conduct books is that, while they sought to regulate behavior, they demanded a certain amount of knowledge on the part of their female readers that was in itself suspect. Although women were not supposed to entertain licentious thoughts, conduct books left unspoken gaps for them to fill. The author of *Etiquette for Ladies* writes, in 1857, that: "At a public ball, it is exceptional for a gentleman to offer to escort a lady home; she is pretty sure to refuse unless – but we need not supply that blank."[84] If the author does not need to "supply that blank," then the reader must already know what is left unspoken, namely that only a woman of suspect morals would go home with a man. Just as Bell posits that a girl's shame is really a sign of her sexual desire, the author of *Etiquette for Ladies* assumes that a woman's modesty indicates what she knows. Similarly, in 1857, Emily Thornwell claims that: "A lady should never seem to understand an indelicate expression, much less use one."[85] To recognize an "indelicate expression" of course, implies that one understands it, and Thornwell's use of the word "seem" suggests that women must merely feign *naïveté*, not actually be ignorant. The system of etiquette, then, depended to some extent on women knowing what they were not supposed to know.

The control of food intake should be contextualized within this larger Victorian management of female behavior. The restrictions placed on women's food intake are akin to more general restrictions on women's speech and manners. Just as codes of conduct assume that women's behavior needs to be regulated, constraints on food consumption assume a certain amount of sexual knowledge or sexual propensity in women that needs to be monitored through their diet. The idea that women should eat only small amounts of food, or particular kinds of food, as a sign of their purity ironically implies that one cannot take women's innocence for granted. Analogously, using diet as a class marker reveals the fear that differences between middle- and working-class women are negligible and must somehow be demonstrated, "performed," through patterns of food intake and body size.

Anorexia nervosa is only the pathological extreme of a continuum on which many Victorian women found themselves. A woman is not necessarily anorexic if she carefully regulates what she eats and if she laces herself into a corset in order to signify her purity and chastity; nevertheless, the woman who exercises control over body fat in the attempt to live up to inflexible standards of feminine beauty does fall within a range of behaviors informed by anorexic logic. Gaskell's Mrs. Gibson, "who was trying to train her midday appetite into the genteelest of all ways," is a parody of the fashionable Victorian woman at the dinner table, but her behavior mirrors popular ideology.[86] Although the women in Victorian literature seldom express their loathing of food as explicitly and comically as Mrs. Gibson, they are nonetheless rarely seen eating. Behind the fictional heroine and the carefully posed woman of the conduct book lived an uncertain number of women whose refusal to eat became disease. Nineteenth-century Britain provided the environment in which anorexia nervosa developed from cultural logic to pathology.

CHAPTER 2

Appetite in Victorian children's literature

It is perhaps unsurprising that Victorian fashion magazines and beauty manuals emphasize the importance of beauty in a woman's life, since they were in the very business that they relentlessly promoted. The authors of books such as *The Science of Dress* or *The Art of Beauty*, and the editors of magazines like *La Mode Illustrée* depended upon women's continued concern over appearance in order to sell their products, and in turn, they reinforced this concern by rearticulating particular ideas of gender and the female body for their readers. Ideologies of body image in literature, on the other hand, are far less overt than in texts that explicitly attempt to convince women to wear particular kinds of dresses or corsets. Nevertheless, the same ideologies that are discernable in non-literary texts – such as the idea that a woman's sexual purity is coded by her body shape – appear in the work of many canonical and non-canonical Victorian authors. Victorian children's literature is a particularly good place to look for evidence of the beginnings of a culture of anorexia within a self-consciously literary discourse because, as children's literature critic Peter Hunt has written: "All books must teach something, and because the checks and balances available to the mature reader are missing in the child reader, the children's writer often feels obliged to supply them."[1] One can easily oversimplify the power dynamics of children's literature; children's literature often resists and parodies hegemonic cultural values, and the utopian and subversive tradition of children's literature has a long and distinguished history. Nevertheless, it is a truism that much literature for children in the nineteenth century, particularly evangelical children's literature, perpetuates prevailing cultural myths. Children's books, after all, are not written by children's peers, but by adults, and, as Julia Briggs writes: "Inevitably the production of children's books is governed by what adults want children to be and to do, and furthermore, it offers an opportunity to induce them to share those adult goals."[2] Although Victorian children's literature is a diverse genre encompassing adventure stories, school stories, fantasy, domestic novels, and religious tracts, to name only a few, much of this literature praises girls for denying their appetites and limiting their consumption of food, often connecting that denial to femininity. Thus, children's books of the period often underpin a culture of anorexia, in which control over the body and its desires are enacted through the control of food intake.

The ideology of the innocent child that informed so much children's literature, particularly secular children's literature, reinforced the frequent admonitions against children's appetite in nineteenth-century culture at large. In her important study of Victorian girlhood, Deborah Gorham argues that, because the middle- and upper-class Victorian woman was supposed to retain aspects of childishness into maturity, the Victorian girl was theoretically already an ideal woman. Unlike the mature woman, whose inescapable sexuality and maternity were incongruent with female purity, the girl did not contain such contradictions. "Much more successfully than her mother," Gorham maintains, "a young girl could represent the quintessential angel in the house . . . a girl could be perceived as a wholly unambiguous model of feminine dependence, childlike simplicity and sexual purity."[3] This valuation of sexual innocence over experience inherently privileges the girl over the adult woman and, in turn, values the *body* of the girl over the *body* of the woman. If "purity" is an essential attribute of female beauty, then maturity must bring with it a fall from the true beauty of the young girl. Such ideas about girlhood dovetail neatly with anorexia nervosa, which, as I have mentioned, many theorists believe reflects a girl's disgust at the impending sexual maturity symbolized by her changing body. "Anorexic girls . . . acknowledge neither hunger for food nor hunger for sex," Deborah Tolman and Elizabeth Debold write, "living within the image of the desireless woman [they] have no sexual feelings to speak of, living out of connection with their bodies."[4] The anorexic girl enacts, then, the persona so often presented in the nineteenth century as the true woman, the one who controls her desires and her body.

This chapter will examine several diverse examples of nineteenth-century children's literature, beginning with the *Girl's Own Paper*, the first widely successful British periodical for girls, and other ephemeral children's literature published in the form of annuals and tracts. These texts reveal the strong emphasis placed on appetite control in nineteenth-century literature and culture, as well as some evidence of the effect that it had on adolescent girls. I will then turn to the works of John Ruskin and Kate Greenaway, both of which reveal the conflation of innocence and eroticism so popular in the nineteenth century, and the valuation of the girl's body over the woman's body. Finally, I will investigate the work of Lewis Carroll who resists, to some degree, the passionless girl and the girl without appetite.

"THE LITTLE GLUTTON"

The *Girl's Own Paper* (*GOP*) was one of the first very successful periodicals for girls: Sally Mitchell cites an 1888 poll in which almost a third of the thousand respondents, girls between the ages of eleven and nineteen, noted *GOP* "as their favorite reading."[5] The *GOP* appealed to a broad group of female readers, from servant girls to the affluent middle class, and readers of the magazine ranged from the ages of twelve to twenty-six, with the majority of readers in their teen years. Judging from reader response in the periodical itself, one of the most popular features of the magazine was the letter column, in which *GOP* editors responded to their readers' requests for advice on varied topics, from needlework and laundry to obeying their parents and poetry writing. Because of the *GOP*'s broad readership base, it is an ideal place to look for evidence that Victorian girls were concerned about their weight, and, in fact, from the first volume, which appeared in 1880, letters attest to the importance of beauty in the readers' lives. Though most of the appearance-oriented letters published in the magazine focus on skin problems and questions about hair, many of them contain fears about growing fat and express the desire to become slender. *GOP* editors consistently take a firm anti-tight-lacing stance, and in general emphasize the need to accept one's natural and God-given shape. Perhaps influenced by late Victorian physicians who argued that girls need a certain amount of fat in order for their reproductive systems to work properly, the editors respond quite sharply to readers' references to common means of losing weight such as drinking vinegar and lemon juice, suggesting instead that girls make peace with and appreciate their plumpness.

The following four letters are representative of the *GOP* correspondence; in each case, we have only the editor's response and so can only surmise the content of the original letter:

We are at a loss to understand why so many girls are demented on the subject of the natural plumpness which nature bestows on youth. It is a sign of health . . . Your suggestion respecting the applicability of vinegar quite shocks us. (I: 272)

You are doing a very rash thing in trying to thin yourself by taking carbonate of soda in daily doses ... Do you wish to look like the poor scarecrows with pipe-stopper waists? (1: 352)

By no means make any experiments with quack medicines, nor by poor living, much less "starvation." You would only thin your blood and produce disease of which you might die early. But you may avoid eating much butter or fat and the drinking of beer or porter, and you should take a walk daily without fail, though not one that would fatigue you. (4: 447)

Do not feel troubled about the silly personal remarks which ill-bred people make. Be thankful that you assimilate, and thrive upon your food ... You are as God made you; be satisfied with the casing in which you are enclosed for a time, and play no dangerous tricks with yourself. (5: 256)[6]

The letters attest to a widespread concern, among pubescent and adolescent girls, about weight, as well as alluding to "the craze which appears to exist among young people to make themselves thin" (1: 272). Contradicting some critics' contention that fear of fatness was not linked to the desire to be slender in the Victorian period, the letters suggest that girls were undertaking diets specifically in order to conform to specific body standards, diets which women's magazines and beauty manuals also make reference to. The content of *GOP* is radically different than that of girls' magazines today. Articles on diet and exercise are non-existent, and the magazine focuses instead on entertaining stories, histories, craft projects, and domestic advice; nevertheless, the responses from editors to readers indicate that weight was a real concern of girls and that many girls very much desired to be slender. Since anorexia nervosa normally develops in girls at the onset of puberty, and since it is characterized by the obsessive hatred and fear of fat, the sentiments evident in many of the *GOP* letters indicate that the climate of nineteenth-century Britain was conducive to the nascence of the disease. As many critics have pointed out, anorexia nervosa does not develop in cultures in which obesity or fleshiness is valued; a cultural denigration of fat is essential to the widespread existence of the disease. Moreover, the correspondence attests to girls' concern with weight at the very age when most girls with eating disorders first develop anorexia nervosa or bulimia.

The focus on weight in the *GOP* is perhaps less surprising after one has examined other Victorian literature written for children. The Victorian culture of anorexia is already apparent in children's literature that associates eating, especially for girls, with traits such as greed, lust, and aggression. In story after story, girls are taught that they must control their appetites and, by implication, their desires and bodies, in order to be "good." As one author writes, in a story called "The Little Glutton" (1860): "A young lady should be ashamed of exhibiting so lively a pleasure at the sight of anything to eat . . . All this discloses a strong disposition to what is called gluttony – an ignoble fault, which degrades us to the level of mere brutes."[7] Here, appetite is explicitly connected with the desires of the body, animalistic desires that have no place in the domestic girl. Usually, the desire to eat in children's literature symbolizes an unattractive trait, such as selfishness or curiosity, that both girls and boys must control. Little Harriet, in *Child Land*, refuses to give one of her apples to her brother, and is chastised by the author – "I am ashamed of you, you greedy girl" – while her virtuous counterpart in literature for children feeds *others*, whether family members, poor children, or even birds, often despite her own hunger.[8] One little girl, in *The Snow*, an earlier (1825) children's story, differentiates herself from a naughty boy by feeding birds, while the boy, in contrast, gives the birds to his cat to be "munched alive."[9] The bad boy kills birds, while the good girl displays her goodness by feeding them. Truly good girls deny their appetites altogether when they notice hunger around them. In "Little Kate's Great Feast" (1860), Kate gives up her delicious pastries when she sees a poor girl, and remarks that "I have not had anything to eat. Well, well! yet it seems to me as if I had never before had a feast I so much enjoyed."[10] Feeding brings more pleasure than eating. Food, then, becomes a vehicle, when given away rather than eaten, for generosity and charity. True pleasure comes both from feeding others and denying one's own appetite.

When eaten in large quantities, food assumes connotations of greed and lack of self control. Usually, girls who eat a lot, and particularly girls who eat in secret, are punished for their crime. Little Helen, for example, likes to "snatch whatever she wanted and go into a corner to eat it" until she falls ill from eating too much fruit and learns to "eat in moderation, of what is given to you; and occasionally, deny yourself anything you are too fond of."[11] Though Helen is punished in part because of her theft, eating when "no one saw her," the lesson that she is taught is not simply to eat publicly, but also to curtail her eating, even renouncing her appetite. As the previous story suggests, the act of eating in all but the most disciplined manner becomes a transgression in much of the literature.[12] Like the Belgian girls described by Lucy Snowe in *Villette*, Miss Lucy Dash, who "spoils [her] pretty mouth by cramming it with food" is a poor student who cheats; her intellectual failings are demonstrated by her propensity to read novels and eat "forbidden fruit."[13] When eating is over and over again associated with negative character traits, and rarely perceived as unambiguously positive and pleasurable, then the very act of eating takes on a negative cast. Rarely, in overtly didactic or evangelical children's literature, is eating portrayed as merely enjoyable. Rather, it is figured as something that must be constantly controlled.

Of course, one could argue that eating is presented as similarly unattractive in boys. Children's stories and poems frequently have a laugh at the expense of the boy who steals a plum tart, or who eats like a glutton. However, there are significant differences between representations of boys' and girls' eating, revealing that male and female hunger have different implications in Victorian children's literature. Most significantly, criticism of girls' appetite focuses on hunger as a sign of sexual desire more frequently than does criticism of boys' appetite. The evangelical "The Stain Upon the Hand" (1859), for instance, tells the story of Kitty, who has stolen butternuts from her parents' "forbidden" pantry and is branded with a sign of her sin in the form of a "dark, ugly stain . . . quite disfiguring the whole palm."[14] Kitty's transgressive appetite is actually imprinted on her body. Throughout the story, the author emphasizes the dark color of the stain against Kitty's white hand, especially while she sleeps in her clean bed, thereby suggesting that her greed threatens her purity and innocence, even implying her vulnerability to more serious transgressions. Like the animalistic hand of Mr. Hyde on Dr. Jekyll's counterpane, the image of Kitty's dark palm suggests a Darwinian degeneration and alludes to Victorian conceptions of the non-white woman, her dark skin a cultural code for voluptuous, unrestrained sexuality; the story, then, represents desire as a breach of domesticity and female chastity. As Kitty's mother chastens her: "When you took the nuts they not only left a dark mark upon your hand . . . but the stain reached your heart and made it offensive to your heavenly Father's eye."[15] Appetite disfigures not only Kitty's body, but also her soul. If the body is a reflection of the soul, moreover, then appetite takes on distinctly moral qualities, so that what and how one eats become extremely important. One must read children's literature that speaks out against female appetite, like "The Stain Upon the Hand," within the larger context of the management of female sexual desire in the nineteenth century. Since men were not subject to the same kinds of restrictions that girls were – specifically, they were not expected to watch their diets in order to demonstrate their incorporeality – denunciations of boys' appetite do not have the same implicit sexual connotations as do denunciations of girls' appetite.

Female appetite was also taken more seriously than boys' appetite. I have been unable to find any children's stories in which female gluttony or obesity is presented humorously. Male fatness, on the other hand, is often cause for laughter. "Limby Lumpy," an anonymous story published *c.* 1840, describes a "great, ugly, fat child" named Limby Lumpy who is so horribly spoiled by his doting parents that, at the end of the story, they actually permit him to ride a saddle of mutton.[16] The story is ostensibly a warning against spoiling one's child, and Limby Lumpy's parents are absurd caricatures of lenient parents, but the story clearly takes great delight in Limby Lumpy's adventures. The association that the story makes between gluttony and aggression (Limby Lumpy throws temper tantrums to get what he wants) are commonplace, but the extreme grotesqueness of the story, and its humorous tone, set it apart from the more earnest evangelical literature. Moreover, though the story mocks Limby Lumpy, and his fatness is unproblematically derided as disgusting, he is never punished in the story and he never reforms. By the end of the story, in fact, he is "as frisky . . . as if nothing has happened, and, about half an hour from the time of this disaster, *cried for his dinner.*"[17] Compare such an ending with the countless stories in which little girls fall ill and solemnly resolve to change their eating habits. The real villains in "Limby Lumpy" are Limby Lumpy's incompetent parents, not the child himself. A lusty male appetite, even when criticized, does not carry as much moral meaning as female appetite, and is even viewed as healthy and typically masculine.

Jane and Ann Taylor's poems, which were popular throughout the nineteenth century, also provide a case in point about the different ways that male and female appetites were understood. The Taylors denounce both male and female gluttony. In "The Plum Cake," for example, George develops a fever from overeating, while Dick, in "The Pigs," eats so many cakes and candies that he is compared unfavorably to a pig, as the title indicates. However, the Taylors provide gendered morals to their poems. In "The Boys and the Apple Tree," William and Thomas encounter the evil consequences of stealing apples when they find a huge trap set under a tree. Thomas concludes: "I learn what may happen by breaking a law, / Although but in stealing an apple."[18] While Thomas's experience teaches him to follow the dictates of law, the girls in "Come and Play in the Garden" learn to obey their mother: they are taught an interpersonal rather than an abstract judicial lesson, a "feminine" rather than a "masculine" lesson. The Taylors' emphasis on behaving well within the context of relationship implies that what a girl primarily needs to learn is how to relate to others within the family. Boys, on the other hand, need to understand concepts of law in preparation for a world of work and extra-familial responsibility. The Taylors' perception of appetite thus reflects the larger ideology of separate spheres, in which a girl's repression of appetite signifies her submission to cultural codes of femininity, including domesticity. A boy's repression of appetite, on the other hand, prefigures his assumption of the masculine role.

The negative representation of eating in much nineteenth-century children's literature was matched by real restrictions on eating in many girls' lives. Most often, girls were urged to eat a bland, unstimulating diet. Colombat de l'Isère, for instance, writes that "the food of a young girl at puberty ought to consist principally of vegetable substances, of prepa-rations of milk, of the tender meats, and of light and easily digestible substances."[19] Girls were supposed to eat only certain foods and in cer-tain quantities, exercise and travelling were to be cut back, especially at menarche, and girls (like boys) were to be watched carefully for im-moral behaviors such as masturbation. Roberta Seid explicitly connects Victorian dietary restrictions with anorexia nervosa, arguing that: "the special diets advocated for children – bland and rife with foods that might not taste good but were 'good for you' – also helped turn eating into a more highly charged adolescent issue than it had been."[20] Certainly, the emphasis on control and discipline in connection with the dinner table is related to the anorexic girl's obsession with the control of her appetite. In addition, the emotional power of food refusal depends upon and varies according to the strictness of rules and rituals surrounding the act of eating. To alter one's eating patterns or even to refuse to eat when eating is a rule-bound activity is a much more rebellious act than refusing to eat when no one will notice. Even if the number of "actual" anorexics was smaller in the Victorian period than it is today, the restrictions that many (though of course not all) adolescent girls were expected to impose on their food intake suggests that the focus on self-discipline normalized the obsessive control of food intake.

Finally, such restrictions are particularly important when they occur at adolescence, because at puberty a girl's ration of fat to muscle typically increases. In a climate in which self-discipline and discipline over one's body are considered important, and when eating itself is represented as suspect, at best, then fat symbolizes losing the battle for control, height-ening the need for further discipline. The letters to the *GOP* indicate quite strongly that fat was viewed by many girls as a personal failure, as a flaw that needed to be corrected. Since anorexia nervosa generally occurs in girls at puberty, when they begin to accumulate fat on their bellies, hips, and thighs, the *GOP* correspondence hints at a struggle with weight and fat that could well have become disease. Although there is no way to tell whether any of the correspondents was in fact anorexic, the letters make it clear that disorderly eating, and most likely eating disorders, existed at the end of the nineteenth century.

CRYSTALS, DANCING GIRLS, AND FEMALE BEAUTY: JOHN RUSKIN AND KATE GREENAWAY

In countless Victorian literature classrooms and critical studies, John Ruskin is presented as the mouthpiece of Victorian gender ideology, and, indeed, *Of Queens' Gardens* remains one of the most important nineteenth-century enunciations of separate spheres ideology. Recent critics, however, have sought to complicate earlier feminist critiques of *Of Queens' Gardens*, examining ways in which Ruskin uses separate spheres ideology to argue for a larger political and social role for women outside of the home, as caretakers of the poor and the environment.[21] Ruskin's assertion that a woman should move "without her gates, where order is more difficult, distress more imminent, loveliness more rare," even suggests that women are natural born leaders in philanthropic and educational work.[22] His ideas about men's and women's fundamentally different natures thus ironically provided an argument for the redefinition of the domestic sphere. Discussion of *Of Queens' Gardens* has, however, largely overshadowed another of Ruskin's works, *The Ethics of the Dust* (1866), a collection of Socratic dialogues on minerology written for children and inspired by Ruskin's visits to Winnington, a progressive girls' school. In *Ethics*, Ruskin alludes to several key arguments that he makes in his other works, touching upon such varied topics as political and domestic economy, theology, and art. Most important for my discussion, however, Ruskin's anthropomorphizes crystals into girls and "geopomorphizes" girls into crystals. His association of girls with crystals enables Ruskin to argue for the importance of girls' physical shapes, contending that, from a young age, a girl should discipline her body into an acceptable form. In addition, Ruskin's association of beauty with youth implies that true beauty is unavailable to the woman.

Ruskin describes the children listening to his lectures as "a lovely group of rosy sugar-candy, arranged by atomic forces."[23] He returns to this identification of girls with crystals again and again in the dialogues, teaching the children how to "play at crystallization" (45), referring to the "crystalline lens" (99) of one girl's eye, and, most important, using crystals to teach the girls moral lessons. Ruskin likens crystals to girls because "their essential virtues are but two; – the first is to be pure, and the second to be well shaped" (87). The crystal is not just a metaphor for girls' natures, then, but for their bodies as well, as the phrase "well shaped" suggests. The idea that girls' figures should be "well-shaped" is particularly important, of course, in the context of a discussion of Victorian body image. Ruskin admits that crystals, and therefore girls, do not have complete control over their forms, citing "time and accident" (87) as influences on a crystal's shape that "the crystal cannot help" (87). Nonetheless, shape is one of the two traits that Ruskin considers fundamental to a girl's makeup, and he contradicts his initial acknowledgment that shape is to some degree out of a girl's control by contending that, like a crystal, a girl should develop slowly and, somehow, purposefully. "A fine crystal seems to have determined that it will be of a certain size and of a certain shape," he writes; "it persists in this plan, and completes it" (89). Though Ruskin does not make explicit the means by which a girl should mold herself into a particular size or shape, he figures the girl's body as an object that needs to be disciplined, and growth as something that needs to be controlled, the same logic that informs anorexia nervosa. There is, of course, a moral dimension to Ruskin's argument. His larger point is that the crystal's purity and shape are a consequence of its goodness; the crystal's appearance reflects its "inherent virtues" (89). Like Dickens, Brontë, and Christina Rossetti, Ruskin views physical appearance as a corporealization of one's "inner" beauty, so that an unattractive, ugly shape offers evidence of a girl's unvirtuous character.

The key quality that contributes to a girl's character and shape, for Ruskin, is her orderliness. Order is at the moral center of *Ethics*. The "nasty ugly" (164) crystal's flaw is its chaotic nature, the fact that it is in "such horrid, horrid disorder" (165). Once again linking girls with crystals, Ruskin writes that "all disorder is horrid, when it is among things that are naturally orderly" (165). In *Ethics*, Ruskin invokes as a model of womanhood the Egyptian goddess Neith, who is able to transform piles of clay into pyramids and snowflakes out of atoms: her power lies in creating order out of disorder, and she thereby exemplifies woman's larger duty to "assist in the ordering . . . of the state" (*Of Queens' Gardens* 95). Orderliness, in the sense of self-regulation, which again and again identifies the good Victorian woman in conduct books, is, as we have seen, also a hallmark of anorexia nervosa, in which the body's disorderliness is contained through the control of food intake. What is important about

Ethics is that Ruskin links the concept of order not simply with a woman's moral duty, but explicitly with the shape of her crystalline body. His emphasis on orderliness suggests, albeit unintentionally, the motivation of the anorexic girl, who sees her body, particularly the growing, maturing body, as a *locus* of disorder.

Besides beauty of shape, Ruskin values a crystal's purity, contending that: "The crystal must be either dirty or clean – and there's an end" (88). In the next sentence, Ruskin specifies that he means cleanliness of "one's hands" and "one's heart" (88), but the word clean, especially in the context of young girls, immediately brings to mind its secondary meaning of chastity and sexual "cleanness." The concept of entirely dirty or clean, however, raises several basic theoretical questions. If to be sexually pure means to be a virgin, how does one interpret adult female sexuality? Is the virtuous married mother still sexually pure, or clean, and if so, what kind of sexual knowledge makes a woman dirty? Does even lawful sexual knowledge pollute? Ruskin conflates his idealization of the child with his distrust of female sexual knowledge. His own life, of course, speaks to Ruskin's deep discomfort with the sexuality of adult women, most notably in his failure to consummate his marriage to Effie Grey and in his hopeless love for Rose La Touche. Pre-sexual girls, however, are easily classified: "clean – and there's an end." Their purity, however, does not make girls unavailable erotically; in fact, it enhances their romantic appeal. Ruskin is keenly aware of the physicality of girls, writing of the "birdies" of Winnington that: "It was beautiful too to see the girls' faces round, their eyes all wet with feeling, and the little coral mouths fixed into little half open gasps."[24] The images of wetness and openness that make this such an erotic description of children underscore Ruskin's preoccupation in *Ethics* with girls climbing on his lap and pressing as closely as possible to him when he speaks, making "themselves into a close circle around me . . . that's to say about two deep, behind & three in front – a cluster of eighteen or twenty altogether."[25] For Ruskin, a girl's purity not only makes her more beautiful, but sanctifies her physicality, making close contact not only permissible but almost sacred. If "purity" is an essential attribute of female beauty, though, maturity must bring with it a fall from the true beauty of the young girl. Ruskin does in fact indicate that growing up threatens to destroy a girl's youthful beauty when he writes that a substance "crystallises as it cools; the more slowly, the more perfectly" (43). He seems to suggest here that early maturation impairs a girl's beauty, implying that the longer a girl can remain a child, the better. The kind of bright, polished crystal that Ruskin admires, without "a flaw in its contour throughout," is an appropriate metaphor only for the smooth and relatively straight body of a girl; during puberty, a girl's awkward developing body more closely develops the "dissolute," "rough-surfaced, jagged" crystal (90) that Ruskin scorns.

Finally, Ruskin's attitude toward the human body in *Ethics* is nothing if not ambiguous. On the one hand, he considers beauty one of a woman's most important traits, an idea that he also proposes in *Of Queens' Gardens*. "Girls ought to like to be seen," the old lecturer of *Ethics* advises his listeners. "Girls should be like daisies; nice and white, with an edge of red, if you look close; making the ground bright wherever they are; knowing simply and quietly that they do it, and are meant to do it, and that it would be very wrong if they didn't do it" (*Ethics* 136–137). Ruskin's admonition corresponds to the rhetoric of Victorian beauty manuals, in which beauty is designated as a peculiarly female virtue, and one that stands women in the same stead as intellect does men. According to Ruskin, girls serve an important ornamental role that, in itself, brings others happiness, and that symbolizes women's wider social roles of ornamenting the home and the state of England.[26] It would be "very wrong," Ruskin warns, for women to reject this ornamental role.

On the other hand, Ruskin engages in a grotesque discussion of the body as crystal, in which he asks the girls to imagine themselves with transparent bodies:

It would not be at all good for you, for instance, whenever you were washing your faces, and braiding your hair, to be thinking of the shapes of the jawbones, and of the cartilage of the nose, and of the jagged sutures of the scalp . . . Still less, to see through a clear glass the daily processes of nourishment and decay . . . Still less if instead of merely inferior and preparatory conditions of structure, as in the skeleton . . . there were actual diseases in the body: ghastly and dreadful. (101–102)

Sharon Weltman has examined this passage in depth, and argues that Ruskin tells the girls "all the wretched truth of their mortal biology. Ironically, they are not bright crystal after all, but flesh and doomed to die."[27] On the one hand, the girls listening to the lecturer's argument might be relieved that their bodies are not crystals, and their biological processes hidden away. However, what is so terrible about the body, finally, is that the body is *not* crystal. Rather, bodies grow old, get horrible diseases, and eventually die, reduced through decay to skulls and bones. The human body, for Ruskin, is finally "ghastly and dreadful," its lovely, ornamental surfaces, its beautiful braids, camouflaging disgusting organs and systems that inevitably collapse. It is worth noting that Ruskin specifies the process of "nourishment" in his description of the crystal body, as though eating symbolizes all the distasteful needs and desires of the body. When Ruskin later explains that the word "wife" derives from the Saxon word for weaver, he distinguishes between house-Wives and house-Moths: "you must either weave men's fortunes, and embroider them; or feed upon, and bring them to decay" (200). Again, Ruskin offers two conflicting visions of woman as ornament and ornamenter, embroidering men's lives, or woman as appetitive body, vampirically feeding upon her husband.[28] Eating, in any case, is figured as gruesome.

Despite the body's fragility, however, Ruskin admired the forms of the Winnington girls. He particularly loved to watch the students dance, informing his father that: "they dance like Dryads. I never saw any dancing at once so finished & so full of life."[29] In his diary entry for 28 December 1885, Ruskin writes of the dances at Winnington as among the "most important" things in his life.[30] Ruskin's vision of girls dancing on the green recalls the flower-wreathed dancing girls, charmingly dressed in mob caps and empire-waist dresses, of his friend Kate Greenaway's wildly popular drawings. Greenaway's illustrations of children were bestsellers in England and America, and on the Continent: *Under the Window*, her 1878 collection of illustrated poems, sold 90,000 copies in England alone. Greenaway was already a well-known artist when Ruskin wrote her for the first time in 1880 and thereby initiated a friendship and correspondence that lasted until his death. Throughout the course of their friendship, he wrote her over five-hundred letters, to which Greenaway responded enthusiastically, sending him perhaps twice that number, often ornamented with drawings of her lithe and langourous girls.

Although Ruskin cherished all the dancing girls of Kate Greenaway's illustrations, he longed and repeatedly requested to see them without their dresses on. At various times in their correspondence, he asked Greenaway to draw children in the nude. Although Ruskin insisted that figure drawing would help Greenaway improve her sense of proportion, his letters suggest that, in addition, he simply took pleasure in representations of child nudity. In one letter to Greenaway, he writes:

As we've got so far as taking off hats, I trust we may in time get to taking off just a little more – say, mittens – and then – perhaps – even – shoes! and (for fairies) even – stockings – And – then . . . Will you (it's all for your own good!) make her stand up, and then draw her for me without her hat – and, without her shoes – (because of her heels) and without her mittens, and without her – frock and its frill? And let me see exactly how tall she is – and how round. It will be so good of and for you – And to and for me.[31]

Ruskin's writing is both restrained and voyeuristic. Engaging in a verbal striptease, he imagines removing a girl's accessories, shoes, and stockings (revealing the normally hidden feet and legs), and finally even her dress. Ruskin's diction indicates a certain reticence about his desires. He qualifies his request with the phrase "I trust we may in time" and three times parenthetically justifies or explains his wishes. The syntax, with its many dashes, suggests Ruskin's struggle between the expression and repression of desire: should he go on? Does he dare ask Greenaway to remove the dress? Ruskin's cousin Joan Severn seems to have glimpsed and recoiled from the sexual implications of the passage, for she penciled a note on the letter that advises Greenaway to "Do nothing of the kind."[32] Greenaway did, in fact, refuse to draw naked girls. While her biographers suggest that Greenaway was merely bored with drawing nudes, a second explanation is that, like Severn, she was uncomfortable with the sexual tone of Ruskin's request.

Ruskin's undisguised attraction to the children in Greenaway's illustrations is tied to his belief in entirely "clean" (*Ethics* 262) girlhood. In *Child-Loving*, James Kincaid theorizes that, in much pedophile literature, "the good child's innocence is figured as shamelessness: like Adam and Eve in the garden, naked and proud of it . . . Modesty, then, is associated with corruption, with the fall. The good child will maintain this innocence, this delightful 'satisfaction' in exposing itself."[33] While Kincaid's analysis most closely matches Carroll's defense of nude photography, it also provides an explanation for the unselfconsciousness of Ruskin's requests to Greenaway. In a lecture on Kate Greenaway that Ruskin presented at Oxford University, he exclaimed, "bursting out like one of the sweet Surrey fountains, all dazzling and pure, you have the radiance and innocence and reinstated infant divinity showered again among the flowers of English meadows by Mrs. Allingham and Kate Greenaway."[34] If children are wholly pure and innocent – even divine – then there cannot possibly be anything corrupt about their nakedness. Propriety therefore rests primarily in the body of the looked-upon rather than merely in the eyes of the looker: to look at a naked adult woman is improper, in certain circumstances, because of the overt sexual potential of her developed body, but to look at a nude child is not. While Carroll and Ruskin were drawn to the innocence of young girls, that innocence ironically served to make girls more beautiful, more "dazzling," than adult women. Carol Mavor writes that:

As both sexual and nonsexual, the body of the little girl marked her as simultaneously different from the male viewer and (according to cultural conventions) lacking the marks of true womanhood. As "pure little girl" she was supposedly nonsexual. Yet given the work of Freud and Foucault, the "cult of the little girl," the artistic treatment of her image, the uneasy law of the period, and so forth, we cannot read her as anything but sexual. She was both woman and not-woman; she played safely and dangerously.[35]

Ruskin's love for young girls clearly underpins his interest in Greenaway's work. His favorite Greenaway book was her illustrated version of Robert Browning's "The Pied Piper of Hamelin," of which he writes, "the Piper is the best book you ever did."[36] In Greenaway's interpretation of Browning's poem, the piper's act of stealing children and confining them in a secret place becomes heroic and loving rather than horrifying. The paradisical garden in which the children play in the book's frontispiece emblematizes the Romantic, upper-class view of childhood as a special time of life during which children should be isolated from the adult world of work and trouble. Greenaway's illustrations thus reenact the piper's kidnapping, segregating children in their own miniature world away from the corrupting power of lazy and dishonest adults. Moreover, the Edenic quality of the garden suggests that the children have reached a heaven of childhood in which maturity will be forever forestalled, in which beautiful children (anticipating Barrie) will never have to grow up. The frontispiece depicts a pastoral scene in which a group of children dance around a blossoming cherry tree, flowers wreathed in their hair. Unlike the stoic children in most of Greenaway's illustrations, these children smile and are portrayed as unequivocally happy. In the front left-hand corner of the painting, the piper sits playing a tune, two little girls embracing him and thereby transforming him from a sinister to a nurturing character. In the background, groups of girls and a few boys dance and lounge about in the grass. Greenaway's portrait depicts a far different scene than that projected by Browning, whose children are swallowed up in a mountain-side and, presumably, trapped in "some subterranean prison."[37] Instead, Greenaway depicts the little lame boy's vision of a land "Where waters gushed and fruit-trees grew, / And flowers put forth a fairer hue, / And everything was strange and new."[38] The reader of the poem knows that the piper's reveries are unreal and function only as a prelude to destruction, but Greenaway de-emphasizes the nightmarish aspects of Browning's poem in favor of a sentimentalized Piper as seen through the eyes of a child.

Greenaway's *Pied Piper* shares with pedophile literature the depiction of "The gentle child [who] lives in a beautiful and tender world, but one that is far away, self-sufficient, and sealed-off. It takes a special invitation to enter."[39] As though beckoning the reader to enter this charming scene, two of the girls leaning on the piper's knee look directly out of the frame at the viewer. The gaze of the children acknowledges their position as the object of the reader's gaze; each girl's passive stare is, as John Berger writes, "a sign of her submission to the owner's [reader's] feelings or demands . . . She is offering up her femininity as the surveyed."[40] By looking, though, and thereby implicitly acknowledging the reader's interest in them, the girls also become, like little Evelyn Hatch in Carroll's most famous nude photograph, aware of their own beauty and feminine appeal, their, in Ruskin's words, "soft eyes and blissful lips."[41]

Can we, however, legitimately discuss Greenaway's illustrations as erotic, or do we thereby risk conflating Ruskin's own love of Greenaway's work, which was surely informed by his romantic fascination with children, with our own? Some historical contextualization is helpful here. Greenaway was far from anomalous in her choice of subjects; many other Victorian paintings and illustrations depict lovely young girls, and some of them clearly contain an erotic element. John Everett Millais's enormously popular 1880 painting "Cherry Ripe," which has been well-discussed in criticism, represents a little girl who is both wholly submissive and yet, as Pamela Tarkin Reis has pointed out, disturbingly sexual in pose. Like Ruskin and Carroll, Millais found the young girl extremely beautiful, writing that: "The only head you could paint to be considered beautiful by everybody would be the face of a little girl about eight years old . . . A child represents beauty more in the abstract . . . I believe that perfect beauty and tender expression alone are compatible and there is undoubtedly the greatest achievement if successful."[42] E. Gertrude Thomson's illustrations of Carroll's poems in the posthumously published *Three Sunsets and Other Poems* depict naked girls as fairies and nymphs in poses – stretched out, supine, or embracing each other – that suggest the traditional poses of women in nude paintings. And, painting a decade after Greenaway, Paul Chabas made a career of portraying beautiful naked young girls bathing themselves in lakes. Bram Dijsktra, who has examined the portrayals of pre-pubescent girls in late nineteenth-century art in detail, writes that some painters:

seem to have come to the conclusion that if woman's grown body soiled the passive purity of her childlike mind, it was better to seek all the positive qualities, all the passive, compliant qualities of woman, in the child itself. The very purity of the child seemed to preclude the threat of a sexual challenge . . . the search for the lineaments of the mother's lost innocence in the features of the child could easily take the form of a rediscovery of the enticements of woman in the physical body of the creature whose mental equal she supposedly already was. As a result, the portrayal of the child in its naked innocence often came to echo the representation of woman in art.[43]

The girl, then, was a substitute – even a superior substitute – for the woman.

My one caveat to Djikstra's persuasive argument is that he rests his analysis upon the notion of some essential "child." The conflation of child and adult in Victorian art that he explores, however, is part of a wider confusion between child and adult in nineteenth-century culture as a whole, particularly in terms of sexual activity: until the Criminal Law Amendment Act of 1885 raised the age of consent to sixteen, the age of consent in Britain was only thirteen years old. In 1861, a man who had intercourse with a child between ten and twelve committed only a misdemeanor, not a felony. It is obvious, from a legal standpoint at least, that thousands of girls and boys – particularly working-class and very poor children – were not considered children in the late twentieth-century Western understanding of the word at all, that they were expected to work, often in horrific circumstances and, often, to be sexually active.

Moreoever, as many critics have pointed out, the pure and innocent child was an ideal reserved for the upper classes. Unlike the half-angels in sentimental Victorian poetry and children's stories, and in Greenaway's work, poor children in Arthur Morrison's *A Child of the Jago* (1896) are un-civilized, bellicose little savages, and the girls "squalid drabs ere they were ripe for the sevenpenny church [fourteen years old]."[44] It was already axiomatic in the nineteenth century that working-class children were sexually promiscuous, if only, as Mayhew and Engels suggest, because of cramped and unsegregated living quarters. In 1882, Ellise Hopkins admitted that: "I fear that there is a great deal more filthy, indecent play, amongst our girls and boys, then we have any idea of."[45] Since working-class children were so often admitted to be sexual, it is not surprising that this acceptance leaked over into the "pure" upper-class child as well: if one child, then why not another?

Greenaway, also, conflates the woman and the child in her illustrations, although it is not absolutely clear whether she models the child upon the woman or the woman on the child. The simple empire-waist, straight dresses in which Greenaway outfits her figures recall the fashions of the Regency period and are very different than the tight-bodiced and sleeved, bustled dresses in vogue during the 1880s, when Greenaway published most of her work. Besides celebrating an idealized, pre-industrial, pastoral world of the kind found in some of Blake's *Songs of Innocence* and in Wordsworth's *Lyrical Ballads*, Greenaway's consciously archaic clothing allows her to elide the differences between girls' and women's bodies that the fashions of her time accentuated. The physical appearance of Greenaway's children change remarkably little as they grow older: whenever Greenaway depicts an adolescent girl or adult woman, her waiflike body is taller but almost identical to the child's in shape. There is little evidence, in most of her female figures, of secondary sexual characteristics like breasts and hips. Her clothing, therefore, posits little distinction between children's and women's bodies except that women are taller and, usually, slimmer. The girl's body, then, becomes the archetypal female body: all signs of the sexual body disappear.

For example, Greenaway's 1890 birthday greeting for John Ruskin, "Many Happy Returns of the Day," depicts three girls, one very young and two pre-pubescent. The three, except for height, appear virtually identical. The same is true when Greenaway draws older girls; even the few mothers in her illustrations, such as the young mothers in "The Pied Piper of Hamelin," do not have bodies that indicate that they ever reached adolescence: even after motherhood, they are really still young girls. By retaining the bodies of girlhood past puberty, Greenaway privileges the pre-pubescent, pre-sexual body both aesthetically (as object of beauty) and symbolically (as emblem of femininity). This emphasis on the pre-pubescent form is significant because, by privileging the body of the girl over the body of the woman, Greenaway, like Ruskin in *The Ethics of the Dust*, implicity privileges the *girl* over the woman, transforming her into the ideal female. It is true, of course, that Greenaway was not obligated to draw voluptuous women. She is certainly not a realist painter, and her sense of proportion is often quite faulty: she often, for example, simply drew dresses and then added feet beneath them without considering the positions of her subjects' legs. However, her work, with its symbolic suspension of maturation, is part of a larger ideology of femininity that presents the girl as the most beautiful and most ideal woman. And, again, this ideology shares with the etiology of the anorexic girl, the idea that the slim girl's body, shaved of its womanly flesh, is more beautiful than the adult woman's body.

In addition, the idealization of girlhood in Greenaway's work goes beyond mere corporeal form. Greenaway's illustration of two young girls sitting in a teacup, entitled "Calm in a Teacup," captures her particular vision of girlhood: even when dancing or playing, her girls are languourous, placid, and reveal very little emotion. Her children are not the rambunctious, argumentative or even woefully sinful children found in much other nineteenth-century children's literature, from Carroll's Alice to Burnett's Mary Lennox, Ewing's Amelia, Rossetti's Flora, and even the mischievous (though wrongheaded) Sherwood children. Rather, quoting the poet Ann Taylor's "For a Naughty Little Girl," which Greenaway illustrated: "My sweet little girl should be cheerful and mild, / And should not be fretful, and cry! / Oh why is this passion? remember, my child, / God sees you, who lives in the sky."[46] Passionlessness and serenity are the keynotes of her drawings.[47] Kincaid has suggested that the gentle child, closely connected to the pure child, is a major "type" of child found in pedophilic literature. Ruskin certainly found the gentleness of her drawings very appealing, responding to the illustration "Calm in a Teacup" with the Wonderland-like wish, "if only I could get imprisoned in the teacup."[48]

Greenaway admitted to finding slender figures more attractive than voluptuous ones, writing to Mrs. Sutton Nelthrope in 1896 that: "I was given the wrong sort of body to live in, I am sure. I ought to have been taller, slimmer, and at any rate passably good looking" (quoted in Spielmann and Layard, *Kate Greenaway* 208). She also kept a notebook in which she preserved sayings that suggest her own profound insecurity about her physical appearance, such as "Beauty unadorned, adorned the most" and "Beauty is but skin deep."[49] The woman who made a career out of drawing beautiful girls, then, felt that she herself was plain and unattractive. One could easily postulate, therefore, that the girls in her drawings are projections of the way that she would have liked to have appeared, had she been born with the right "sort of body." Greenaway may have identified more closely with the old witch riding a broomstick in *Under the Window*, which Ruskin chastised as "mere ugly nonsense" (quoted in Spielmann and Layard, *Kate Greenaway* 109) and which, following Ruskin's advice, Greenaway removed from later editions of the book. Ruskin's hostility toward the witch, combined with his admiration of Greenaway's lovely young women, of course suggests Ruskin's preference for sentimental visions of passive girls over

Greenaway's glimpse of threatening, chaotic womanhood. Since Greenaway once signed an angry letter to her friend Frederick Locker with a
witch on a broomstick – the way, therefore, that she represented herself –
she may well have felt that Ruskin's insistence that she remove the witch
from the book constituted a rejection of her.

Greenaway's relationship with Ruskin, though it provided her with
some mentoring and support, also brought her considerable pain, as
her increasing feelings of love for the older man were rebuffed. In his
biography of Greenaway, Rodney Engen has discussed Greenaway's love
for Ruskin, and his disinterest in her, at length. Though Ruskin, for
example, had suggested that they play a game of "love letters," he then
chides Greenaway that: "I can't write such letters as you would like me
to write . . . I cannot make out why women ever care for men at all!" Two
days later, on 6 November 1883, he adds: "How I wish I could write you
a real love-letter! and to think of all the foolish girls everywhere that get
them . . . and poor Kate Greenaway – not one – only lectures and teasers
and dreadful silences."[50] Her age was, certainly, an issue with Ruskin,
who admitted that "you are mixed child and woman, – and therefore
extremely puzzling to me."[51] It is clear from his ecstatic responses to her
illustrations that Ruskin much preferred children. Despite his disinterest,
however, Greenaway continued to send him illustrations and letters, in
which she begged him to write to her. By essentially using her drawings to
keep Ruskin interested in her, Greenaway, out of her own insecurity and
unhappiness, must have wished that she herself had more in common,
at least in terms of her appearance, with her illustrations.

In a letter to a friend, Lady Maria Ponsonby, Greenaway explains that
art should not be wholly realistic:

I can never define what art really is – in painting, I mean. It isn't realism, it isn't
all imagination, it's a queer giving of something to nature that is possible for
nature to have, but always has not – that's my idea. It's what Burne-Jones does
when he twists those roses all about his people in the Briar Rose. They don't
often grow like that, but they could, and it's a great comfort to like such things,
as least I find it so. (Quoted in Spielmann and Layard, *Kate Greenaway* 209)

Greenaway's own work closely conforms to her artistic ideal. Her children dwell, like Wordsworth's naive children in an agrarian realm far
removed from the troubles of nineteenth-century Britain. This world, in
which Ruskin, piper-like, would have liked to abide, presents the lives of
girls as so calm, so beautiful, so free from despair, that any maturation,

and therefore entry into the adult world, would constitute a fall from grace. No wonder that Ruskin, who idealizes the "simplicity" and "sexual purity" of young girls in *Ethics of the Dust*, loved the captured female forms with which Greenaway populated her drawings. Even here, though, maturation threatens to rob children of their beauty and to make them as uninteresting, physically, as Greenaway herself was to Ruskin; he writes, albeit playfully, of one young girl in a Greenaway drawing, that: "she's just three days and a minute or two too *old* for me." Still, he concludes, "they're all ineffable! – I think you never did a more marvellous piece of Beauty and it's a treasure to me like a caught dream" (quoted in Spielmann and Layard, *Kate Greenaway*, 135).

LEWIS CARROLL'S HUNGRY DREAM-CHILD

Turning from the hundreds of interchangeable girls in Kate Greenaway's drawings to Carroll's Alice is to turn from stillness to frenetic movement. Unlike Greenaway's passive girls, Alice is aggressive, curious, and hungry, three closely interrelated traits. At the trial of the Knave of Hearts, for instance, she greedily eyes the suspect plate of tarts: "they looked so good, that it made Alice quite hungry to look at them – 'I wish they'd get the trial done,' she thought, 'and hand round the refreshments.' "[52] Alice's hunger makes her bold: she rudely nudges her way into the Mad Hatter's tea party (where her hunger is ignored and frustrated) and slices through the plum pudding at the final banquet despite being formally introduced. Alice's enormous appetite clearly and hilariously subverts the conventional Victorian heroine's lack of hunger, and serves to set Carroll apart, among many other reasons, from most Victorian writers of children's literature. However, the problem with appetite, according to the *Alice* books, is that it is always associated with physical change and, symbolically, with a girl's maturation and her concurrent loss of childhood identity. Since maturation and Wonderland are finally incompatible, growth itself becomes frightening and eating undesirable, if not downright grotesque. By linking a disdain for sexual maturation with the consumption of food, Carroll's writing shares qualities with the logic of anorexia nervosa, since the anorexic girl often first rejects food at puberty or at adolescence. For the anorexic girl, and to a milder degree for Carroll, eating becomes a potentially disruptive and dangerous activity. Carroll's writing is therefore a good example of the ways that anorexia becomes a symbolic system in a text that is not directly "about" anorexia.

One of the first things that Alice does in Wonderland is consume. When she sees the bottle with the label "Drink Me" on it, she carefully checks to make sure that it does not contain poison, for:

she had read several nice little stories about children who had got burnt, and eaten up by wild beasts, and other unpleasant things, all because they would not remember the simple rules their friends had taught them . . . and she had never forgotten that, if you drink much from a bottle marked "poison," it is almost certain to disagree with you, sooner or later. (22)

Carroll situates his brilliant skewering of the "awful warning" school of children's literature within the context of eating because, as I have discussed, female appetite is a primary target of many "nice little stories" that aimed to teach children how to behave, and is linked to such emotions as aggression, jealousy, and lust. In "The Little Glutton" (1861), for instance, Helen's aunt secretly poisons a box of chocolates in order to punish her niece for stealing them, a sadistic act never criticized by the story.[53] Alice, apparently, has not read "The Little Glutton," for she eagerly "finished . . . off" the bottle and savors the taste of "cherry-tart, custard, pine-apple, roast turkey, toffy, and hot buttered toast" (22). Unlike most Victorian children's book authors, then, Carroll does not condemn his heroine's enjoyment of eating.

Instead, Carroll juxtaposes Alice to the sisters who, in the Dormouse's tale, live at the bottom of a well and eat only treacle. Elsie, Lacie, and Tillie, with their tiny appetites, are opposed to Alice, "who always took a great interest in questions of eating and drinking" (71), and who informs the Dormouse that the sisters "couldn't have done that . . . They'd have been ill" (71). Elsie, Lacie, and Tillie parody the women so often lauded by Victorian pundits, shut away in their prison-like well/home where they are essentially starved. Treacle, with its secondary meaning of excessive sentimentality, is Carroll's comment on the idealized conception of girls as sweet and gentle darlings of the home; he implies that women are restricted by such ideology, that, at least metaphorically, it makes them "*very* ill" (71). The three sisters also take the sort of polite drawing lessons recommended for middle-class girls. The subjects of their drawings – "mouse-traps, and the moon, and memory, and muchness" (73) – are a strange *mélange* of aggression against their captor (mouse-traps could not have been a pleasant image for the Dormouse, their artist–creator and prisoner), the kind of nostalgic art (moon and memory) that was considered appropriate for female artists, and wish fulfillment (since the girls have no muchness either of food or of freedom). Alice, however, responds angrily to the seemingly benign Dormouse's fantasy of female enclosure and starvation, insisting that: "There's no such thing!" (72) as a treacle well and soon leaving the mad tea party "in great disgust" (73). One can only presume that she experiences pleasure at the sight of the Mad Hatter and the March Hare stuffing the Dormouse into the teapot in an enactment of his own story. Alice's rejection of the Dormouse is akin to her observation that the Bread-and-butter-fly, subsisting on the frugal fare of Victorian women – "Weak tea with cream in it" (153) – always dies. Although Alice's orality is a general sign of her curious and pugnacious personality, in part her appetite signifies Carroll's refusal to contain her within an anorexic conception of femininity. Carroll may have seen enough food refusal to want his heroine to be different, or have seen enough hungry little girls to want to portray a girl's appetite realistically.

To be hungry means to be ferocious. As Nina Auerbach has pointed out, Carroll links Alice's hunger with her aggression, for she "is almost always threatening to the animals of Wonderland."[54] Alice constantly talks about eating other animals: she frightens the swimming mouse by alluding to her cat Dinah and later sings a song about a panther ruthlessly devouring an owl. Similarly, in *Through the Looking Glass,* Carroll relates an incident in which Alice "had really frightened her old nurse by shouting suddenly in her ear, 'Nurse! Do let's pretend that I'm a hungry hyaena, and you're a bone'" (128)! Directed against a maternal figure, Alice's hunger is particularly unfeminine and predatory, demonstrating her fundamentally animal (rather than spiritual) nature. Alice is no ethereal fairy, but a serpent and a hyena whose appetite needs to be fed. The disturbing aspect of hunger – at least for carnivorous little girls – is that it involves victims. Carroll does not depart from the Victorian conflation of appetite and aggression, but he recasts those attributes not as moral failings but as part of the normal makeup of the girl.

Carroll's positive interpretation of girlhood appetite thus represents a significant departure from most Victorian literature for children, and one that makes Carroll something of an anomaly in the field of nineteenth-century children's literature. However, he was not perceived as particularly subversive in his own time. Contemporary reviews of the *Alice* books indicate that, while the novels were considered original, most critics did not find them inexplicable or bizarre. *The Publishers Circular,* for instance, found *Alice in Wonderland* "most original and charming"; the *Reader* called it "a glorious artistic treasure . . . a book to put on one's shelf as an antidote to a fit of blues."[55] *Through the Looking Glass* received similarly glowing reviews. *The Illustrated London News* notes it is "quite as rich in humours whims and fancy, quite as laughable in its queer incidents, as lovable for its pleasant spirit and graceful manner as the wondrous tale of Alice's former adventures underground."[56] "Charming," "glorious," "pleasant," and "graceful" are hardly the words that one would apply to a work that challenges widespread and deeply held assumptions about girlhood. Only Christina Rossetti, by rewriting Alice's gluttony as a sin in *Speaking Likenesses,* seems to have perceived the subversive elements of *Alice,* and even she politely thanked Carroll for "the funny pretty book you have so very kindly sent me."[57] Carroll's books appealed to a large segment of the Victorian reading public (including conservative readers such as Rossetti and Charlotte Yonge) and so it is difficult to view his portrayals of Alice as quite as radical as some critics have assumed.

Balancing his generally positive and good-humoured portrayal of Alice's appetite, Carroll, like Greenaway, symbolically attempts to capture Alice's childhood by placing her in a world in which the normal physiological laws of growth do not apply. In Wonderland, with its lack of linear time, Alice does not have to grow up. *Through the Looking Glass*, a more pessimistic book than *Wonderland*, on the other hand, suggests that Alice's maturation is inevitable and prompted in part by Alice's desire to be a queen. Images of appetite are among both books' most important semiotic signs because Carroll uses them to denigrate the process of maturation. In *Wonderland*, food dramatically changes the size of Alice's body and usually leads to disfigurement: in the rabbit's house, for instance, she sees yet another bottle and muses: "I do hope it'll make me grow large again, for really I'm quite tired of being such a tiny little thing" (39). Alice, expressing a child's desire to grow up, then proceeds to grow to such immense proportions that she fills up the house. Carroll's nightmarish illustration of the scene in *Alice's Adventures Under Ground*, the initial version of *Alice in Wonderland* that Carroll wrote for and presented to Alice Liddell, portrays Alice squeezed claustrophobically in a box, her knees pushed all the way up to her chin: "'I'm grown up now,' she added in a sorrowful tone: 'at least there's no room to grow up any more *here*'" (40). The scene expresses Carroll's belief (already encountered in the Dormouse's tale) that maturation entails imprisonment in the home and that growth is a "sorrowful" occurrence. If maturity and growth are associated with the consumption of food, and if maturation is viewed ambivalently, then appetite necessarily becomes a more ambiguous feeling in the *Alice* books than it first appears to be. Carroll's work underscores the ambivalence about maturing women that Victorian culture shares with the victims of anorexia nervosa: significantly, the best food that Alice finds in Wonderland is the mushroom, which allows her to *control* the changes in her body and, theoretically, can be used to keep her from getting any larger. After telling the Caterpillar that she finds "being so many different sizes in a day . . . very confusing" (47), she discovers that the mushroom on which he sits will allow her to regulate her own growth. After some experimentation, she is able to nibble from both sides of the mushroom and bring herself back to the "right size" (55), and then shrink herself down to a mere nine inches tall. This validation of control again associates Carroll's ideas about girlhood appetite with Ruskin's, and with wider Victorian proscriptions about appetite, as well as with the etiology of anorexia.

At the end of *Through the Looking Glass*, Carroll depicts Alice's maturation, symbolized by the confining crown/marriage band that appears on her head after she jumps over the river (perhaps a menstrual symbol), with unabashed regret and uncharacteristic pathos. Terry Otten argues that "the journey through the looking-glass marks the final passage from a rapidly fading innocence to an assertive self-hood," a movement that, in Blakean fashion, "portrays the consequences of a fall."[58] Carroll's aversion to maturation is well-documented in his letters. In a typical letter to one of his many child-friends, he writes that: "Some children have a most disagreeable way of getting grown-up: I hope you won't do anything of that sort before we meet again."[59] Carroll feared girls' maturation largely because social conventions, personified in his letters as "Mrs. Grundy," restricted his friendships with women; to one friend, he writes that: "I shall keep [your letter] for years and years – till you are old and sign yourself 'yrs truly,' and give me a cold little bow when we meet."[60] Similarly concerned with protocol after gaining her crown, Alice immediately lectures herself "in a severe tone" that "it'll never do for you to be lolling about on the grass like that! Queens have to be dignified, you know" (218). Since Alice begins *Wonderland* by lying in the grass with her sister, her "stiff" (218) behavior in this scene signals the artificiality of womanly decorum. Margaret Homans has argued that Carroll emphasizes the randomness of Alice's queening. Unlike Ruskin, who views "queenliness" as the intrinsic essence of the middle-class woman, Carroll suggests that "to become a queen is to arrive arbitrarily at a certain position that may be designated by a sign such as the crown and spoken of in the conditional."[61] The behavior associated with maturation is, as Homans indicates, false and, like the heavy crown, oppressive.

However, maturation *itself* is, unfortunately, inevitable, making a fleeting childhood more precious. Throughout *Through the Looking Glass*, Alice moves around the chessboard with very little agency or volition: she floats, must run to stay in place, and ends up in places that she never meant to enter, such as the Sheep Shop. "Things flow about so here!" (175), she muses, referring as much to her own movement as to that of the objects on the shelves. The book's chess-game structure highlights the orderliness underneath the seeming disorder of Alice's adventures and underscores, again, the inevitability of Alice's growing up; she has little control over whether or not she will become a queen. James Kincaid interprets Humpty Dumpty's enigmatic comment that, "[w]ith proper assistance, you might have left off at seven" (184) as "[offering] a whole world of help to Alice in remaining a child," but Humpty Dumpty's sly reference to death requires external interference with the life cycle ("One ca'n't [*sic*] help growing older" but "*two* can") and annihilation.[62] The choice offered to Alice is not the rather romantic "whole world of help" that Kincaid posits, but death as a child or death-in-life – expulsion from Wonderland and Looking-Glass land – as an adult.

Carroll may have concluded Alice's story at the moment of maturity because, while he adored the pre-pubescent girl, he could not represent the woman positively in his work. Mature women in the Alice books – particularly the Duchess with her screaming pig-baby and the Queen of Hearts – are grotesque figures associated with death and chaos. In her discussion of Tenniel's illustrations, Nancy Armstrong distinguishes "two kinds of women in Wonderland – pretty little girls who control themselves and hideous women who do not."[63] She points out, also, that Alice "grow[s] up without ruining her figure. For even though her size increases at the story's end, she retains the pre-pubescent shape distinguishing her from the other women in that story."[64] While Armstrong's argument is applicable to parts of *Alice's Adventures in Wonderland*, the end of *Through the Looking-Glass* blurs the distinction between "little girls" and "hideous women." Carroll associates Alice with the two queens throughout the entire last section, particularly at the moment when the two queens take a nap in Alice's lap and the Red Queen croons: "When the feast's over, we'll go the ball – / Red Queen, and White Queen, and Alice, and all" (224). The three women now form a triumvirate: through maturation, Alice has taken her place among the queens and duchesses, or mature women, of the text. Moreover, because Alice is moved across the chessboard without agency, and because the crown is simply popped upon her head, Carroll suggests that she really has no choice but to become a queen.

Although Carroll permits Alice freedom of language and appetite as a child, these same qualities become repulsive in womanhood. Alice's propensity to speak her mind, for instance, is exaggerated by the adult Queen of Hearts, who "shouted" and "roared" (78) as evidence of her maniacal aggression. Likewise, the chaotic scene in the Duchess's kitchen suggests that adult appetite, unlike Alice's hunger, is repellent. After taking a cauldron of soup off the fire, the Cook explodes in a fit of violence against the Duchess and her child. Here, Carroll depicts adult women's appetite unfavorably because it threatens Alice; once Alice becomes a queen, however, Carroll also refigures *her* hunger negatively. The final banquet, which celebrates Alice's rite of passage into adulthood, is one of the book's most ambiguous scenes. Like the sadistic walrus and carpenter, Alice turns to eat her own guests, slicing off a piece of the plum pudding, who angrily retorts, "What impertinence! . . . I wonder how you'd like it, if I were to cut a slice out of you, you creature!" (201). Food becomes animated and humans become food: the leg of mutton takes the chair of the White Queen and the White Queen dissolves into soup. "Alice turned again," Carroll writes, "just in time to see the Queen's broad good-natured face grinning at her for a moment over the edge of the tureen, before she disappeared into the soup" (231). Alice panics, realizing that "[t]here was not a moment to be lost" (231) before all distinctions between eater and eaten disappear. Already, the soup-ladle ominously works its way to Alice's chair, suggesting that she, too, will be devoured. The processes of natural selection and survival of the fittest to which Carroll has alluded throughout the books now threaten to overwhelm Alice. "I can't stand this any longer!" (231) she screams, ripping the cloth from the table and exorcising looking-glass land.

Where, in this scene, do Carroll's sympathies lie? Are they with Alice, suddenly turned upon by the creatures who should serve and nourish her? Or does Carroll turn upon Alice because, as a woman, she has become threatening to the world of Wonderland? The outbreak of mayhem at the banquet occurs directly after Alice finds herself lifted in the air – "she really did rise as she spoke, several inches" (231) – a symbolic growth spurt that initiates "dreadful confusion" (231). In her work on anorexia nervosa, Susan Bordo writes that: "the body is the *locus* of all that which threatens our attempts at control. It overtakes, it overwhelms, it erupts and disrupts" (145). The newly grown-up Alice now takes her place with other disruptive females, and Carroll expels her from Wonderland and from the text. A child's aggression and a woman's aggression are perceived differently in the novel, and, while the former is acceptable, even positive, the latter is not. In the final scene, female power is subjugated to male power. The scene begins with a moment of phallic assertion as "[t]he candles all grew up to the ceiling, looking something like a bed of rushes with fireworks at the top" (231) and ends when the Red Queen "suddenly dwindled down to the size of a little doll" (231), her threat miniaturized and made comic. All three of the queens are contained: the White Queen melts, the Red Queen turns into a harmless kitten, and Alice leaves Wonderland forever.

The extravagance and humor of Alice's appetite notwithstanding, Carroll does not completely escape anorexic logic in the *Alice* books. Hunger emblematizes growth, and since maturity and sexual desire are presented negatively, then hunger must ultimately be a negative sign as well. It is not surprising, therefore, that the apocalyptical last scene takes place at a feast. In the final banquet scene, hunger becomes grotesque *because* it is associated with the celebration of Alice's maturity. Once she becomes a queen, Carroll responds to her bold appetite with a mutiny of food and dinnerware. Additionally, Carroll suggests (perhaps somewhat sadly) that Alice, because she is now a sexual being, has become food, an object to be consumed, and must be erased from the text. Denigrating the sexual woman in favor of the pre-sexual girl, and representing appetite differently for the girl and for the woman, Carroll's *Alice* books thus share in the discomfort with female appetite found in so much Victorian children's literature, despite Carroll's enthusiasm for some of the qualities that it symbolizes.

Carroll's own life demonstrates his often contradictory ideas about appetite. His nephew Stuart Dodgson Collingwood writes that "the healthy appetites of [Carroll's] young friends filled him with wonder, and even with alarm."[65] On the other hand, Carroll's own description of the food that he planned for a child's dinner included "two courses, meat and sweets."[66] A similar contradiction informs Carroll's abstemious eating habits – he skipped midday meals and kept detailed journals of his meals – and the following joking letter that he wrote to a young friend:

And what do you think I am going to have for my birthday treat? A *whole plum-pudding!* It is to be about the size for four people to eat: and I shall eat it in my room, all by myself! The doctor says he is "afraid I shall be ill": but I simply say "*Nonsense.*" (Letters 451–452).[67]

The last word of Carroll's letter – "Nonsense" – is perhaps one way out of the contradiction, namely that Carroll could view appetite positively only within the boundaries of nonsense and fantasy. Stephen Prickett has explained that, "so far from being 'free' or formless, [nonsense] is the most highly organized and, in many ways, the most rigidly controlled of all forms of fantasy."[68] Within the logical framework of nonsense, then, Carroll is able to manipulate and control Alice's hunger and growth in ways that he obviously could not manipulate girls' bodies in his own life.

In the garden of live flowers, the Rose informs Alice that: "You're beginning to fade, you know – and then one ca'n't [*sic*] help one's petals getting a little untidy" (140). The Rose speaks for Carroll, who suggests that as Alice moves closer to the brook, she begins to lose her girlish beauty and approaches the "untidiness" of adult sexuality. In a letter to the artist A. B. Frost, Carroll admits that: "I had rather not have an adult figure (which always looks to me rather in need of drapery): a girl of about 12 is my ideal of beauty *in form*.[69] Like Ruskin, Carroll finds girls' bodies most beautiful when they are poised on the cusp of maturity, their youthful beauty at its most vivid before, like the dream rushes that Alice frantically tries to pick, being forever lost. In his photography, and in Greenaway's drawings and paintings, both artists attempted to freeze – or crystallize, to use Ruskin's metaphor – girls before maturity diminished their fleeting beauty.

At first glance, the letters to the *GOP* about weight and body size may have little in common with such disparate texts as girls' birthday books, Ruskin's *The Ethics of the Dust*, Greenaway's illustrations, and the two *Alice* books. As I have indicated, these texts do differ in significant ways; for example, Carroll grants girls far more latitude in their hunger than does most Victorian literature for children, with its disproportionate emphasis on the denial of appetite. However, by addressing weight concerns among adolescent girls, the letters attest to a culture in which fatness, and, by extension, appetite, were widely represented as undesirable in girls. If eating heartily is connected to greed and aggression, then fat itself becomes a sign of badness, while the small appetite, especially in a girl, signifies self-control, docility, and goodness. Through literature written specifically for them, then, children were explicitly taught the importance of restraining their appetites as an aspect of gender performance. In this sense, Ruskin's *The Ethics of the Dust* and much popular children's literature are surprisingly closely allied. Relatedly, the cultural validation of the "pure" non-sexual woman found its way into children's literature through the cult of childhood innocence, which is connected to the slender body insofar as such an ideology turns the child into the ideal woman and therefore makes the child's body more beautiful than the sexual adult body. Here, Greenaway's work intersects with both Ruskin's and Carroll's. Because maturity was generally thought of as a treacherous time in a girl's life, menarche making a girl particularly vulnerable to mental and emotional disturbance, and because adolescence often brought with it increased restrictions on a girl's life, it is no surprise that self-control would be so much emphasized in literature for children. The letters to the *GOP*, when contextualized within nineteenth-century children's literature and culture, suggest that one reason for girls' dislike of their plumpness is that fat was already being viewed as a moral weakness which girls and women should eliminate in any possible way.

CHAPTER 3

Hunger and repression in Shirley *and* Villette

Although they wrote as contemporaries, Charlotte Brontë and Charles Dickens never met, nor did they hold high opinions of each other's work. Brontë enjoyed *David Copperfield,* but she criticized those portions of *Bleak House* narrated by Esther as "too often weak and twaddling."[1] Even her compliments of Dickens are noticeably strained. When commenting on *David Copperfield,* she only commends Dickens for his "varied knowledge of men and things," tepid praise when juxtaposed with her summation of Goëthe, in the same paragraph, as "Great, powerful, giant-souled" (*Correspondence* III: 20).[2] Dickens was even less enthusiastic about Brontë, reportedly announcing in 1860 that "he had not read *Jane Eyre* and . . . never would as he disapproved of the whole school."[3] Probably, like so many other Victorian readers, Dickens would have found the character of Jane coarse and vulgar and would have distinguished his own more rarefied and conventional heroines from those of Brontë's "school." Despite the many differences between Dickens's and Brontë's novels, however, the two authors share a proclivity for slender female heroines that runs throughout both of their works: Jane Eyre, Frances Henri, Caroline Helston, and Lucy Snowe have the same slim, contourless bodies as do Agnes Copperfield, Rose Maylie, Mary Graham, and Amy Dorritt, to name only a few.

Dickens typically employs the slender female body as a marker of his heroines' selflessness and lack of sensuality, going so far as to sentimentalize hunger and starvation. This sentimentalization of hunger is precisely where Brontë's images of slenderness depart from his. In Brontë's work, hunger is always painful. Moreover, women's lack of appetite (or inability to eat) is not an innate sign of feminine "nature," as it is in Dickens's work, but represents in large part a criticism of women's social roles, most specifically women's inability, because of constructions of femininity, to speak their desires. Unlike Dickens's heroines, who do not eat because they do not have appetites, Brontë's heroines have desires but learn to repress them: the narrator of *Shirley*, advising Caroline Helstone on "sealing the lips," conflates silence, starvation, and sexual repression within one image.[4] In Brontë's novels, the fasting body is always a physical presence in the text; it is never, like Agnes's, absent or, like Nell's, erased.

Although repression and starvation are painful, however, Brontë's work resembles Dickens's in that Brontë does not go so far as to validate appetite unequivocally. Rather, she repeatedly favors suffering over the easy pleasures of appetite and dissolute sexuality. Since repression is signified by starvation, then it should come as no surprise that the licentious women in Brontë's novels – Bertha Mason, Blanche Ingram, Ginevra Fanshawe – are all plump. Brontë's negative representations of the corpulent female body demonstrate her ambiguous and complicated position toward women's desires and her qualified acceptance of the Victorian aesthetic ideal of the slim woman.

DICKENS AND FEMALE HUNGER

Gail Houston and Patricia Ingham have written at length about Dickens and women's hunger, precluding a protracted discussion here; nevertheless, a brief introduction to Dickens's poetics of anorexia provides an excellent foil for Brontë's work because the two authors' semiotics, though they involve the same slim bodies, are finally incompatible. As I have just noted, throughout his work, Dickens sentimentalizes women's hunger, depicting the "feminine" woman as naturally abstemious. At the same time, like the good girl in Victorian children's literature, she is obsessively concerned with feeding others: we rarely see the Dickens heroine eating, but she presides over meals and tea and her ability to do so is one mark of her correct adherence to gender roles. The fat female body in a Dickens novel either corporealizes the comic grotesque of a Mrs. Gamp – whose girth also suggests an earthy sexuality – or a maternal type like Peggotty, bursting buttons in extravagant love for her adopted child. The young Dickens heroine, however, is never fat, and her lack of appetite suggests an absence of sexual desire and, more generally, her overall selflessness.

Agnes Wickfield and Little Nell are two of Dickens's most widely known (and widely derided) heroines, and both are models of abstentious eating. Agnes, once sneeringly dismissed by Orwell as a "legless angel," is often considered one of Dickens's least successful creations.[5] David Copperfield never describes Agnes's body, focusing instead on her voice and on her "beautiful serene eyes," but from the moment that he sees her, David associates Agnes with "the soft light of the coloured window in the church."[6] Of course, David's association of Agnes with a stained-glass window underscores her position as angel in the house, making the places in which she moves "sacred" (632) with her quiet, modest, nurturing demeanor. However, the window is also an emblem of Agnes's body itself, transparent because unrepresented; David sees through Agnes's body (in a way that he never sees through Dora's) and, consequently, the reader does not "see" her body at all.[7] Michael Slater writes, of Dickens's heroines, that "the domestic ideal cancels out their sexuality."[8] Agnes's bodilessness, along with the keys jingling at her invisible waist, emblematize her role as David's spiritual sister, guiding star, and domestic angel, but precludes her from being viewed, at least by the reader, as passionate wife. Because she has no body, Agnes necessarily has no appetite. Though she serves tea to others, we never observe her eating, and this in a novel in which food, especially for the young David, plays a very conspicuous role. David describes his desire for food – between the expensive and inexpensive puddings, for instance – in great detail, but ladies' (as opposed to women's) appetites in Dickens remain unwritten.

Whereas Agnes is middle class, Nell is poor, so the reader might expect her fasting to derive directly from her poverty. Gail Houston, however, has correctly called Nell "self-starved"; the phrase is important because, despite her poverty, Nell's starvation is a function of her hungerlessness rather than her pennilessness.[9] Over and over again, Dickens points out Nell's lack of appetite. Fleeing London with her grandfather, Nell "had no thought of hunger or cold, or thirst, or suffering."[10] She is sometimes too exhausted to eat, but even when she experiences hunger, she first offers her portion of food to others, whether "selecting [the] best fragments for her grandfather" (178) or proffering her meal to a hungry circus dog. By the end of the journey, Nell has developed "[a] loathing of food [which] prevented her partaking even of this poor repast" (426). Nell abstains from food, then, not merely because of poverty and lack of sustenance (her grandfather continues to eat "greedily" [426]) but because appetite is alien to her nature.

Dickens is contradictory about Nell's size in the beginning of the novel. Quilp describes her as "chubby, rosy, cosy, little Nell" (125), clearly linking her attractiveness to her plumpness and therefore reinforcing the link between fat and sexual availability. However, Master Humphrey calls her "slight" (55) and Dick Swiveller dismisses her as: "Fine girl for her age, but small" (103). She is, as Master Humphrey has noted, "so spiritual, so slight and fairy-like a creature" (55), an incorporeality underscored by her lack of hunger and born out in the novel by her eventual death. Houston and James Kincaid argue that Nell's starvation and death result from Dickens's desire to prevent Nell's imminent sexual maturity, for despite her small size, Nell is fourteen years old and already an object of desire for both Kit and Quilp.[11] Death saves her from maturation and sexual violation, leaving her "tranquil" (654) child's beauty unchanged. Dickens's biographer John Forster writes, of Dickens's decision that Nell should die, that:

He had not thought of killing her when, about half-way through, I asked him to consider whether it did not necessarily belong even to his own conception, after taking so mere a child through such a tragedy of sorrow, to lift her also out of the commonplace of ordinary happy endings, so that the gentle *pure little figure and form* should never change to the fancy.[12]

It would, of course, be reductive to suggest that Dickens kills Nell because he does not want to envision, or even allow, the maturation of her body from "pure" and "little" to womanly and, presumably, sexually mature. However, Forster's association of innocent childhood with a child's "figure and form," the precise shape of her body, suggests that the woman's body, no longer marked by littleness, is less beautiful than the child's body. The death of the pre-sexual child is better, more satisfying, than the "ordinary happy ending" of the romance plot that would conclude with Nell's growth and eventual marriage.

Dickens does not precisely name the cause of Nell's death, but after her long journey she "is perishing of want" (429) and never fully regains her strength. She has, essentially, starved to death. Throughout the novel, Dickens views this starvation sentimentally, as evidence of Nell's remarkable selflessness. After waking up from her swoon at the schoolmaster's feet, for instance, she thanks her rescuer because, had she died, "[her grandfather] would have been left alone" (434). Even in her weakest moments, when her "pale face and wasted figure" (434) bring tears to the gentle schoolmaster's eyes, Nell's thoughts are primarily with her grandfather. Her "wasted figure" highlights her position as tragic but heroic figure of child–womanhood: she has entirely neglected her body in her effort to bring her grandfather to safety and to keep their little family together. Dickens, then, uses Nell's body as a sentimental prop within his ideology of self-sacrificing female love. Her death, one of the most mawkish in Dickens's work, deifies the starved female body by comparing the night of Nell's death to the night of the birth of Christ, complete with the resonant hymnal phrase "solemn stillness" (652).

Of course, one could argue that Dickens employs sentiment in his depiction of Nell's death in order to heighten the power of the event for the reader over and above the emotional power of realistic characterization; as is well known, little Nell's death profoundly affected members of the Victorian reading public. Dickens himself found the writing of the deathbed scene extraordinarily painful and, in an odd reversal of the plot of *The Old Curiosity Shop*, confessed to feeling "pursued by the child" as he neared the dreaded narration of her death.[13] He had conceived of Nell's death as a way to comfort those members of the reading public who had lost loved ones, explaining that: "I resolved to try and do something which might be read by people about whom Death had been, – with a softened feeling, and with consolation" (*Letters* 188).[14] For that reason, he asked the illustrator George Cattermole to depict Nell in "the most beautiful repose and tranquillity, and to have something of a happy look, if death can" (*Letters* 172).[15] In his study of Victorian sentimentality, Fred Kaplan explains that sentiment allowed Dickens to personify moral virtues through idealized character types and thereby to "arouse his readers' innate moral sentiments, reminding them that the more emotionally sensitive they are to death the more morally attentive they will be to the values of life."[16] Nevertheless, Nell's moral type – that of the all-loving and self-sacrificing woman – is inscribed upon a wasted body. Her body becomes the symbol of her femininity so that, in Dickens's poetics of anorexia, her starved body on its deathbed is beautiful; it *must* be beautiful if it is to represent those traits that Nell embodies. At the same time, Nell's starvation is erased from her body once she dies and becomes an image of "peace and perfect happiness . . . tranquil beauty and profound repose" (654). Dickens no longer needs starvation as an emblem of Nell's selflessness once her self has been extinguished by death.

SHIRLEY: GENDER, CLASS, AND THE STARVING BODY

[T]he first dish set upon the table shall be one that a Catholic – ay, even an Anglo-Catholic – might eat on Good Friday in Passion Week: it shall be cold lentils and vinegar without oil; it shall be unleavened bread with bitter herbs, and no roast lamb.[17]

Like Dickens's works, Brontë's novels emphasize food, and how much is consumed, in detail. *Shirley*, for example, begins with the portrayal of three curates greedily devouring dinner:

The curates had good appetites, and though the beef was "tough," they ate a great deal of it. They swallowed, too, a tolerable allowance of the "flat beer," while a dish of Yorkshire pudding, and two tureens of vegetables, disappeared like leaves before locusts. The cheese, too, received distinguished marks of their attention; and a "spice-cake," which followed by way of dessert, vanished like a vision, and was no more found. (5–6)

In addition to underscoring the clergy's selfishness and lack of restraint, the curates' dinner establishes the gender and class dynamics of the novel: *Shirley* is a novel in which men consume and women – or feminized, working-class men – are consumed. Both Caroline and Shirley undergo starvation and, like the food that the curates eat, begin literally to "disappear" and "vanish" in the course of the novel. By not eating, they are themselves consumed by the men who ostensibly love them. Brontë thus suggests that Caroline and Shirley's disordered eating proceeds in large part from their emotionally destructive romantic relationships. Caroline, suffering under Robert's indifference, and Shirley, repressing her autonomy in order to become Louis's wife, cease to eat and are thereby metaphorically devoured by the men they love. In love, Brontë suggests, women are consumed like so much roast-beef and spice cake. Eating is, however, not only a gender privilege, but a class privilege as well. Because Shirley initially enjoys far more economic autonomy than Caroline, the two women's starvation does not proceed identically; at times, Shirley's appetite allies her more with the men in the novel than with her friend Caroline. In elucidating the power dynamics between her characters, Brontë repeatedly uses detailed food and eating imagery to illustrate the enmeshment of gender and class, so that in the rapidly industrializing culture that she depicts, eating symbolizes the political, economic, and social oppression of both women and the working classes by educated, upwardly mobile people who are largely, but not exclusively, male.

Because the curates eat gluttonously in the opening scene, Brontë likens them to "locusts . . . thick on the hills" (3), the biblical archetype of the destructive insect. The chapter, appropriately titled "Levitical," associates the greedy consumption of food with obnoxious, boorish behavior in general, and, more specifically, with the industrial destruction of the landscape that the characters in *Shirley* witness throughout the novel. Brontë does not immediately juxtapose the negative depiction of eating in the chapter to a portrayal of "good" consumption, only to its opposite in the hungry wailing of Abraham Gale. In a world of limited resources, when one person eats, Brontë suggests, another person does not.

The curates eat without consideration for little Abraham's hunger. Their consumption, rather, is totally individualistic and egotistical, since they are concerned only with their own personal appetites rather than with the appetites, or needs, of the community. How, Brontë seems to ask, can one trust one's soul to curates who have no concern for the hungry bodies of society's most vulnerable members, its children? Brontë later contrasts the curates' meal to the generous allowance of currant-buns and tea given to children during the school feast. Here, eating is shared among a community, is given unselfishly, and, because the children eat at a religious festival, symbolizes the ideal fusion of soul and body. Brontë distinguishes, then, between shared eating and individualistic eating, between exploitative eating and nurturant eating. Gilbert and Gubar, who have discussed hunger in *Shirley*, astutely claim that because Brontë links food with the curates, Caroline and Shirley's later self-starvation "reflects male hatred of the female and fear of her sustaining or strengthening herself."[18] I would add that starvation reflects the hatred of the "haves" for the "have-nots." Eating, particularly who eats and who does not, emblematizes who has economic and social power and who does not. Women and working-class men, who have less power, are rarely satiated: they either starve themselves or are starved by others. Middle-class and affluent men, on the other hand, satisfy their hunger and feel little anxiety about food. Discussing Virginia Woolf's *Jacob's Room*, Allie Glenny has written that, in Woolf's work, "domination continues to be enacted through control over the food supply, and subordination effected through starvation."[19] The same dynamic is at work in *Shirley*. Although the curates are not wealthy, they are educated, professional, and socially respected, and Donne and Sweeting, by the end of the novel, have become quite affluent. Their eating thus signals their social status. Perhaps most fundamentally, Brontë, as narrator, expresses a disgust with appetite in the novel's opening scene that reverberates throughout both *Shirley* and *Villette*. While Brontë associates gluttony with middle-class men and condemns it throughout the novel, starvation (though not romanticized, as it is in Dickens) does not register equal moral disgust.

One question that comes to mind during an analysis of hunger in *Shirley* is whether Caroline Helstone is anorexic. She begins the novel as one of Brontë's only pretty heroines, a young woman with a shape "girlish, light, and pliant; every curve was neat, every limb proportionate" (56). However, her disappointed love for her cousin Robert Moore changes her from a hopeful, healthy girl to a depressed and alarmingly thin invalid. After Robert perversely changes overnight from warm and "lover-like" to merely "brother-like, friend-like" (79), Brontë intrudes into the narrative with the injunction: "You expected bread and you have got a stone: break your teeth on it, and don't shriek because the nerves are martyrised; do not doubt that your mental stomach – if you have such a thing – is strong as an ostrich's; the stone will digest" (79). The repression of love and desire and the repression of hunger, Brontë implies, fall along the same continuum of denied appetite: to refuse to eat is to corporealize sexual and emotional repression. As the passage demonstrates, Caroline does not suffer merely as a result of Robert's fickle attentions, but because of her inability to express anger or sadness at his capricious temperament, for "a feminine lover can say nothing" (79) without losing her self-respect and the respect of her lover. Caroline's illness, Athena Vrettos has noted, "arises out of a cultural demand for feminine quiescence."[20] Since repression consists of the inability to voice one's desires, and since women must necessarily keep silent if they are to be considered feminine, hunger (another repression of desire) becomes a peculiarly female state. Caroline's stomach, which can take in and digest even a rock, is akin to her mind, which will overcome the disappointment of Robert's rejection. Brontë's tone suggests that a woman should be proud of her ability to repress, because that ability suggests her inner strength, the fact that she is strong enough to silently crush a rock. There is, after all, strength in martyrdom, and, according to Brontë, strength in renunciation. Moreover, what choice does Caroline have but to submit to her fate?

"Sealing the lips" (79), then, refers not only to Caroline's silence in the face of Robert's cruel rejection but to her subsequent self-starvation, which Brontë describes in painful detail. When Caroline asks her uncle Helstone for permission to find employment as a governess, he notes for the first time that her "bloom had vanished, flesh wasted; she sat before him drooping, colourless, and thin" (144). Her change from "rose" to "mere snowdrop" reveals her starvation's roots in the denial of her love for Robert: from a full summer blossom that signifies passionate love, she has turned into a tiny, pale flower that blooms in the snow. Rather than trying to understand the cause of his niece's illness, however, Helstone cavalierly suggests that she cheer herself up by buying a new dress, at the same time expounding on the ridiculous nature of women:

Today you see them bouncing, buxom, red as cherries, and round as apples; tomorrow they exhibit themselves effete as dead weeds, blanched and broken down. And the reason of it all? That's the puzzle. She has her meals, her liberty, a good house to live in, and good clothes to wear, as usual. A while since that sufficed to keep her handsome and cheery, and there she sits now a poor, little pale, puling chit enough. Provoking! (145)

The ideal woman, for a man like Helstone, is an object to be devoured, an apple or a cherry, much like Nell is for the despicable Quilp. He understands a woman's roundness not as symbolic of lack of control (Caroline is not, after all, obese or stocky, but "light," "neat," and "proportionate"), but as symbolic of contentment, domesticity, and femininity. Caroline's "meals," like her "good house" and "good clothes," indicate her class privilege, so that her refusal to eat signifies a rejection of her bourgeois social position. The material perks that Helstone bestows upon Caroline no longer "suffice" to give her life meaning. Again, Brontë associates the act of consumption with men and, more explicitly than in the opening scene, the object to be consumed with women. The reader knows that Helstone has already metaphorically consumed his own wife, Mary Cave, who declines as a result of his neglect until she is only a "still, beautiful-featured mould of clay left, cold and white, in the conjugal couch" (39). Like Caroline, Mary Cave becomes a snowdrop, "cold and white," as if Helstone had vampirishly drained her of blood as well as life. Moreover, her last name suggests hollowness, both mentally/emotionally and physically. The phrase "conjugal couch" is particularly resonant, suggesting that Mary is the victim of Helstone's purely sexual love, consumed like fruit and afterwards rendered insignificant. Like Caroline, Mary is a silent woman whose silence masks despair, but, unlike Caroline, her anguish eventually kills her. She dies a lovely mold – or "cave" – after her metaphorical starvation in marriage.

Helstone prefers a round woman who feels content with her circumscribed life, her "good house" and "good clothes." He expresses contempt, on the other hand, for Caroline's thin body, dismissing her as "provoking" because she upsets the smooth and established grooves of his life, in which women play the role of cheerful decorative objects; her depression is as unfeminine to Helstone as her wasted body. The phrase "exhibit themselves," with its suggestion that Caroline is merely showing off, also indicates that Helstone considers her change of appearance and temperament a feminine caprice. He echoes, here, those Victorian physicians and commentators who blamed women's self-starvation or disorderly eating on a stubborn, needy temperament, what physician John Ogle called "a morbid indulgence of temper and desire for sympathy and attention."[21] Contrary to Helstone's insinuations, though, Caroline's renunciation of food, along with her unhappiness in his poem, signal her resistance to his traditional conception of femininity. Not eating disrupts the routine patterns of behavior that Caroline, as a woman, is expected to maintain, signaling her unhappiness within those routines. At the same time though, as Mary Cave's death demonstrates, such starvation is ultimately self-destructive and ineffective.

It is thus tempting to view Caroline's disordered eating as an act of rebellion against social constraints, an attempt to "provoke" Helstone into letting her do what she wants. Critics have read Caroline's behavior as a sort of proto-feminist rebellion. Gilbert and Gubar, for instance, interpret her starvation as a "hunger strike" and "kind of protest . . . against growing up female," claiming that "Caroline has good reason to believe that the only control she can exert is over her own body, since she is completely ineffectual at altering her intolerable lot in the world."[22] Similarly, in her important essay on hunger in *Shirley*, Deirdre Lashgari writes that:

Caroline and Shirley have both struggled against gender roles and relationships that are "killing" them. When each in turn finds herself blocked from any effective overt protest and barred from speaking her pain, she asserts control over her life in the only arena available, inscribing her hunger on her own body in a desperate plea to be "read aright."[23]

We know that Brontë was familiar with the uses of the hunger strike from her own life. Around Christmas 1836, the Brontës' servant Tabby fractured her leg in a fall; the sisters refused to eat until their Aunt Branwell allowed them to nurse the elderly woman back to health.[24] It seems at first reading that Caroline's refusal to eat is just such a conscious decision. Seeing her friend's illness, for example, Shirley begs Caroline to: "Eat something – you eat nothing. Laugh and be cheerful, and stay at home" (181). Shirley, like Helstone, associates food with domestic contentment and complacency. Ironically, of course, staying at home and masquerading as the laughing, cheerful hostess only contribute to Caroline's sickness. Caroline clearly resents her confinement in her uncle's home when she wants a profession to give her life some purpose and to answer her desperate question: "What was I created for, I wonder? Where is my place in the world?" (133).

Ultimately, though, a casting of Caroline's hunger as conscious rebellion exaggerates her subversiveness by conflating disease with social protest. Rather, Caroline can be read as a figure of anorexia because her starvation enacts the same feminine self-renunciation that keeps her imprisoned in the first place. An interpretation of her hunger can thus take into account Caroline's desire for control over her life, a cardinal aspect of anorexia nervosa, without turning her into an emblem of overt rebellion; self-denial, not protest, is at the heart of her fasting. Though she feels frustration and anger over the lack of opportunities in her life, Caroline does not *set out* to starve herself in order to make a political point, to achieve a specific goal, or even to draw attention to her dissatisfaction. When Helstone refuses to allow her to become a governess, Caroline keeps starving in silence, "keeping her pale face and wasted figure as much out of sight as she could" (147). Unlike the goal-oriented or political hunger strike, with which Brontë was personally familiar, Caroline's fasting is seemingly out of her control. She "missed all sense of appetite. Palatable food was as ashes and sawdust to her" (311). When Mrs. Pryor tries to feed her during her breakdown, Caroline insists that: "I cannot eat" (313). At her recovery, the narrator writes that: "All descriptions of food were no longer equally distasteful; she could be induced, sometimes, to indicate a preference" (329). Her hunger is more disease than public protest, and Caroline does not consciously "choose" food refusal.

Susan Bordo writes that "[a]norexia could . . . be seen as an extreme development of the capacity for self-denial and the repression of desire," while Marilyn Lawrence, who has connected anorexia nervosa to asceticism, argues that self-denial is particularly important for women because they have traditionally been viewed as "more inherently prone to badness and moral weakness."[25] Since women have, in Judeo-Christian culture, been considered more physical, more "embodied" than men have, it has been particularly important for them to discipline their bodies. Fasting has historically been one means for doing so, as I will discuss in the context of Christina Rossetti's work. More specifically, self-denial, and particularly control of one's sexuality, was closely tied to feminine virtue in the nineteenth century. Anorexia nervosa thus represents, as pathology, the self-denial enshrined within the Victorian ideology of femininity. Self-denial also lies at the heart of Caroline's fasting. "Is there not a terrible hollowness, mockery, want, craving, in that existence which is given away to others, for want of something of your own to bestow it on" (133), Caroline asks herself, clearly associating the repression of her life with starvation through images of "hollowness," "want," and "craving." Although she hungers, desires, and has emotional appetites, Caroline's life has been rendered as "hollow" as a starving woman's body. Her self-denial takes several forms (including the forced repression of her desire to leave home), but much of the self-denial associated with Caroline's hunger is sexual and affectional. After the narrator informs the reader that Caroline "wasted, grew more joyless and more wan," we learn that "her memory kept harping on the name of Robert Moore" (141).

Significantly, this passage occurs at the close of the chapter in which Caroline visits the "spinsters" Miss Mann and Miss Ainley, the two figures associated with the most rigorous self-denial in the novel and both connected with the wasting of the body. Miss Mann, for instance, "exercised rigid self-denial" and simultaneously endures "slow-wasting... sufferings" that leave her "corpse-like" (137). She is "extenuated" and both metaphorically and physically "ahungered and athirst to famine" (138). The second "old maid," Miss Ainley, "talked never of herself, always of others" and "straitened herself to privation" (139). Because they are single women, these spinsters are meant, like the nun in *Villette*, to symbolize sexual and emotional repression and thus the larger repression of the female self within patriarchy. Through images of "slow-wasting" hunger, Brontë links that repression to Caroline's starvation and provides an image of what Caroline might become both physically and emotionally. Miss Mann's self-control brings to mind Caroline's day-to-day repression, while Miss Ainley, like Caroline, has given herself away to the degree that there is nothing left for herself. In the context of the novel's eating imagery, Miss Mann and Miss Ainley function as foils to the curates. While the curates are all appetite, the two women are all refusal. While the curates eat selfishly, the older women are selfless to the point of self-destruction. Eating and not eating are, in Brontë's vision, gendered activities that signify the curates' and women's respective social positions. Educated, professionally respectable, and members of the more powerful gender, the curates assert their right to eat what and when they want. Spinsters, or redundant women, on the other hand, can make no claim for nourishment, either literal or metaphorical. However, neither group offers an admirable model of behavior. The curates are, of course, selfish and rude, while the women, whom Brontë likens to corpses, live a death in life existence that brings them little joy or fulfillment.

The lives led by Miss Mann and Miss Ainley, however, are no worse than the unhappy situations of married women like Mary Cave and Mrs. Pryor, who also epitomize self-denial: for the women of *Shirley*, female sexual desire either leads to the protracted starvation of spinsters or to abuse or death in marriage. In fact, the only females in the novel who do not practice extreme repression in one form or another are presexual girls. The most outspoken female in the text is Rose Yorke, a girl of twelve. Rose uncannily summarizes Caroline's character and vocalizes what the older woman has learned to repress, coolly observing that she plans to travel in her life, not suffer Caroline's "long slow death . . . in Briarfield rectory" (299). Like Brontë's friend Mary Taylor, on whom the character of Rose was based, Rose emigrates in order to be free from the social conventions that already constrict her, forcing her to quietly sit and sew by her mother's side. Rose can speak with the freedom of a girl who has not yet learned to bite down on the stone of her sorrows. Many therapists, taking their cue from Hilde Bruch, theorize that puberty burdens girls with a bewildering sense of loss of control and autonomy, both physiologically and socially. The anorexic girl, they argue, fasts in order to avoid maturation because she is unable to cope with the "issues about autonomy, independence, and self-esteem" that confront her at adolescence.[26] As one anorexic girl explains: "I did not want what it [the body] stood for – to live like a mature woman. It had been a good body – but it was too much for me and the safest thing was to 'forget about it.' "[27] This sense of the mature body as "too much," literally and metaphorically, is often repeated by women who suffer from anorexia. Caroline's self-starvation can thus be read as a denial of the adulthood that robs women of the freedom of speech that girls like Rose still enjoy. The body that is gendered as an adult female, as Caroline's and Shirley's are, is a body that must deny speech, desire, and appetite in a way that the girl must not. Maturation, ironically, gives a woman less freedom of expression than she experienced as a child.

Of course, Caroline is not the only woman who suffers from hunger in the novel: Shirley also undergoes self-starvation. Shirley's hunger brings Brontë's biography to bear on the novel, since critics have long maintained that the character of Shirley was based on Emily Brontë. Elizabeth Gaskell first mentions Shirley's origins in her biography of Brontë: "The character of Shirley herself, is Charlotte's representation of Emily . . . [she] tried to depict her character in Shirley Keeldar, as what Emily Brontë would have been, had she been placed in health and prosperity."[28] Brontë based the incident of Shirley cauterizing a mad dog's bite with a hot iron, for instance, on an event in Emily's life, when, "taking up one of Tabby's red-hot Italian irons to sear the bitten place," Emily told "no one, till the danger was well-nigh over."[29] More significantly, Shirley and Caroline's self-starvation may be rooted in Emily's wasting death of consumption. During her sister's slow dying, Charlotte emphasized her shrinking frame. In one letter, she writes: "A more hollow, wasted, pallid aspect I have not beheld."[30] A month later, she alludes to Emily's "extreme emaciation" (*Life and Letters* II: 11).[31] When she died,

Emily's coffin measured only seventeen inches in width, the narrowest adult coffin the carpenter had ever made."[32]

Brontë's biographer Lyndall Gordon has suggested that Emily was anorexic, claiming that, when she left the Moors, Emily suffered "self-starvation and pining illness."[33] Katherine Frank goes into more detail about Emily's fasting behavior, chronicling her refusal to eat both as a pupil at the Roe Head school and as a teacher at the Law Hill school. Of Roe Head, for instance, Frank writes: "her refusal to eat was, in fact, a kind of utterance. By pushing her plate away at breakfast, dinner and tea, day after day, she was clearly, if silently, speaking her mind: *I hate it here. I will not eat. I want to go home.*"[34] Frank argues convincingly that today Emily Brontë would have been diagnosed as suffering from anorexia nervosa: "Not merely her refusal to eat and her extreme slenderness and preoccupation with food and cooking, but also her obsessive need for control, her retreat into an ongoing, interior fantasy world, and her social isolation are all characteristics of the 'anorexic personality.' "[35] A note written by Charlotte to her sister's doctor also suggests that Emily may have suffered from anorexia; Brontë writes that:

Her appetite failed... In appearance she grew rapidly emaciated... Her resolution to contend against illness being very fixed, she never consented to lie in bed for a single day – she sits up from 7 in the morning till 10 at night. All medical aid she has rejected... Her diet, which she regulates herself, is very simple and light. (*Life and Letters* II:IIn)

Brontë's professed (though perhaps not actual) lack of appetite, her stubbornness, high energy level and insistence on controlling her own meager diet, are all characteristics of anorexic behavior. However, in her definitive biography of the Brontës, Juliet Barker does not discuss the possibility of Emily's anorexia at all, probably since, as Barker points out, so little biographical information on Emily exists. In her introduction, Barker writes that: "it is impossible to write an authoritative biography of either of the two youngest Brontë sisters. The known facts of their lives could be written on a single sheet of paper; their letters, diary papers and drawings would not fill two dozen."[36] Most importantly, it is most likely that Brontë's tuberculosis *caused* her lack of appetite. Faced with this dearth of biographical evidence, therefore, one can not definitively conclude that Emily was anorexic, though Frank's argument is intriguing based on the sketchy information that is available. In either case, the physical fact of Emily's deteriorating body surely had an effect on the depictions of Caroline and Shirley.

Shirley's starvation, like Caroline's, originates from the repression of desire, in this case for her former tutor Louis Moore. After Moore's arrival, the previously energetic and healthy young woman begins literally to pine away; Shirley grows so thin that: "The ring dropped from the wasted little hand" (376). Louis quickly establishes the cause of Shirley's despair when she admits to him that she has been bitten by a dog and that she fears contracting rabies. However, when one considers that Shirley takes ill shortly after Louis rebuffs her attempts to be friendly, it becomes obvious that Shirley suffers from her love for her former master and that, like the dog who tries to take a bite out of Shirley, Louis has started to consume her. One early incident that defines their relationship takes place when Shirley offers Louis grapes from her basket: "From the rich cluster that filled a small basket held in her hand she severed a berry and offered it to his lips. He shook his head, and turned aside his flushed face" (356). In this erotically charged encounter, Shirley plays the role of aggressor, boldly holding the berry up to Louis's lips. Her assertiveness disconcerts him; though his "flushed face" suggests a return of her passion, he is unable to accept Shirley as aggressor. In order for them to marry, he must regain the role of her master and she must accept a submissive role in their relationship. Her self-starvation, then, can be read as a symptom of the denial of self and autonomy that marriage with Louis entails.

Louis's courtship of Shirley involves a struggle for dominance over the pupil who is now wealthier and more autonomous than he. To tip the balance, therefore, Louis infantilizes her, calling her childish and musing: "It was unutterably sweet to feel myself at once near her and above her – to be conscious of a natural right and power to sustain her, as a husband should sustain his wife" (388). Louis's "natural" male "right and power" diffuses the economic power that Shirley holds over him and shifts the unconventional power dynamic of their relationship back to what it "should" be. While Louis enjoys Shirley's tendency to strain against his dominance, claiming that he would rather marry a "young lioness or leopardess" (390) than a lamb, he ultimately desires to "curb her" (391), to turn her from a carnivorous animal to one that can be fed out of his hand. Feline images of Shirley continue through the disturbing scene of Louis's proposal (reminiscent of William Crimsworth's equally disturbing proposal to Frances Henri in *The Professor*), during which he wishes for: "Something to tame first, and teach afterwards; to break in and then to fondle . . . to establish power over and then to be indulgent to the capricious moods" (462). Louis conceptualizes his courtship and marriage in terms of domination and submission, so that Shirley, "some*thing*," must be captured, tamed, and taught like a domestic beast. The reader knows that he has succeeded in "breaking" her in when she humbly calls him "My master" (463). Henceforth, there will be no more scenes in which Shirley provocatively offers Louis berries.

Shirley's capitulation to Louis does not come as much of a surprise to the reader, for she has already admitted her masochistic tendencies to Caroline, musing that she wants a master to "hold me in check" (409), to obey and to fear. After her engagement, though, Shirley's struggle to repress her autonomy costs her both health and happiness. "Conquered" and "bound" (475), she becomes totally dependent on Louis. Caroline notes that in his absence she "sat or wandered alone, spoke little, and *ate less*" (475, emphasis mine). Louis's love does not alleviate Shirley's self-starvation; rather, her continued refusal to eat, acting as a metaphor for female silence, symbolizes the fact that her once powerful voice has become mediated through her tutor's. We only read of Louis's proposal and Shirley's response through the words of his diary, thereby circumventing the narrator of the rest of the novel. More explicitly, Louis autocratically informs Shirley's uncle that "any further observations you have to make may as well be addressed to me" (467). Just as Caroline's earlier silence led to her illness, so too Shirley's continued fasting is intimately connected to Louis's cooption of her voice. She becomes "melancholy or nonchalant" (476), her glances "half wistful, half reckless" (476). Shirley's starvation, linked to the loss of her autonomy, represents a self-destructive and unsuccessful resistance to power. Rather than actively opposing Louis, Shirley turns her depression inward, allowing her body to grow as extenuated as her voice. By the end of the novel, she has been effectively silenced.

Women, however, are not the only characters in *Shirley* who starve. Gilbert and Gubar, in *The Madwoman in the Attic*, and, more recently, Sally Shuttleworth, in *Charlotte Brontë and Victorian Psychology*, have argued that starvation links the women of the novel to the unemployed workers, who "ate the bread and drank the waters of affliction" (23). The parallels between the mill hands, who riot for food, and Caroline are especially strong. Both the workers and Caroline have been cruelly ignored by Robert, both of them seek a trade that will sustain them, and both of them initially suffer silently. Brontë describes William Farren, after his unsuccessful plea to Robert for help, as "haggard with want . . . and yet there was no ferocity, no malignity in his countenance; it was worn, dejected, austere, but still patient" (105). Similarly, Caroline, "feeling ready to perish with craving want, turns to philosophy, to resolution, to resignation; calls on all these gods for aid, calls vainly – is unheard, unhelped, and languishes" (263). The traits that Farren and Caroline share – sadness, depression, hopelessness – connect the two of them in suffering. The working classes and women, Brontë implies, are both oppressed politically and socially within a capitalist patriarchy. The voices of both groups are ignored, discounted, and rejected, and their physical, political, and social needs are unattended to, even mocked. Starvation thus functions in the novel on both literal and metaphorical levels. Those whom society values, society feeds. Those whom society does not value, by extension, are allowed to starve.

In contrast to the workers, Robert and Malone have access to food whenever they want it. For example, in "The Wagons," Malone prepares a pork chop while callously discussing the workers and women with Robert. In the same chapter, Robert boasts of his independence from his sister and female domestic help, explaining to Malone that he often eats alone so as "not to be dependent on the femininity in the cottage yonder" (19). Like the curates, his solitary eating demonstrates his lack of engagement with the wider community. Malone's and Robert's political and economic empowerment, and the social privileges that derive from their gender and class status, are symbolized by the comfort and security in which they eat, as opposed to the anxiety that surrounds the procuring or consumption of food for others in the novel. Similarly, Robert breaks off his meeting with the starving Farrell when the bell rings to signal the dinner-hour. Robert's appetite comes first. As someone who does not worry about food, who enjoys the predictability of a dinner bell and a prepared dinner, Robert has no empathy for Farrell's hunger or, by extension, the slow starvation of his family.

However, there are also fundamental differences between the starvation of women and working-class men. While Caroline turns her hunger inward, starving and remaining silent, the workers eventually revolt against Robert, first attacking machinery and then the mill itself. Working-class men's hunger, then, is not identical to Caroline's: the objects of hatred for starving men are machines and mills, but starving middle-class women hate their own bodies.[37] Working-class men reject their class status, or at any rate how their labor is exploited by the owners of capital, but they do not reject their maleness, and they can therefore externalize their hatred through violence against others. Theirs is, after all, a class, not a gender, rebellion. Caroline, and later Shirley, are hemmed in because of their gender, their femaleness, so they reject the bodies that represent their gender. Their violence is completely turned inward. One should not, therefore, merely conflate the class and gender oppression in the novel, since Brontë carefully distinguishes between the two.

Also, though starvation constitutes a shared experience for Caroline and the workers, Caroline's class identity remains intact throughout the novel. She is not solely identified with her gender, but with her class as well, which keeps her from an alliance with working-class men or women. Helplessness and starvation make men metaphorically female: Farren, for instance, is portrayed crying at the hearth, while Robert, like Caroline, becomes "hopelessly weak" (434) and "a mere ghost" (434) during his illness. However, starving does not identify Caroline or Shirley with the working classes. Ironically, Brontë uses Caroline's slim body to *differentiate* her from laboring women. Robert tells Caroline that, while walking through his mill: "I seemed to see a figure resembling yours. It was some effect of doubtful light or shade, or of dazzling sunbeam. I walked up to this group. What I sought had glided away; I found myself between two buxom lasses in pinafores" (191). Here, a glimpse of Caroline's body becomes entirely incorporeal, merely "light" and "dazzling sunbeam," the angel in the mill. She obviously has little in common with the "buxom," wholly physical bodies of the female factory workers. Even though Caroline protests against Robert's sentimental "illusions" (191), these are the only representations of working-class women in the text, and they conform to Victorian stereotypes of robust working women. Though starvation puts working men in the suffering position of women, then, it does not put women into the same category as workers.

Shirley also carefully distances herself from the working classes throughout the novel because of her own alliance with land and property owners. She sympathizes with the workers' starvation, but only so long as the mill hands remain non-violent and essentially passive. Her charity ceases at the possibility of open rebellion. "If once they violently wrong me or mine," she informs Caroline, "and then presume to dictate to us, I shall quite forget pity for their wretchedness and respect for their poverty, in scorn of their ignorance and wrath at their insolence" (200). Her identification with Robert and with patriarchal industrial power – seeing the poor as "they" as opposed to "us," for example – is not surprising, considering her own economic autonomy, as indicated by her masculine name. Replacing Helstone as "the first gentleman in Briarfield" (249) the night of the raid on Robert's mill, Shirley asks for a pistol with which to protect herself: in order to take Helstone's place as patriarch, she needs a metaphorical phallus. She also declares to Caroline, directly after taking the pistol, that "now I am really hungry" (250), identifying herself with figures like Robert and Malone, who eat heartily while discussing the starvation of the poor. This night, Shirley has, metaphorically, become a man, complete with a phallus and its corresponding appetite. This acceptance of the "male" role is also reflected in the dynamics of her friendship with Caroline. Shirley twice physically restrains Caroline from running to Robert, to which Caroline finally protests: "Am I always to be curbed and kept down?" (261). Although Caroline subsequently feels thankful that she did not confront Robert, her gratitude does not negate Shirley's role as the authoritative and restricting figure of masculinity who, like Helstone, forbids Caroline both physical freedom and freedom of expression.[38] Of course, the power that Shirley takes on with her "maleness" is temporary and illusory, and her assumption of a male body and social role early in the novel starkly contrasts with her later self-starvation. Louis forces her to accept the submissive role of the woman, to accept her gendered body, after she has become accustomed, with Caroline, to playing the man. Frustrated, she then takes out her anger on her own flesh. The repression of independence that Louis demands at their marriage turns her into a woman socially and legally and suddenly her corporeality, the outward sign of her womanhood, begins to disappear.

When she describes the precarious state of Robert's business near the opening of *Shirley*, Brontë writes that, because of the Orders of Council that forbade trade with France: "Minor foreign markets were *glutted* [with cloth] and would receive no more. The Brazils, Portugal, Sicily, were all overstocked by nearly two years' *consumption*" (23, emphasis mine). By using metaphors of eating to describe the wool trade, Brontë suggests that consumption is at the very heart of capitalism: nations and people consume goods, the rich consume the poor, capitalists consume labor, men consume women. As the similarities between women and the working class in the novel suggest, class and gender reinforce each other in cementing the power of wealthy white men. Robert, however, is not a blustery, swaggering type like Yorke or Helstone. When we first meet him, he is in an insecure financial situation, close to ruin, with a slender body and a "hollow, somewhat haggard outline of face" (20). During his illness, he becomes a "thin, wasted figure" (432) like Caroline herself was earlier in the novel. His starvation temporarily renders him weak and dependent, and thus "feminine"; as Deirdre Lashgari writes: "Through his experience of suffering, of 'hunger' in the broad sense of desire and lack, Robert has begun to unlearn the patriarchal hardness that determined his treatment of Caroline before. His 'not eating' constitutes a dis/ordering of his masculinist assumptions, his taking for granted that he will be fed."[39] After such a feminizing experience, the reader might hope that he and Caroline could enjoy a mutually supportive, respectful, and nurturing marriage in which Robert better understands Caroline. During the proposal, for instance, Robert alludes to the fact that he caused Caroline great "sickness of body and mind" (478), and that he never visited her on her sickbed. Brontë also suggests that, finally, Caroline might be satiated, when she writes that Caroline "devoured [Robert's] words" as he speaks.

However, Brontë does not allow the reader such a positive reading. While sick, Robert refers to himself as "unmanned" (434), but, once recovered, he is presumably once more "manned," and able to take possession of Caroline. The novel's conclusion leaves the reader with images that emphasize the division between Caroline and Shirley and their husbands. "The two Mr. Moores" (482) now constitute a partnership responsible for a new mill and the hideous industrialization of the once green Hollow with a "cinder-black highway" and "a chimney ambitious as the tower of Babel" (482). Just as the female Hollow, with its "last fairish" (482), has been colonized by masculine industrial power, Shirley and Caroline have been "colonized" by their husbands: they have lost their names and identities and metamorphosed simply into Mrs. Louis and Mrs. Robert. The novel offers little hope for the happiness of the protagonists' marriages. Robert's proposal to Caroline is anything but romantically satisfying, considering his admission that just the night before he had planned to leave her and emigrate to Canada. As for Shirley, after being "mastered" by Louis, the once-passionate heroine is now described mundanely as one "who wore such handsome dresses" (482): the powerful Nature goddess Eve has been starved out of her.

VILLETTE: CORPULENCE, SEXUAL PROMISCUITY, AND CATHOLICISM

Like *Shirley*, *Villette* is a novel about hunger. When Lucy Snowe wakes up at La Terrasse after her breakdown, she: "looked spectral; my eyes larger and more hollow, my hair darker than was natural, by contrast with my thin and ashen face."[40] Here and throughout the novel, Lucy's emaciation symbolizes the lovelessness of her emotionally repressed life, while her simultaneous longing for food, particularly sweet food, attests to her need for affection.[41] Despite such metaphors of hunger and appetite, however, Lucy does not figure hunger negatively and fullness positively.

Rather, her desire to eat is often compromised by her scorn for corpulent women, whose obesity she repeatedly equates with promiscuity and with an irrational mind. Brontë's use of the body as an emblem of character is in keeping with her interest in phrenology and physiognomy. Most explicitly in *The Professor* but in her other novels as well, Brontë alludes to the popular sciences of phrenology and physiognomy to provide evidence of a character's real nature and to demonstrate her protagonists' abilities to analyze each other's dispositions.[42] When Lucy first arrives at the Pensionnat, for instance, Paul examines the features of her face to recommend her for employment; Paul also "reads" Lucy best throughout the novel. Brontë applies the fundamental basis of these pseudosciences, that character can be established by physical type, to the analysis of women's bodies, in general favoring the slim woman – what physiognomist Alexander Walker called a "thinking beauty" – because of her supposedly reasonable, intellectual character.[43] Lucy's acceptance of the connection between body and character inclines her toward interpreting fat as a sign of a woman's slavish attention to her appetite; underlying her disdainful description of the Cleopatra portrait is the assumption that women should maintain control over their appetites both for food and sexuality. While the repression of passion is difficult, Lucy prefers it over the wallowing in passion that characterizes Cleopatra. Brontë's emphasis on the suffering of hunger and sexual repression implies that a woman's small appetite is not simply a natural, essential characteristic of her gender. Nevertheless, Brontë validates her female characters' control over their desires and presents the slim body as a symbol of regulated appetite, thereby reproducing an anorexic logic.

Lucy's love for Graham is a central *locus* of appetite images in the novel, for Brontë consistently describes their correspondence by using tropes of hunger. Waiting for his infrequent letters, Lucy wonders if: "animals kept in cages, and so scantily fed as to be always on the verge of famine, await their food as I awaited a letter" (260). Lucy is, of course, trapped in the small and confining spaces of the Pensionnat and watched over like any beast in the zoo by Madame Beck. Graham's letters are her only food, but their infrequency keeps her on the "verge of famine." On a deeper level, the cage in which she is trapped can be read as her own body, which Graham never finds beautiful enough to love, and her soul the hungry animal within; as I have mentioned, the image of the soul as trapped or imprisoned in the body is often used in literature about anorexia to describe the anorexic woman's hatred for her body.[44] Mary Jacobus and Sally Shuttleworth have already shown that Graham's letters can be read as a focal point of Lucy's repression: Lucy encounters the mysterious nun when she reads one of his notes, and her decision to bury his letters under the pear tree echoes the burial alive of the legendary nun "for some sin against her vow" (103).[45] After writing Graham a letter that speaks of her "closely-clinging and deeply-honouring attachment" for him, she rips it up, afraid to express her love lest it not be returned. "Reason" (248), which forces Lucy to "erase, tear up, re-write" (248) her affectionate letter, also torments her with "her stint, her chill, her barren board" (224). Lucy's emotional repression is thus conflated with starvation; like Caroline, her lips are sealed and she consequently suffers the pangs of hunger.

Initially, Graham's letters satisfy Lucy's hunger: his first letter is a "bubble – but a sweet bubble – of real honey dew" (239). His correspondence, however, proves fickle and ultimately unsatisfying, as beautiful but as transient as a bubble. Lucy eventually describes her collection of five letters, which she returns to again and again, as merely a "crust" (261). Having lost even their initial quality of sweetness, Graham's letters "did not nourish me: I pined . . . and got as thin as a shadow" (261). Lucy's starvation continues despite Graham's few friendly but dispassionate letters because she realizes that Graham neither loves nor is capable of loving her. Dismissing Lucy as "a being inoffensive as a shadow" (308), or essentially lacking a body, he does not recognize her hunger and therefore cannot feed her. Moreover, while Lucy gets thin, Graham grows fatter. Mrs. Bretton cheerfully tells him to: "not neglect your own size: which seems to me a good deal on the increase . . . He used to be slender as an eel, but now I fancy in him a sort of heavy-dragoon bent – a beef-eater tendency" (182). Brontë corporealizes the dynamic between Lucy and Graham: like Helstone and Mary Cave and Louis and Shirley, Graham vampirishly siphons off Lucy's energies and passions and grows fat on them while she starves from lack of return. Eating is, again, a sign of male privilege and power and starvation a sign of female powerlessness.

Paul Emanuel, on the other hand, both recognizes and helps satiate Lucy's hunger, though he initially criticizes her proclivity for sweet food:

"You look," said he, "like one who would snatch at a draught of sweet poison, and spurn wholesome bitters with disgust."
"Indeed, I never liked bitters; nor do I believe them wholesome. And to whatever is sweet, be it poison or food, you cannot, at least, deny its own delicious quality – sweetness. Better, perhaps, to die quickly a pleasant death, than drag on long a charmless life." (227)

Lucy, who understands and suffers the pain of starvation, craves its opposite, the sweetness of shared love. The embodiment of repression herself,
she nonetheless recklessly promotes the merits of sweetness, even at the
risk of death. Better die "a pleasant death," she urges, than continue a
loveless life. In this passage, she seems to speak for the mythical nun,
whose unnamed pleasure led to her supposed burial alive. Better than
anyone else in *Villette*, Lucy realizes that the bitterness of repression is
not "wholesome." She does not wish to become a Miss Mann or a Miss
Ainley, and still aspires to satiety. In his contradictory way, Paul validates
her need, surreptitiously stuffing chocolates into her desk.

Paul also feeds Lucy after locking her in the attic to learn her part in
the vaudeville. Lucy, trapped in the hot, dusty room, begins longing for
a *paté à la crême*: "as my relish for these dainties increased, it began to appear somewhat hard that I should pass my holiday, fasting and in prison"
(132–133). Shut up in the attic, "excessively hungry" (132), the scene epitomizes Lucy's position at the Pensionnat, imprisoned within its walls and
starved for love. Again, one can read her imprisonment as metaphor
for her sense that she is trapped within her body and its inescapable
femaleness, both because her gender and class restrict her movement and because her corporeality itself makes many demands upon
her, including its need and desire for food. However, unlike Graham,
who lets Lucy grovel on the floor of the garret in search of the letter that
represents the "famished" (239) woman's only food, Paul is no "tyrant
and Blue-beard, starving women in a garret" (134); instead, he finds
Lucy the cake that she so desires and then: "superintended my repast,
and almost forced upon me more than I could swallow" (134). The food
that Paul feeds her is sugary, rich, and sensual, food that throughout
the Victorian era was often associated with sexual desire.[46] Alexander
Walker (1841), for example, warned parents to abstain from giving their
children chocolate because it "accelerate[s] precocity"; Colombat de
l'Isère (1845) claimed that "pastry" "exaggerate[s] the limits of the appetite," and Edward Clarke famously proclaimed, in 1873, that: "We
live in the zone of perpetual pie and doughnut; and our girls revel in
those unassimilable abominations."[47] Because Paul encourages Lucy to
gorge herself, "almost" forcing her to eat more than she is able, her
miniature feast suggests the anorexic's desire to binge after a period of
starvation. Paul represents the food that Lucy has been starving for; he is
the binge that she desires. Though the word "forcing," in the context of
food, also brings to mind the forced feedings administered to Victorian
hysterics who did not eat, the word "almost" modifies Paul's behavior,

and Lucy clearly enjoys the experience. Whereas Graham soon leaves off feeding Lucy, the "nourishing and salubrious meat" (234) of his first letter drying up into an unappetizing crust, Paul and Lucy eventually share a paradisaical supper of "cherries and strawberries bedded in green leaves" (476), the verb "bedded" lending the meal an erotic tone. Paul's letters, moreover, replace the sweet food that they share during their last meeting, for he gives her "real food that nourished, living water that refreshed" (482). Though Lucy grows thin on Graham's food, Paul's food sustains her. Through Paul and Lucy's relationship, Brontë rewrites *Shirley*'s admonition to women to bite down on the stone of disappointment; in his letters Paul "would give neither a stone, nor an excuse" (482). For a brief moment near the close of *Villette*, Brontë envisions the satiation of Lucy's hunger and desire for love.

However, Brontë, like Lucy, was no hedonist. In *Villette*, she stops short of unequivocally condoning appetite by presenting several derogatory images of body fat, most notably, Lucy's famous encounter with the painting of Cleopatra:

I calculated that this lady, put into a scale of magnitude suitable for the reception of a commodity of bulk, would infallibly turn from fourteen to sixteen stone. She was, indeed, extremely well fed; very much butcher's meat . . . must she have consumed to attain that breadth and height, that wealth of muscle, that affluence of flesh. She lay half-reclined on a couch: why, it would be difficult to say . . . she appeared in hearty health, strong enough to do the work of two plain cooks . . . She ought likewise to have worn decent garments; a gown covering her properly, which was not the case: out of abundance of material – seven and twenty yards, I should say, of drapery – she managed to make inefficient raiment. (195–196)

The Egyptian's large size fills Lucy with self-righteous revulsion. Her supposition that Cleopatra has been fed "very much butcher's meat," together with her joke about the size scale that one would need in order to weigh her, implies that Cleopatra herself is just a huge slab of meat, a commodity to consume. Lucy's association of Cleopatra with meat recalls her own experience when, at the wharf, a waterman: "offered me up as oblation, served me as a dripping roast, making me alight in the midst of a throng of watermen" (47). As in *Shirley*, women's bodies in *Villette* become metaphorical food, pieces of meat for the visual and sexual consumption of a male audience: once again, men consume and women are consumed. However, while Lucy implicitly criticizes the treatment that she receives at the hands of the watermen, describing herself as "a dripping roast" in order to critique the men's ungentlemanly behavior, she suggests that Cleopatra's large size justifies viewing her as sexual object and as object to be eaten. Furthermore, Lucy herself takes on a male perspective while eyeing Cleopatra, first figuring her as food and then metaphorically devouring her by studying the painting.

Cleopatra's size signifies her irrepressible sexuality, for even if Brontë had not identified the subject of the painting, her size, lack of clothing, and supine posture during "broad daylight" (195) would have marked her as a concubine. Since the respectable lady was expected to consume only small amounts of food in order to downplay her corporeality, one can posit that large women, because of their prodigious appetite for food, were often considered more sexual than slim women. In fact, Jill Matus points out that: "Victorian studies of prostitution point repeatedly to grossness, stoutness, and excessive weight as characteristic of profligate women," a fact which I will discuss at greater length in chapter 4.[48] Like the large and dark Bertha Mason with her "giant propensities," or Zola's curvaceous, sexually voracious courtesan Nana, Cleopatra's appearance as a "huge, dark-complexioned gipsy-queen" suggests her position as highly sexual female.[49] Brontë here calls attention not just to Cleopatra's size, but to her dark skin, further allying Cleopatra to the highly sexed non-white woman. By reducing her to meat and by lavishing attention on her size, then, Lucy responds to Cleopatra using familiar Victorian symbolic constructions of the body that equate both the consumption of meat and body fat with sexual appetite.[50]

Some critics have unproblematically accepted Lucy's opinion that the painting is "coarse and preposterous."As de Hamal and the other "worshipping connoisseurs" (195) gazing at the painting make clear, Cleopatra is indeed a fantasy woman, both completely passive and wholly sexual. However, Lucy's attack on Cleopatra's corpulence also constitutes part of a wider denigration of fat within the novel. For, though fat can function as a symbol of maternity, sexuality, or a number of other things, it is also *just fat*, and again and again is used by Brontë as a negative sign. When Lucy describes her invariably ignorant students, for example, she also mentions their weight. Just as reason (as opposed to emotion) is associated with starvation throughout the text, Brontë uses Lucy's students to link the *lack* of reason with a greedy appetite. Of two students who "ought to have been in the first class, but whose brains had never got them beyond the second division" (209), one is a glutton: "the quantity of household bread, butter, and stewed fruit, she would habitually consume at 'second déjeuner' was a real world's wonder – to be exceeded only by the fact of her actually pocketing slices she could not eat" (210). Lucy thus presents her students' eating habits as "proof" of their stupidity, their inability to "rationally" (210) complete their assignments, thereby suggesting that the body somatically expresses intellectual capability.

Of course, the girls' stupidity is also a function of their nationality and religion, and Lucy's unintelligent students evoke the stupid and preco-ciously sexual female students of *The Professor*, a novel that exceeds even *Villette* in its virulent anti-Catholicism and xenophobia. The students of the Pensionnat are not "quiet, decorous English girls" (75) but "insolent" (76) Belgians, unable to do the work of even "an English girl of not more than average capacity and docility" (80) because of their inherent lazi-ness and lack of self-discipline. The Labassecouriennes demonstrate the same lack of discipline over their bodies as they do over their school work. Lucy comments that even young aristocratic women "boasted contours as robust and solid as those of a stout Englishwoman of five-and-twenty" (209). Brontë thus generalizes the meaning of female fat from one or two students to an entire nation of people, and her interpretation of female corpulence ultimately supports the theory of English ethnic and cultural superiority. The inherently greater intelligence of the English woman is reflected in her sylph-like body.

Such examples in the novel can be multiplied. For instance, the other "fat women" (195) whom Lucy sees portrayed in the gallery's paintings are "complacent-looking" (195), suggesting, once again, that fat signifies lack of intelligence. Even more intriguing, Lucy calls the insipid char-acter whom she portrays in the vaudeville a "fat" (132) because of his "emptiness, frivolity, and falsehood" (132). The word "fat" (from fatuous) came to connote a foppish person in the mid-nineteenth century. Though fatuous and fat (meaning corpulent) have different etymologies, it is sig-nificant, and surely not coincidental, that their meanings converged in the Victorian era.[51] The word fat, in Brontë's novels and in the larger Victorian culture, acts as a semiotic sign of foolishness even where it does not physically exist: when Lucy plays an idiotic man, she symboli-cally becomes fat. Lucy's derogatory comments about heavy women and about fat finally lead one to the conclusion that she considers fat *itself* distasteful.

In part, Brontë denigrates corpulence because she associates it with Catholicism: the Labassecouriennes' appetites are a natural outgrowth of their religious faith. Madame Beck, who plots with Père Silas to prevent Paul and Lucy's love relationship, is "an undenied sensualist" (543) who "take[s] sedatives and meats, and drinks spiced and sweet" (543), and the reader's only glimpse of Catholic laity, excepting Père Silas, is "an *obese* and aged archbishop" (516, emphasis mine). Catholicism, like the Cleopatra herself, is "grossly material" (516), made up of extravagant costumes, sweet-smelling incense, "flowers and tinsel" (516). Most importantly, according to Lucy, the Catholic Church's ritual and hierarchy replaces a personal relationship with God, while its emphasis on feeling replaces individual responsibility and reason. "The CHURCH," Lucy proclaims, "strove to bring up her children robust in body, feeble in soul, fat, ruddy, hale, joyous, ignorant, unthinking, unquestioning. 'Eat, drink, and live!' she says. 'Look after your bodies; leave your souls to me. I hold their cure – guide their course: I guarantee their final fate'" (196). As in the Cleopatra section, Lucy contrasts fat with spirit, a dualism in which the "ruddy" and "fat" body indicates a starved, "feeble" soul and intellect. Catholics, according to Lucy, do not think for themselves because of their "unquestioning" trust in the Church; they abandon thought and reason for the pleasures of the senses. Protestants, on the other hand, rely not on "a sect" (514) but on the Bible alone, prompting Paul's accusation that they are "strange, self-reliant, invulnerable" (512).[52] Brontë's portrayals of Catholicism are in line with much Victorian anti-Catholic rhetoric. In her 1852 novel *Beatrice*, Catherine Sinclair's heroine watches a Catholic Mass and "felt that the whole was a solemn pantomime, in which all the mental faculties were suspended, instead of being exercised, – a well-got-up melodramatic representation, dazzling to the eyes, but most prostrating to the intellect. Such finely adorned, busy, and fussy ceremonies appeared . . . no better than the flowers and fruit brought to Cleopatra, which concealed a deadly asp lurking underneath."[53] In *Beatrice*, as in *Villette*, Catholicism signifies the abandonment of reason to superficial ceremony and to the sensual temptation of "flowers and fruit." Both Brontë and Sinclair split the mind from the body. Catholicism appeals to the body, including the senses of sight and smell, but Protestantism appeals to the mind. Both authors, then, subscribe not only to the body/soul split, but to the sense that the body is degraded and fallen, so that appealing to the senses at all indicates moral weakness. Catholicism itself becomes the appetite that must be starved.

Confession is the essence of all that is wrong with, and yet all that is seductive about, Catholicism for Lucy. For, if the repression of Lucy's emotions is signaled in the text through painful starvation, the confessional is all about letting go of emotion, the "pouring out of some portion of long accumulating, long pent-up pain" (234). Here, Brontë employs the language of purgation, the flip-side of the bulimic binge, thereby framing the confessional episode as one of starvation, eating, and purging. Lucy turns

to the church because she "was perishing for a word of advice or an ac-
cent of comfort" (234), once again employing the starvation/repression
metaphor that she uses throughout *Villette*. The experience of sitting in
the cool and dark church nourishes her "as bread to one in extremity
of want" (233), and she decides that confession might calm her troubled
mind. Though the confession helps Lucy, its tremendous flood of emotion
is excessive and overwhelming. By using the language of binging and purgation, Brontë suggests that confession is dangerous for the same reason
that overeating is dangerous: both Catholicism and gluttony are associated with the senses and with materialist and emotional excess rather
than with reason. The confessional's very virtue and pleasure constitute
its danger, its potential ability not only to seduce the fiercely Protestant
Lucy into a convent, but to unleash painful feelings and passions that
she attempts to repress.[54] Anti-Catholic literature about convents emphasizes the power of the priest in the confessional, and his ability to
compromise women's modesty by drawing out their most intimate se-
crets. While Père Silas does not pose any sexual danger or temptation
to Lucy, such fears about the inappropriate utterance of emotion are
certainly in line with Brontë's overall depiction of the confession and
Catholicism. Although Lucy must eventually learn to reconcile feeling
and reason, her attraction to the confessional alerts her to the dangers
of expression and how easy it is to lose control over her emotions.

In contrast to Cleopatra and the other large women in *Villette*, Brontë
offers the actress Vashti, based in part on Queen Vashti of the biblical
Book of Esther and in part on the actress Rachel, whom Brontë watched
perform in London.[55] The Book of Esther contains no description of
Vashti, but the actress's "wasted" (251) body in *Villette* is an important
index of her character. Vashti's slenderness is not a sign (as it often is in
Dickens) of conventional femininity. Remarking on Vashti's appearance,
Lucy invokes Paul Rubens to "wake from the dead . . . and bring into
this presence all the army of his fat women," claiming that "that slight
rod of Moses" (252) could conquer the whole host. By comparing the
actress to the rod of Moses and "the scimitar [sword] of Saladin" (252),
Brontë immediately associates Vashti with patriarchal male power and
righteousness; Laura Ciolkowski writes that "the figure of Vashti threatens to defraud Victorian fictions of masculinity and femininity of their
absolute authority."[56] Graham's denunciation of the actress, for example,
hinges on the fact that her extreme passion falls outside the boundaries of
conventional feminine behavior, and her body, characterized by strength
rather than beauty or grace (252), is more typically masculine than

feminine. On the other hand, however, Vashti is profoundly female, for, like Lucy and the wasted women in *Shirley*, she is figured as food. When Lucy first sees her, she describes her as "half-consumed" (251); later, she calls her a "condiment for a people's palate" (251). In both *Shirley* and *Villette*, the trope of being consumed either marks a character as female or (in the case of Robert's illness) as undergoing an initiation into the experience of femaleness. Like Caroline, Shirley, and Lucy, Vashti's wasted body is a sign of her struggle with anger, pain and desire; indeed, she "hushed Desire" (253) in Lucy.

The difference between "the full-fed flesh" (252) of Cleopatra and the slender Vashti depends, according to Lucy, on each woman's willingness to be consumed. Lucy concurs that Cleopatra is merely "flesh"; her body brands her as sexual object and, as odalisque, she seems to welcome that objectification. Like the biblical Vashti, who refused to display herself for her husband Ahasuerus's court, Vashti's body, on the other hand, suggests that she resists consumption, and this makes her, for Lucy, a figure to be respected, even if her rebelliousness is also frightening. Both Cleopatra and Vashti represent excessive kinds of passion, but, while Cleopatra gives in to sexual desire, yielding her body to others, Vashti resists any form of domination or power; an "empress" (339) like Cleopatra, she "resisted to the latest the rape of every faculty" (254). Brontë's use of the word "rape" as metaphor for larger violation here underscores Vashti's denial of her body's sexuality and desires. So, while Vashti is, on the one hand, a monitory figure, a sign of the potentially fiery dangers of passion and its repression, on the other, Lucy admires her power and takes some of that power away with her. After watching the performance, Lucy recognizes Graham's narrow-minded rejection of the actress as "almost callous" (342), initiating the process of her separation from a man who could never understand her own passion.

Lest Brontë's dichotomy between corpulence and slenderness seem too simple, however, two of the secondary characters in *Villette*, Paulina Home and Ginevra Fanshawe, modify the negative depiction of female appetite found elsewhere in the novel. Paulina's and Ginevra's sexual drives and intellects are clearly reflected in their contrasting physical types: Paulina is tiny and almost bodiless whereas Ginevra is full and fleshy. Surprisingly, however, Brontë draws a largely positive rendition of Ginevra side by side with a highly conflicted portrait of Paulina. To claim that Brontë favors Ginevra is, of course, to go against much of the text's own evidence, for Lucy several times points out Paulina's superiority to her cousin. However, Lucy is not always a reliable narrator, given that she has already misled the reader by initially concealing the identity of Dr. John. Most important, whereas the portrayal of Ginevra, even when sarcastic, is fairly straightforward and transparent, Lucy frequently employs parody in her descriptions of Paulina. By plainly pointing out Ginevra's flaws but veiling Paulina's in satire, Lucy distances her narrative voice from judgment of Paulina.

To start, Paulina and Ginevra's names underscore their characters, dividing them into figures who predominantly (though not wholly or reductively) represent soul and body. The name Paulina suggests St. Paul, whose negative assessment of sexual desire underscores Paulina's own sexlessness. Paulina's name also links her with Paul Emanuel, who, despite his nurturance of Lucy, remains a patriarchal figure in the text. Ginevra's name is more complicated. According to the *OED*, the prefix "gin" has several meanings. One, dating from the Middle English period to the late eighteenth century, is a scheme or trick; Ginevra, of course, tricks Lucy and the Pensionnat during her flirtation with the "nun" de Hamal. The word also signifies a snare or trap for catching game: again, Ginevra almost traps the infatuated Graham with her beauty. Finally, Brontë may have been playing with the prefix "gyn," signifying not only woman but, more technically, the female reproductive organs. Such an interpretation is certainly in line with the flirtatious and sensual Ginevra, who is in large part defined by her physical appetites and body. Because these two characters do not fully integrate their souls and bodies, neither is a model of ideal womanhood.

Brontë considered Paulina the novel's biggest failure. She confessed to her publisher George Smith that: "the weakest character in the book is the one I aimed at making the most beautiful . . . I felt that this character lacked substance; I fear the reader will feel the same. Union with it resembles too much the fate of Ixion, who was mated with a cloud" (*Correspondence* IV: 23).[57] Brontë's comment is telling, for Paulina *is* a strangely ethereal and cloud-like creation, lacking both a substantial physical body and a character of "substance"; Brontë revealingly refers to her as "it" rather than "she." "Exceedingly tiny" (6) and "a mere doll" (6) as a six-year-old girl, Paulina eerily seems never to grow. When Lucy meets her eleven years later, she is still "a small, delicate creature" (257) whom Graham mistakes for a child. Like the Dickens heroine, Paulina's child-like body suggests that she has not developed the desires of an adult woman, but that she has instead retained a child's innocence and sexual purity. She is also spirit-like. Lucy calls her an "airy, fairy thing – small, slight, white – a winter sprite" (267): she reminds Lucy of a "spectral illusion" (267). These images of paleness and transparency essentially turn Paulina into a ghost, denying her corporeality in much the same way as comparison with a stained glass window denies Agnes's corporeality. As the "angel" of La Terrasse, moreover, Paulina personifies the sentimental Victorian woman, the "half doll, half angel" that Shirley derides. Her intense dependence on and identification with men, through which she embodies the virtues of passivity and submission to male authority, further identify her as the ideal guardian of the hearth.[58] Although critics have already noted Paulina's resemblance to the middle-class housewife, they have neglected the way that Brontë uses images of food and appetite in her depiction of this strange character. Examining Paulina's relationship to eating and to the preparation of food reinforces her position as tragically stunted Victorian woman.

Paulina's "slight" body is a sign of her renunciation of appetite. As a child, she assures Mrs. Bretton that "girls – such as me and Miss Snowe – don't need treats, but *he* [Graham] would like it" (22); already, she has internalized the denial of her appetite, even speaking for the perpetually hungry Lucy. Both times that we see Paulina eating, she consumes very little, as though instinctively aware that the feminine woman moderates her appetite. After bringing "whatever was best on the table" (20) to Graham, she shares his breakfast but refuses to touch the marmalade "lest . . . it should appear that she had procured it as much on her account as his" (20). Paulina believes that men naturally deserve "whatever was best" and that her own duty in relationships with men is to serve their desires rather than satisfying her own. These "delicate instincts" (20) remain consistent as Paulina grows older. "Your old October was only desirable while forbidden," she demurs after tasting a sip of Graham's ale, "Thank you, no more" (275). Although Paulina suggests that she desires the "forbidden," her rejection of ale, a hearty and masculine beverage, highlights her intense femininity. Paulina's lack of (or repression of) appetite underscores her tendency to live only through the men in her life; her desires become submerged into theirs so that her only concern is that *they* are fed, that *they* are satiated. We never see Paulina crave food the way that Lucy does.

Since Paulina's identity depends upon taking care of men, the preparation of food constitutes one of her main activities. Lucy describes the child serving tea to her father and wryly comments: "Throughout the meal she continued her attentions: rather absurd they were. The sugar-tongs were too wide for one of her hands . . . the weight of the silver cream-ewer, the bread and butter plates, the very cup and saucer tasked

her insufficient strength and dexterity . . . Candidly speaking, I thought
her a little busy-body" (13). Paulina is a satire of the ideal Victorian
wife, dutifully presiding over family tea. Her behavior mimics the advice to young wives found in marriage manuals like the 1851 *Etiquette of
Courtship*: "Remember that husbands are men . . . and that they must eat;
and that the way to peace and quietness . . . lies down their throats."[59]
While the tone of this particular etiquette manual is a bit menacing,
suggesting that women should stuff food down men's throats just to shut
them up, Paulina's compulsive serving of food, which echoes the ideology of the manual, is far from subversive. Too little and weak to even
manipulate the sugar-tongs, the child–housewife is contemptuously and
cruelly dismissed by Lucy, who will never adopt that role, as "a little
busy-body." The negative language with which Lucy describes Paulina's
attentions to her father – "absurd," "insufficient strength and dexterity,"
"busy-body" – refer not only to the under-sized Paulina, but to the whole
sentimental ideal of woman as angel of the table that Paulina represents.

Lucy's nastiness suggests that we should not entirely trust her narrative
voice. After all, there is something touching in Paulina's eagerness to
serve her loving father that Lucy herself comes to appreciate when she
meets Paulina as a young woman. Even as a seventeen year old, however,
Paulina has not outgrown her intense dependence on men. As befits a
woman who waits on her beloved as though he were "the Grand Turk"
(21), Paulina's love for Graham verges on the idolatrous. She views him
as a sort of Greek god, confiding to Lucy that: "To me he seems now
all sacred, his locks are inaccessible, and . . . I feel a sort of fear when
I look at his firm, marble chin, at his straight Greek features" (414).
While Lucy is finally repelled by the coldness of the "half-marble" (352)
Graham, Paulina feels drawn to him as the personification of "sacred"
and "inaccessible" classical patriarchy. She wants a husband whom she
can humbly serve and look up to "like a tower . . . on the whole, I would
rather not have him otherwise" (424). The tower symbolizes not only
Graham's phallic masculinity, but his legal and social power over Paulina:
she will be confined in that tower as his wife. Such an idealized, non-
human view of Graham leaves little room for sexual passion, as Paulina's
own sprite-like body has already implied. Paulina is "not an opaque vase,
of material however costly, but a lamp chastely lucent . . . a flame vital
and vestal" (269). The vase, which might have been a symbol of female
fertility is here completely desexualized. Paulina's is not the flame of
sexual desire. Instead, her transparent lamp is "chaste" and its flame
"vestal" and "pure" (366). This "vestal" flame brings to mind the vestal

vow that the legendary nun has broken: both the nun and Paulina are buried alive, the nun under the pear tree and Paulina in Graham's tower. Paulina epitomizes the woman as light of the home and, like a vestal virgin, will keep the hearth flame lit.

At several points in the novel, Paulina does hint at her own sexual desire. For instance, discussing a letter from Graham, she describes her heart upon reading it as "the pant of an animal athirst" (364); significantly, her thirst is quenched by the purest of water, "not a mote . . . no moss, no insect, no atom in the thrice-refined golden gurgle" (365). The water – Graham's letter – bears no traces of anything organic; everything alive has been refined out of it. Again, Brontë emphasizes the lack of physicality in Graham and Paulina's love, a love more intellectual and spiritual than of the body.

Despite the differences between Lucy and Paulina, critics have established that, in terms of repression, Paulina functions as Lucy's double.[60] Even as a child, Paulina suppresses her pain, so that, whereas her father openly sobs at their parting, she hides her suffering in a strange, "most unchildlike" (7) way. Like Lucy, she "contended with an intolerable feeling; and, ere long, in some degree, repressed it" (19), but, unlike Lucy, who struggles with repression throughout the novel, Paulina leads a charmed life. "These two lives . . . were blessed," Lucy says of Paulina and Graham's marriage, "like that of Jacob's favorite son" (426). For one thing, Paulina is rich and beautiful and does not need to come to terms with plainness and poverty like Lucy does. Paulina's beauty seduces Graham, whereas Lucy's plain exterior renders her invisible, easily ignored. It is thus no surprise that Lucy later says to Paul: "I am not pleasant to look at – " and adds that "the point had its vital import for me" (471). Lucy needs to know that, unlike Graham, Paul finds her attractive. Secondly, Paulina has a father's name and therefore a fixed identity, whereas Lucy's identity is fluid. Because she has neither father nor husband with whom others can identify her, nobody really knows who Lucy is or to which social class she belongs, prompting Ginevra's confused question: "Who are you, Miss Snowe?" (299). And, finally, Paulina's repression is ultimately more successful than Lucy's. Lucy notes that as a result of Paulina's repression as a little girl, she "grew more passive afterwards" (19): Lucy's self-denial may render her outwardly calm, but she never grows passive.

Paulina's unsuccessful rival for Graham's heart is Ginevra Fanshaw, whom Lucy scorns but who is ultimately a more faithful friend than Paulina. Though critics have branded her an "idiot beauty," "worthless," and trivial, such epithets do not take into account her many positive characteristics.[61] Lucy's sardonic description of "bearing on my arm the dear pressure of that angel's not unsubstantial limb" (369) reveals that whereas Paulina lacks "substance," Ginevra is "not unsubstantial." Certainly, she is no "angel" in the house. Sensual rather than self-denying, "unsparing[ly] selfish" (54) rather than selfless, and almost thoroughly uninterested in intellectual achievement, Ginevra's character (like Blanche Ingram's) is embodied by her fleshy figure. While Paulina and Lucy have in common the quality of self-denial, Ginevra and Lucy's symbiotic friendship is founded on their shared appetite. Both women crave food, but, unlike Lucy, the hedonistic Ginevra does not repress her appetite. Instead, she "fed on creams and ices like a humming-bird on honey-paste: sweet wine was her element and sweet cake her daily bread" (139). Although this description paints the schoolgirl as somewhat cloying, a "child of pleasure" (139) who takes no part in Lucy's suffering, Ginevra's fondness for sensual delights actually allies her with the older woman. The two regularly share their food, a form of intimacy that Lucy only participates in with Ginevra and Paul. Even though they argue constantly, Lucy admits that she and Ginevra "were never alienated" (229). For Lucy and Ginevra, eating becomes a form of social intimacy: shared consumption creates a bond between them.

Ginevra's indulgence of appetite symbolizes her ripe sexuality. No "vestal flame," she spends her free hours scheming to illicitly meet Alfred de Hamal. Although her giddy, romance-centered life is well within the bounds of stereotypical female behavior, she is far less a darling of patriarchy than her cousin Paulina. She rejects, for instance, Graham's paternalistic treatment of her, snapping, "[a]lways preaching . . . always coddling and admonishing" (144). In contrast to her cousin, Ginevra does not want a father-figure for a husband, even one who pampers her. She therefore dislikes Graham's notion of love, which she associates with "fettering" (88) herself. Her chosen husband Alfred, on the other hand, is feminine, "pretty and smooth and trim as a doll" (143). With the dandy De Hamal, Ginevra enjoys a playful, mischievous, and undoubtedly sexual relationship of "les joies et les plaisirs" (89). Her dislike of Paulina, while largely based on jealousy over Graham's defection, is also a rejection of the patriarchal family epitomized by the de Bassompierres or, to use their appropriately symbolic name, the Homes. She finds their family "quite sickening," especially Graham's cool insistence on "prohibiting excitement" (263), which, not incidentally, was standard medical advice handed down to Victorian women because of their supposedly weaker constitutions.[62] Graham echoes, for example, the author of *Health for the Million* (1858), who claims that "immoderate emotions ... disorder the body in various ways, chiefly by their impression upon the nervous system."[63] Graham's stereotypical view of women annoys Ginevra, for she realizes, as does Lucy, that Graham is incapable of "reading" women correctly: "He thinks I am perfect," she complains, "furnished with all sort of sterling qualities and solid virtues" (88).[64] Ginevra rejects Graham's tendency to idealize her, on the one hand, and restrain her, on the other. Though no rebel against Victorian gender discourse, she nevertheless finds those gender codes stifling. She says and does exactly what she wants, and her frankness endears her to Lucy. Moreover, whereas Paulina disappears from the text after her marriage to Graham (except in a hasty summary of her future life, in which Graham figures more prominently than she), Ginevra does not forget Lucy, writing to her for many years. In our final vision of Ginevra, "she got on – fighting the battle of life by proxy" (466). Ginevra is finally more active and energetic than Paulina, as well as a more faithful friend to Lucy. Lucy's friendship with the schoolgirl suggests that, at least in Ginevra's case, Lucy tempers the dislike of corpulence that she manifests throughout the novel.

Matthew Arnold dismissed Charlotte Brontë as "hunger, rebellion, and rage," a slight that contains much truth.[65] *Villette* and *Shirley* are companion pieces in their portrayal of women's self-denial and, particularly, in the complicated and sometimes contradictory connections that Brontë draws between self-denial and starvation. While, on the one hand, Caroline, Shirley, Lucy, and Paulina's varying degrees of hunger illustrate the intense suffering of women forced into silence about their emotions, Brontë also denigrates an "affluence of flesh" (*Villette* 195) as an emblem of a grotesque sexuality. Brontë's novels thus reflect on and depart from Victorian anorexic ideology; while they can be read within the Victorian tradition of denouncing female appetite, they are at the same time subversive in their depiction of female anger and ambition. Brontë does not, like many nineteenth-century writers, critique appetite in favor of the etherealized and spiritual woman; rather, in Paulina, she suggests that such a woman is little more than a helpless child. Her heroines are, returning to Matthew Arnold's insulting summation of Brontë herself, closer to "past thirty and plain."[66] Whether single like Lucy or married like Shirley, Brontë's heroines go hungry in silence because Brontë could finally not conceive of a romantic union in which women's appetites would be filled.

CHAPTER 4

Vampirism and the anorexic paradigm

While visiting her old lover Mr. Holbrook, Miss Matty Jenkyns, the heroine of Elizabeth Gaskell's *Cranford* (1851–1853), faces the problem of how to eat a plate of new peas without the proper silverware. Describing this dilemma, Mary Smith notes that: "Miss Matty picked up her peas, one by one, on the point of the prongs, much as Aminé ate her grains of rice after her previous feast with the Ghoul."[1] Gaskell alludes to a tale in the *Arabian Nights* in which Sidi Nouman discovers that his wife Aminé, who eats only a few grains of rice with a pin for dinner, is really an enchantress who clandestinely devours the flesh of corpses; the apparently delicate woman without an appetite turns out to be a monster who gorges upon gruesome and forbidden food at night. An allusion to Aminé also appears in Thackeray's *The History of Pendennis*, in which the narrator describes Blanche Amory's deceptive eating habits: "When nobody was near, our little syphide, who scarcely ate at dinner more than the six grains of rice of Amina, the friend of the Ghouls in the Arabian Nights, was most active with her knife and fork, and consumed a very substantial portion of mutton cutlets."[2] In Blanche's case, the split between her private and public dining indicates her general untrustworthiness and falseness, while the comparison of Miss Matty with Aminé is more clearly ironic, its humor relying on the obvious gulf between the two women, one malevolent, the other gentle and completely unthreatening. However, the intrusion of an exotic Eastern figure of evil into the relatively snug and quotidian worlds of London and Cranford connects Gaskell's and Thackeray's works with later Victorian thrillers like Bram Stoker's *Dracula* (1897), Sheridan Le Fanu's *Carmilla* (1872), and George Du Maurier's *Trilby* (1893–1894). In these three works, a literal or metaphorical (in the case of Svengali) vampire from an unfamiliar or unexplored region (Transylvania, Styria, Germany) brings horrible sickness or death to Britain or to a British family. In *Dracula* and in *Carmilla* (as in the *Arabian Nights* story), cruelty and horror center around the act of eating: eating is the means by which a grotesque creature sets itself apart from the norm, and symbolizes the monster's overweening lust and desire for domination. Vampires can be male or female, but, except for the figure of Dracula himself, the female vampire, not the male, dominated the late nineteenth-century literary imagination, thereby placing female hunger at the center of literature of horror. As I will explore in this chapter, the female vampire illustrates, in hyperbolic form, cultural anxieties about women and hunger, in which hunger is symbolically related to women's predatory sexuality and aggression. In addition to their anti-maternal proclivity for feeding upon children, female vampires are overtly and aggressively sexual, using their beauty and seductiveness to prey on both men and other women; in each case, the female vampire's hunger is inseparable from her sexual desire. The vampire's hunger thus positions her on one end of a continuum on which normative nineteenth-century women's hunger also falls. This chapter will examine, first, the female vampires in Stoker's and Le Fanu's work, and then turn to Du Maurier's *Trilby*, in which the vampiric Svengali destroys the title character. Like Stoker and Le Fanu, Du Maurier uses imagery of the thin, sickly female body as evidence of Trilby's purity and decency and suggests that the destruction of her body indicates a goodness compromised earlier in the novel by her appetitive body.

Female vampires can symbolize any number of negative traits or types, depending upon the particular cultural moment in which they appear. In Rudyard Kipling's misogynist poem "The Vampire," the titular vampire represents all women who do not appreciate their husbands, wearing them down through work because of their lust for material possessions: "Oh the toil we lost and the spoil we lost / And the excellent things we planned / Belong to the woman who didn't know why / ... / And did not understand" (lines 18–22).[3] Using the vampire metaphor in medical discourse, the American S. Weir Mitchell writes that: "An hysterical girl is, as Oliver Wendell Holmes has said ... a vampire who sucks the blood of the healthy people about her" ([1887]; 355); possibly influenced by Mitchell and Holmes, Julien Gordon entitled his 1893 novella about a sick girl who grows healthy at her husband's expense *Vampires*.[4] In short, vampires can symbolize any needy, parasitic, energy-draining woman (or man, as epitomized by the evil Svengali), and, by the end of the nineteenth century, vampires became a common part of the artistic landscape. Writing about female evil at the turn of the century, Bram Dijkstra writes that: "By 1900 the vampire had come to represent woman as the personification of everything negative that linked sex, ownership, and money. She symbolized the sterile hunger for seed of the brainless, instinctually polyandrous – even if still virginal – child–woman. She also came to represent the equally sterile lust for gold of woman as the eternal polyandrous prostitute. She was the absinthe drinker . . . She was the woman cloaked in darkness who beckoned man to his death."[5] As the wealth of critical material on *Dracula*, in particular, demonstrates, the vampire myth can and has been contextualized within discourses of gender, sexuality, race, class, capitalism, foreignness, colonialization, and industrialization. The vampire is a fluid figure, one that can be deployed for many symbolic purposes.

However, although the vampire's blood-feasting is, as many critics have explored, highly metaphorical, it is also a *literal* act of eating: the act of consumption is at the very center of vampire legend and literature. The vampire myth therefore takes on a new significance in a culture, like nineteenth-century Britain, that denigrates female appetite in favor of self-discipline and self-control. In addition to reading in the female vampire a general fear of the independent, rebellious, or sexual woman, one can read in both *Dracula* and *Carmilla* a disgust with the act of female consumption that is emblematic of these other characteristics. Female hunger in these works is always suspect and usually grotesque, hunger itself becoming a negative sign. By connecting the vampires' overt sexuality with their insatiable hunger, Stoker and Le Fanu imply that women's hunger, as a sign of transgressive desires, is fearful in and of itself, and that women's bodies reflect their sexual propensities.

Consequently, the vampire's body in both *Dracula* and *Carmilla* is emblematic of its nightmarish nature, though the meanings of its fatness and thinness are ever-shifting. On the one hand, fatness in *Dracula* appears as a sign that the vampire has satiated its hunger for blood, and is therefore a token of evil and excessive sexuality. Dracula's fatness, for example, occurs after he has been feeding on his victims. On the other hand, the vampire is often portrayed as very thin, in which case emaciation can be read either as a sign of the monster's excessive and unfillable appetite or, conversely, as a sign of virtuous suffering in the victim who, like Lucy at her death, has conquered the vampire's evil embraces. The meanings of thinness and fatness in vampire literature, therefore, depend entirely upon context.

Carol Senf and others have already pointed out the disreputable sexuality of Lucy's question, upon getting three marriage proposals in one day, of: "why can't they let a girl marry three men, or as many as want her, and save all this trouble?"[6] The "exultation" that Lucy expresses in her letter to Mina connects her to the three "gloating" vampire women in

Dracula's castle, who act out Lucy's secret polyandrous desires.[7] Because the vampire's sexuality is expressed entirely through appetite, the novel's vivid descriptions of sexual arousal always occur within the desire to eat or (metaphorically) be eaten; appropriately, the three vampire women refer to devouring a victim as kissing him. Stoker dwells in detail on the female vampires' desire to consume. "There was a deliberate voluptuousness which was both thrilling and repulsive," Jonathan Harker writes, "and as she arched her neck she actually licked her lips like an animal, till I could see in the moonlight the moisture shining on the scarlet lips and on the red tongue as it lapped the white sharp teeth . . . I could hear the churning sound of her tongue as it licked her teeth and lips, and could feel the hot breath on my neck" (39). Monstrous female sexuality, in which a predatory woman prepares to penetrate the passive, helpless Jonathan, is figured as the "animal" desire to eat. Stoker dwells in detail on the vampire's mouth, her red lips, red tongue, and canine teeth all emphasizing the impending act of oral consumption. This mouth, moreover, blurs gender distinctions. On the one hand, the "voluptuous" vampire's wet "scarlet lips" are an obvious vaginal symbol, but, on the other hand, the "hard dents" of her "sharp teeth" are clearly, and hyperbolically, phallic. Eating thus becomes the emblem in the novel not only of carnality, but of a carnality that is especially repulsive in female vampires who behave, through the act of eating, like men. It is significant, therefore, that Mina writes, of tea with Lucy, that: "I believe we should have shocked the 'New Woman' with our appetites!" (94). Since vampires are defined by their monstrous appetite for human blood, obviously symbolizing erotic appetite, Mina and Lucy's large appetites hint at the same sorts of desires, albeit genteely repressed. These two ostensibly proper women reveal their latent physical appetites through eating and thereby demonstrate their innate tendencies toward vampirism.

Not surprisingly, Dracula first visits Lucy the same day as she has expressed her physicality through her lunch with Mina. Later, Lucy describes her encounter with Dracula in detail:

Then I had a vague memory of something long and dark with red eyes, just as we saw in the sunset, and something very sweet and very bitter all around me at once; and then I seemed sinking into deep green water, and there was singing in my ears, as I have heard there is to drowning men; and then everything seemed passing away from me; my soul seemed to go out of my body and float about the air . . . I came back and found you shaking my body. I saw you do it before I felt you. (104)

During this key scene, Lucy's contradictory responses to Dracula, who is both "very sweet" and "very bitter" stem from the split between her soul and body.[8] Her soul, the "good" Lucy which is eventually saved after her staking, recognizes Dracula's "bitter" evil, but her body, the "bad" Lucy, seems to enjoy her meeting with the phallic "long and dark" Dracula. By splitting her soul and body, Stoker leaves Lucy some possibility of redemption, but in so doing he locates the body as the site of lust, desire, and appetite (hence the gustatory adjectives "sweet" and "bitter") that must be controlled by the soul/will. When the soul, for whatever reason, loses control of the body, the body falls into the morass of sin. Lucy's repressed impulses are given gratification through her encounter with Dracula; however, these impulses clearly existed in her before she met him. If Lucy had learned, as does the protagonist of an 1864 children's story, not to "spoil a pretty mouth by cramming it with food," her own mouth might not have become so "bloodstained, voluptuous" (225).[9]

In Mina's case, Dracula does not only feed upon her, but forces her to drink blood from a wound in his chest. Although Mina is terrified and repulsed by Dracula, the vampire plays upon her appetite in the same way as he did upon Lucy's, for when the men burst in upon Mina and Dracula, "[t]he attitude of the two had a terrible resemblance to a child forcing a kitten's nose into a saucer of milk to compel it to drink" (298). Although the metaphor is one of violation and rape, kittens *like* milk; Dracula forces Mina to do something that she on some instinctual level desires; indeed, Mina admits that: "strangely enough, I did not want to hinder him" (304).[10] Dracula thus reveals and exploits Mina's *own* appetite: female hunger signifies female sexual desire which, in Stoker's novel, literally makes women monsters.[11] Just as the female vampires elide gender distinctions through their voracious eating, so, too, does Dracula. As C. F. Bentley and Christopher Craft have argued, the scene between Mina and Dracula symbolizes both fellatio and breast-feeding, as Dracula simultaneously orally impregnates Mina with his "seed" and gruesomely feeds his newest infant. The wound itself, Craft points out, is both phallic, spurting blood/semen at Mina, and a "bleeding vagina."[12] In this scene, Craft writes, "anatomical displacements and the confluence of blood, milk, and semen forcefully erase the demarcation separating the masculine and the feminine."[13] Eating, a culturally gendered activity, is the *locus* through which vampirism disrupts gender norms more broadly.

After the men have rescued her, Mina leans her head against Jonathan's chest and then realizes, with horror, that "his white night-robe was stained with blood where her lips had touched, and where the thin open wound in her neck had sent forth drops" (300). Her own summation of herself as "Unclean, unclean!" (300) alludes not only to "ancient primitive fears of menstruation," as C. F. Bentley has noted, but to the Levitical ban against eating blood.[14] According to Leviticus: "the life of every creature is the blood of it; therefore I have said to the people of Israel, You shall not eat the blood of any creature" (Leviticus 17: 14). Mina has, in effect, broken a dietary law, and her use of the word "unclean" stems directly from Levitical language. Eating is therefore at the center of *Dracula* not only as metaphor but as literal activity. Eating the wrong kinds of food, at the wrong times, and in the wrong amounts is a transgressive behavior that places a person outside of civilized society and its behavioral norms. Appropriately, after this scene, Mina must be excluded from her husband's full confidence, since she is no longer fully human; through her eating, she has become an outsider.

By associating hunger with desire, a debased carnality, and loss of control, as opposed to mind, will, and self-control, Stoker accepts traditional binaries that are also implicated in anorexic logic. Women's hunger, as a sign of irrepressible and predatory sexuality, debases them from true womanhood to "devils of the Pit" (*Dracula* 55). The fleshy female body therefore comes under suspicion as evidence of the ascendance of carnality over spirituality. Stoker uses the word "voluptuous" repeatedly in his descriptions of vampire women, a word that connotes not all female bodies, but specifically the curvaceous, fleshy body. When he first encounters the three vampire women, Jonathan Harker immediately notices their "voluptuous lips" (39), a metonymic symbol of their sexual hunger. Later, Van Helsing describes the vampire women's "swaying round forms" and, once again, "voluptuous lips" (388). Their beauty is dangerous and potentially fatal, for before Van Helsing destroys the women at the end of the novel, he is almost tempted not to do so by their "exquisitely voluptuous" (392) appearance. In *Dracula*, the fleshy body is simultaneously beautiful and dangerous, its beauty ultimately undercut by the rampant sexuality that it symbolizes. Like Cleopatra in *Villette* or the prostitute Nana in Zola's *Nana*, fat is a sign of woman's sensual and sexual appetite, although in *Dracula*, the "fat" woman becomes not merely contemptible but deadly.

Stoker reveals one possible source for his association between fat and monstrosity when Mina, describing Dracula, tells Van Helsing and Dr. Seward: "The Count is a criminal and of criminal type. Nordau and Lombroso would so classify him, and *qua* criminal he is of imperfectly formed mind" (361). Judith Halberstam has convincingly argued that

Stoker drew from Nordau and Lombroso's theories of degeneracy and criminality in his portrait of Dracula, whose physical appearance and character have much in common with anti-Semitic nineteenth-century representations of Jews.[15] However, the Count is not the only figure who illustrates some of the assumptions of criminal anthropology. In *The Female Offender*, Lombroso analyzes the body types of female criminals, concluding, based on his own and others' research, that: "weight appears more often equal to or above the medium in thieves and murderesses, but especially in prostitutes."[16] More specifically, he elaborates that "60 per cent of female poisoners, 59.4 per cent of prostitutes, 50 per cent of female assassins, and 46 per cent of female thieves, have a weight above the average" (53), while only a minority of criminals, including prostitutes, are below normal weight. Lombroso focuses the most upon the weight of prostitutes (arguing that they tend to have larger thighs than normal women), assuming it a matter of common knowledge that prostitutes tend toward obesity: "This greater weight among prostitutes is confirmed by the notorious fact of the obesity of those who grow old in their vile trade, and who gradually become positive monsters of adipose tissues" (50). The fat body, Lombroso argues, is a visible sign of criminality or criminal tendencies, especially indicative of promiscuous sexuality and "unchastity." Excessive weight goes so far as to turn prostitutes into "monsters" of fat. Lombroso blames the supposed obesity of criminals, particularly prostitutes, not just upon their living and eating habits but upon atavism. The weight gain observed in prostitutes connects them physiologically to "savage" and "primitive" women, who are also likely to be fat. Lombroso notes that prostitutes are physiologically comparable to African women, who are well known, in comparison to "civilized" white European women, for their heightened virility. To support his point, he draws upon his own experience with the criminal and insane: "in prisons and asylums for the insane, the female lunatics are far more often exaggeratedly fat than the men. In Imola there is a girl of 12 years with hypertrophy of the breasts and buttocks . . . so that she is fatter than a Hottentot woman, and has to wear special stays" (114). Lombroso, then, inextricably links fatness, sexuality, criminality, and racial "primitivism" in a closely connected web. For a woman to be fat indicates her large sexual propensities, which suggests either an active or latent criminality, and therefore her close connection with non-European women. Lombroso would, of course, not have argued that all fat women were "unchaste" or criminal, but he clearly reads fatness as a likely physiological marker of both, essentially criminalizing fat. Although his perception of fat is more negative than representations of fat in, for example, beauty manuals, Lombroso is only on one extreme of an anti-fat continuum; his science reinforces more general cultural beliefs.

Stoker's use of body type, and especially of fat, is best analyzed through the figure of Lucy in her degeneration from virtuous woman to vampire. Upon becoming Dracula's victim, Lucy begins to lose blood and pine away. Mina notes that she "gets weaker and more languid" (101) and, later, that she becomes "thin and pale and weak-looking" (110). However, after meeting Dracula, Lucy briefly recovers the appetite that indicates her vulnerability to vampirism when she writes to Mina that "I have an appetite like a cormorant . . . Arthur says I am getting fat" (113). The word "cormorant," which is synonymous with "glutton," derives from the name of a bird which captures fish and stores them in a pouch underneath its bill. Like Alice's reference to the hyena, Lucy's comment links eating with carnivorous aggression. Moreover, the cormorant is an appropriately vampiric bird, since the fish in its pouch briefly remain, like the vampire's victims, in a liminal space between life and death. Here, then, Lucy's thinness, weakness, and pallor initially indicate illness and suffering, while her subsequent fatness suggests renewed health. However, Lucy's appetite is deceptive and does not, in fact, demonstrate the recovery that Arthur hopes it does; rather, Dracula has already sown the seeds of vampirism in Lucy, and her decline becomes inevitable as long as he remains alive. Lucy's temporary vigor thus refers back to and underscores the hunger that Mina has mentioned in her diary, foreshadowing Lucy's deadly vampiric hunger, when she will suck the blood of little children and attempt to seduce Arthur.

Lucy also grows fatter upon her transformation, after death, to a member of the un-Dead. When the men encounter Lucy in her tomb, her appearance has changed from illness to one of "voluptuous wantonness" (222), and she reveals both "a voluptuous smile" (223) and "voluptuous grace" (223). Although Stoker does not explicitly discuss Lucy's body, his almost obsessive use of the word "voluptuous," in addition to allusions to her reddened cheeks, suggests that her nocturnal feedings have fattened Lucy up in the same manner as eating changed Dracula's appearance at the beginning of the novel, making him "swollen" and "bloated" and his "cheeks . . . fuller" (54). Alluding back to the theories of Lombroso, Lucy's fatness indicates her exaggerated, carnivorous sexuality. Only when Arthur kills her in a metaphorical and extremely brutal rape does Lucy regain her former appearance: "True that there were there, as we had seen them in life, the traces of care and pain and waste; but these were all dear to us, for they marked her truth to what we knew. One and all we felt that the holy calm that lay like sunshine over the wasted face and form was only an earthly token and symbol of the calm that was to reign forever" (228). The thin, "wasted" body that Lucy recovers, though indicative of great suffering, is finally more beautiful than the fatty female body because it indicates, especially in the case of the dead body, purity and submissiveness. Her "wasted face and form" signify her "holy calm," the recovery of her soul through the destruction of her evil and appetitive body: in order for Lucy's soul to be redeemed, her body must be mutilated and destroyed. As Elizabeth Signoretti writes: "Lucy's sexuality is 'corrected.'"[17] After death, her body is "corrected" as well, and Lucy takes her place with other properly passive – and slender – Victorian heroines.

Not all vampires, however, are fat. Rather, both male and female vampires are often depicted as excessively thin, even emaciated.[18] Although she never completely becomes a vampire, Mina reveals her slide toward vampirism when she starts waking up at night and, simultaneously, stops eating. Stoker never describes Mina's body type, so we do not know whether or not she is thin, but her refusal to eat certainly suggests her slenderness. Her lack of appetite concerns Van Helsing tremendously, for the nearer that Mina gets to Dracula's castle, the less she eats:

Then when I return to the fire she have my supper ready. I go to help her; but she smile, and tell me that she have eat already – that she was so hungry that she would not wait. I like it not, and I have grave doubts . . . She help me and I eat alone; and then we wrap in fur and lie beside the fire, and I tell her to sleep while I watch . . . I find her lying quiet, but awake, and looking at me with so bright eyes . . . And I am afraid, afraid, afraid! (386)

Mina's behavior concerns Van Helsing because vampires never share meals with humans. Mina therefore displays the same behavior as Dracula does at the beginning of the novel and as Le Fanu's Carmilla does when she "take[s] a cup of chocolate, but eat[s] nothing."[19] Such behavior is disturbing because, as Caroline's self-starvation does, it unsettles norms and disrupts the routine of orderly and regimented eating. Moreover, Van Helsing suspects that Mina has lied about eating and has therefore begun to take on the deceptive character of the vampire (and the anorexic girl). By not eating at the appropriate, customary times, Mina and Carmilla reject domestic routine; not eating with the family is of a kind, in *Carmilla*, to not praying or not rising with the family. Many Victorian physicians believed that eating bizarre foods or eating in an unusual manner were actually signs of insanity. The phrase "morbid appetite" could mean any number of strange food-related behaviors, from eating chalk and drinking urine, to simply not eating with the proper decorum.[20] Mina and Carmilla's disorderly eating, therefore, betokens their abnormality and indicates that they receive nourishment elsewhere.

The vampire Carmilla is thin, a "slender girl" (253) with a "slender pretty figure" (258); elsewhere, Le Fanu notes that "she was slender and wonderfully graceful" (238). Laura even wonders, upon listening to Carmilla's extravagant and highly erotic speeches, whether "a boyish lover has found his way into the house" (265), suggesting that Carmilla's figure resembles the slim body of a boy. In Carmilla's case, however, thinness is not a sign of passivity or spirituality. She is certainly no angelic woman in the house, but a hungry and devious demon who literally sucks the life out of young women. Carmilla is not thin because she is not hungry (like the petite Dickens heroine), but because she can never eat enough. The one time we witness Carmilla after feasting, she has gorged on Laura's blood and is "standing, near the foot of [Laura's] bed, in her white nightdress, bathed, from her chin to her feet, in one great stain of blood" (283). Smallness and slenderness, in Carmilla's case, signify the voracious female, the one with unfillable and unsatiable appetites. And though Carmilla, in her attractive form, is physically small, she also takes on other forms, including a huge black cat and "a large black object, very ill-defined, [that] crawl[ed] . . . over the foot of the bed, and swiftly spread itself up to the poor girl's throat, where it swelled, in a moment, into a great, palpitating mass" (311). Here, Carmilla becomes thoroughly grotesque, "ill-defined" and merely "a great, palpitating mass," like some sort of vegetative blob. Her true but disguised nature, then, is that of Cleopatra-like fleshliness thoroughly out of bounds, undisciplined, shapeless, and not even human.[21] Her thinness is merely a deceptive veil.

Carmilla and Mina's thinness suggests that they can be read as figures of anorexia nervosa. Vampires are personifications of anorexia in that they, like the disease, cause emaciation and, eventually, death, by disrupting their victims' normal eating habits, as Mina's "morbid appetite" and Lucy's wasting body demonstrate. Within an anorexic paradigm, the vampires' insatiable desire for blood can be read as a metaphor for the enormous appetite with which the anorexic girl struggles. As in "Goblin Market," in which Lizzie and Laura are two halves of the anorexic persona – Laura the urge to binge and Lizzie the virtuous

repression of appetite – the female vampire is a grotesque personification of a woman's hunger, the hunger that the good woman resists. Lucy,
for example, wavers between two different personas, the sweet and pure
young lady and her monstrous, ravenous double. Van Helsing explains
that Lucy leads a sort of "dual life" (211): "this so sweet that was when she
not Un-Dead she go back to the nothings of the common dead" (211).
The vampire is always only half of Lucy's character; even as a vampire,
she returns to the "good" Lucy in sleep. Nevertheless, the two Lucys
do fit into an anorexic scheme: the evil Lucy feasts; the good Lucy, at
least usually, does not. The evil Lucy lusts for men's blood and wantonly
tells Arthur that: "My arms are *hungry* for you" (223; emphasis mine),
while the good Lucy thanks Van Helsing for keeping Arthur from her
polluted lips: "Their eyes met instead of their lips; and so they parted"
(169). *Dracula*'s validation of woman as the spiritual, non-sexual helpmeet
of a woman – versus the voraciously sexual siren – fits into the logic of
anorexia, a logic that denigrates female appetite and desire in favor of
the mind and the soul. Of course, as I have argued, Stoker complicates
such easy dualisms by revealing Lucy's tendencies toward vampirism
(her appetite and her flirtation) in her normal life. All women, Stoker
suggests, harbor tendencies toward uncontrollable appetite and desire;
nevertheless, evil and disorder, in the novel, are signified by appetite, a
paradigm that conforms to anorexia nervosa.

The same anorexic dynamic informs *Carmilla*, in which female characters are divided into the lustful lesbian vampire Carmilla and passive,
obedient Laura. Both Carmilla and Laura stem from the Karnstein family: Carmilla is actually Mircalla, Countess Karnstein, while Laura is a
descendant of the Karnsteins through her mother's side, though English
through her father's family. The Karnsteins as a family, then, are divided into the "bad family," with their "atrotious lusts" (305), and the
good Karnsteins, consisting of Laura and her mother, who died when
Laura was a child but who, in a voice "sweet and tender, and at the same
time terrible" warns her daughter to "beware of the assassin" (283).
The mother's brief presence in the text represents her attempt to save
her daughter by overcoming the darker forces in Laura's own family
and, by extension, in Laura herself. The familial doubling of Laura
and Carmilla, along with the simultaneous feelings of attraction and
repulsion that Laura experiences in Carmilla's presence, suggests that
Laura (like Lucy and even Mina) already harbors tendencies toward vampirism and that Carmilla and Laura are to some degree doubles; however, Carmilla and Laura clearly represent evil and innocent goodness,

a doubling that makes even more appropriate an anorexic reading of the story. Evil resides in Carmilla, whose eating is highly transgressive in terms of both when and what she eats, while goodness is centered in the girl whom we never witness eating (but who, unlike Mina, is not in fact becoming a vampire).[22]

Finally, it is worth noting that the mysterious Carmilla comes from a "lonely and primitive place" (Le Fanu, *Carmilla* 244) and Dracula from "one of the wildest and least known portions of Europe" (Stoker, *Dracula* 2). By depicting the East as an "imaginative whirlpool" (ibid., 2) of folklore, unmapped territory, and ruined villages inhabited by super-stitious peasants, Stoker and Le Fanu suggest, not subtly, that sexuality is allied with the irrational, the primitive, and the non-British.[23] It is there-fore not surprising that Jonathan Harker describes the peasant women of Transylvania as "very clumsy about the waist" (3), since a slender body is associated, in nineteenth-century culture and today with self-discipline and self-control, not qualities normally assigned to the poor. The vampires that infiltrate British families in *Dracula* and *Carmilla* arrive from the disorderly East and bring with them disorderly eating carried to its pathological and grotesque extreme. However, the central fear for Stoker and Le Fanu is that vampirism is inherent in women, that their appetites and lusts are easily stirred up, and that vampires need only ex-ploit tendencies present in the seemingly good woman. Or, as Dracula triumphantly tells the men of *Dracula*: "Your girls that you all love are mine already" (324).

Du Maurier's villain Svengali, like Dracula and Carmilla, also comes from east of England. Although Germany in the nineteenth century was not as mysterious and uncharted a territory as Transylvania, Svengali's Jewishness makes him ethnically "other" both within his native Germany and in the other countries in which he travels. Like the archetypal wan-dering Jew, he belongs nowhere and is hated wherever he goes. Sven-gali's villainy is inextricable from his Jewishness, because Du Maurier employs common, long-standing anti-Semitic stereotypes to emphasize Svengali's difference from the novel's non-Jewish characters: he is dirty, manipulative, cunning, greedy, and cowardly, all traditional insults ap-plied to Jews. Svengali's metaphorical poisoning of Trilby's mind, and her eventual death, can be traced back to medieval accusations about Jews poisoning wells and murdering Christians.[24] Svengali's control over Trilby is thus all the more sinister because she is a racially superior Englishwoman being corrupted by the member of, in the language of nineteenth-century criminal anthropology, a degenerate race.

Although he is not literally a vampire, Du Maurier uses so much vampiric imagery to describe him that Svengali belongs alongside Dracula in a discussion of nineteenth-century vampires. For example, Trilby compares Svengali to a "big hungry spider" (47) and he will, of course, suck life and energy from her. Using language found both in *Dracula* and *Carmilla*, the narrator writes that Svengali is "most unclean; a sticky, haunting, long, lean, uncanny, black spider-cat, if there is such an animal outside a bad dream."[25] Not only does Svengali, with his "long" and "lean" figure, look like Dracula, but the words "unclean" and "haunting" come directly from vampire lore, and the odd image of a "spider-cat" recalls Carmilla's manifestation as a black cat. A "dread powerful demon" (82) with vampire-like "big yellow teeth baring themselves in a mongrel canine snarl" (82), Svengali ultimately kills Trilby from beyond the grave via the mysterious photograph of him that arrives (much like Dracula) "out of some remote province in eastern Russia – out of the mysterious East! The poisonous East – birthplace and home of an ill wind that blows nobody good" (239). At the moment when Svengali indirectly kills Trilby, he is no longer associated with Germany, but with "remote . . . eastern Russia," an even more alien and "primitive" place, and a fitting birthplace for a figure as evil, "mysterious," and "poisonous" as Svengali himself. Svengali is, finally, strong enough to kill Trilby after his own death, making him an almost supernatural figure. Thus, Svengali, made monstrous by his Jewishness and by his diabolical powers of mesmerism, is very much within vampire tradition, a tradition that allows Du Maurier to focus throughout the novel on the changes that Trilby's body undergoes as she falls under his spell.

Like Lucy, Mina, and Carmilla, Trilby's body symbolizes her moral state. At the beginning of the novel, Du Maurier emphasizes both his heroine's large size and her moral dubiousness, particularly her sexual promiscuity. Trilby is beautiful but morally flawed, which makes her an inappropriate wife for Little Billee. By the end of the novel, when Trilby has completely repressed her sexuality, repented of her unrespectable behavior, and become Svengali's slave, her body has wasted away and grown thin, if not emaciated. The dichotomy between body and soul is at the philosophical center of *Trilby*. Trilby's soul finally wins out over her body, and reveals its ascendancy in the destruction of the body that houses it. Trilby's new thinness represents her acceptance of selfless, passive femininity. Evoking Brontë's depiction of Belgium, Du Maurier further elaborates on this body/soul dichotomy through the juxtaposition of

France and England, in which France represents the corruption of body and soul that Trilby must reject in order to be morally redeemed.

Du Maurier spends a great deal of time in his novel describing Trilby's body. Like the three vampires in Dracula's castle, Trilby is quite voluptuous. The reader immediately learns that Trilby is "very tall and fully developed" (11), with a large mouth, "massive" (12) chin, and "beautiful big chest" (47). Her largeness, combined with her short hair and the fact that she appears for the first time wearing a soldier's uniform, lends her a masculine appearance. "She would," the narrator reflects, "have made a singularly handsome boy" (12). Her behavior, down to her gestures and ways of moving, is masculine as well: she sits cross-legged, smokes, watches men box, and eats heartily. Her eating is an important sign of masculinity (or, in her case, androgyny) because of the great deal of attention that Du Maurier pays to men eating in the novel. When we first meet Little Billee, the Laird, and Taffy, they lounge together on a divan, "three well-fed, well-contented Englishmen" (4). Taffy is the most physically massive and bulky of the men, but all three, even delicate Little Billee, eat with gusto. They "stare with greedy eyes" (23) at elaborate displays of pastries and candies, eat enormous meals in French cafés and British pubs, and cook for each other. It is difficult to recall many other nineteenth-century novels in which so much attention is paid to the minute details of food and how much is eaten:

Then they found something else – namely, that the sting of healthy appetite was becoming intolerable; so they would betake themselves to an English eating-house in the Rue de la Madeleine (on the left-hand side near the top), where they would renovate their strength and their patriotism on British beef and beer, and household bread, and bracing, biting, stinging yellow mustard, and heroic horseradish, and noble apple-pie, and Cheshire cheese, and get through as much of these in an hour or so as they could for talking, talking, talking; such happy talk! (24)

Not only do the men enthusiastically eat "as much" food as they can, but the food that they consume is almost hyperbolically manly, "bracing" and "noble" food that makes them stronger. Their appetites mark them as good, healthy British men (more so than if they simply desired luxurious but effeminate French foods, like "charming . . . delicately frosted sweets" [23]). As in Brontë's novels, eating is coded as a male prerogative, and marks a particular character as masculine. The meals in *Trilby* are communal, generous (especially when the men cook for each other), and a serve as an affectional bond between them. When Trilby comes into their apartment, then, and immediately begins to eat, Du Maurier signals that she is a masculine woman, "one of the boys," who coopts the privileges of masculinity.

The meaning of masculinity translates, in Trilby's case, into sexual desire and into a bohemian freedom of lifestyle. Although the reader never learns much about Trilby's sexual past, and although we never really witness Trilby actively desiring anybody, we know that "she had all the virtues but one; and the virtue she lacked (the very one of all that plays the title-role, and gives its generic name to all the rest of that goodly company) was such a kind that I have found it impossible so as to tell her history as to make it quite fit and proper reading" (32). Trilby's sexual past does not consist of one great, doomed love affair, or of a betrayal that the reader might be able to integrate into a traditional model of the tragic heroine (like Gaskell's Ruth); rather, she simply "followed love for love's sake only . . . as she would have followed art if she had been a man – capriciously, desultorily, more in a frolicsome spirit of *camaraderie* than anything else" (33). Even her sexual exploits are not feminine, as femininity was constructed in the nineteenth century. Rather, her affairs are fleeting, not serious, and not particularly important to her. As they do in *Dracula*, appetite for food and sexual appetite come together in Svengali's extraordinary description of Trilby's mouth:

"Himmel! The roof of your mouth is like the dome of the Pantheon; there is room in it for 'toutes les gloires de la France', and a little to spare! The entrance to your throat is like the middle porch of St. Sulpice when the doors are open for the faithful on All Saints' Day; and not one tooth is missing – thirty two British teeth as white as milk and as big as knuckle-bones! and your little tongue is scooped out like the leaf of a pink peony." (46)

Most obviously, the large size of Trilby's mouth suggests her large gustatory appetite. However, Svengali's observation that Trilby's mouth is big enough for the glories of France, and the metaphor of her throat as open doors, seems to allude, in veiled fashion, to fellatio. Appetite for food and sexual appetite merge here with sacred imagery – the Pantheon, St. Sulpice, and All Saints' Day – as though Trilby herself is saintly. The sexual and sacred imagery in fact indicates the struggle between body and soul that Trilby undergoes throughout the novel, but particularly near the end. Which will prove preeminent in Trilby, her beautiful, if stained, soul or her corrupt body? Svengali's religious images also indicate Trilby's deep, essential innocence. Despite her sexual maturity, she is frequently referred to both as a child and as an angel. She seems to have stumbled upon sexual experience without even understanding it, and without realizing the implications that sexual experience has upon a woman's place in society. This fundamental innocence ultimately allows her to be redeemed.

However, Du Maurier is not suggesting that Trilby's sexual experience is unimportant. Little Billee does rail, briefly, against the sexual double standard, dramatically declaring: "what a hideous shame it is that there should be one law for the woman and another for the man" (122), but the novel does not bear out this point of view. Rather, from the time that Little Billee meets Trilby, he: "divined far down beneath the shining surface of those eyes . . . a well of sweetness; and floating somewhere in the midst of it the very heart of compassion, generosity and warm sisterly love; and under that – alas! at the bottom of all – a thin slimy layer of sorrow and shame" (27). While it is true that Trilby is composed largely of "sweetness," "compassion," and "generosity," and while she is undoubtedly the heroine of the novel, the "thin slimy layer of sorrow and shame" connotes the corruption and decay that remain at her center despite her many positive qualities. And, though her lack of shame – "she was equally unconscious of self with her clothes on or without" (60) – underscores her *naïveté* and childishness, she does eventually regret and renounce her modeling. To be the novel's true heroine, Trilby must learn to be ashamed of her body and, specifically, of the freedom with which she has displayed and shared it. She must, in other words, carry her body like a virtuous woman: hide it and deny its desires. Trilby's problem is that she has approached her body as though she were a man. "It seemed as natural for me to sit as for a man," she writes the Laird, "[n]ow I see the awful difference" (76). By recognizing this "awful difference," Trilby rejects androgyny and recognizes the distinction between men's and women's relationships to their bodies. Miserably, even pathetically, ashamed of her modeling and the other "dreadful things" (76) that she has done, Trilby accepts a body that is gendered female, which is to say that she begins to reject and deny her fleshly embodiment.

Once Trilby determines to mend her ways, she stops smoking cigars, takes on the more suitably feminine occupation of washing laundry, and obediently spends every Sunday darning the Laird's socks. In short, she becomes a true, selfless woman, accepting her womanly birthright. Trilby changes in another important way as well: she immediately begins to lose weight. "She grew thinner," the reader learns, "especially in the face, where the bones of her cheeks and jaws began to show themselves, and those bones were constructed on such right principles . . . that the improvement was astonishing, almost inexplicable" (79). Her fat, symbolizing her sensuality, melts away, her thinness indicating that she is now eating less and, metaphorically, denying her body's appetites as she did not do before. The good Englishman may be "well-fed," but the virtuous Englishwoman, the one whose life is "constructed on . . . right principles," renounces food and becomes more beautiful, the "improvement" in her now slender body "astonishing."

Du Maurier frames Trilby's changes as the triumph of her Englishness over her bohemian Frenchness. Her bilingualism has always symbolized two Trilbys. Trilby's English "was more or less that of her father, a highly educated man" (59) while her French "was that of the Quartier Latin – droll, slangy, piquant, quaint, picturesque . . . in which there was scarcely a turn of phrase that would not stamp the speaker as being hopelessly, emphatically 'no lady!'" (59). In short, her English is that of a respectable, educated (albeit not wealthy) person, while her French is that of someone who spends time primarily with men, dances the cancan, and sheds her clothes for various artists. When Little Billee walks in upon Trilby modeling and immediately bolts from the room in horror, Trilby first wonders, in French, why he might have reacted so strongly to seeing her naked. It is not until she thinks about the situation in "nice clean English . . . her father's English" (74) that an understanding of her behavior breaks in upon her mind with a "new-born feeling of shame" (74). The dichotomies here are clear: English/French, middle class/lower class, angel/whore, femininity/androgyny. England and the English language symbolize the orderly, "clean," self-disciplined, patriarchal (hence the reference to her father) paradigm that Trilby adopts. All of Du Maurier's fondness for bohemian French life does not obscure the fact that Trilby's Englishness saves her virtue. When she adopts her femininity, she does so specifically as an English woman, giving up her risqué French slang. In the company of her three friends, Trilby "grew more English every day; and that was a good thing" (58).

When Trilby reappears as "La Svengali," the changes in her body become even more apparent. Du Maurier dwells upon her thinness as a sign that Trilby has been completely redeemed from her earlier sexual looseness. When Little Billee, the Laird, and Taffy first see her perform, they note that: "Her face was thin, and had a rather haggard expression . . . but its contour was divine" (189). Trilby's face is "divine" *because* it is thin; her thinness signifies the triumph of soul over body, selflessness over selfishness, dependence over independence, femininity over androgyny. When the reader was first introduced to Trilby, she was eating. Now, she muses that: "It made [Svengali] quite unhappy when I wouldn't eat, so I used to *force* myself" (236, emphasis mine). Her appetite seems to have completely disappeared. While this lack of appetite stems from her sadness over the loss of her brother and from her abuse by Svengali, it is nevertheless a virtue, because it shows how much Trilby has starved her sensual desires. Her new thinness is lovely to her old friends: "Day by day she grew more beautiful in their eyes, in spite of her increasing pallor and emaciation – her skin was so pure and white and delicate, and the bones of her face so admirable" (244). Later, the narrator writes: "And then Trilby's pathetic beauty, so touching, so winning, in its rapid decay . . . her childlike simplicity, her transparent forgetfulness of self" (248). Like a fasting saint, Trilby's thinness corporealizes the fundamentally good and decent soul that even the evil Svengali had glimpsed in the contours of her mouth. Her "emaciation" and the "decay" of her body code Trilby's body as feminine in a way that it was not feminine at the start of the novel. Now, her "pure" and "delicate" skin signifies that she is a true woman: passive, weak, obedient, helpless, and completely selfless. Like her hands, which grow "almost transparent" (238), her thin body signifies the "transparent forgetfulness of self" that is so much more beautiful than her earlier appetite and desire. Du Maurier's repetition of the word "transparent" (the ill Trilby even stops to look in a laundry with "transparent blinds" [241]) underscores the dissolution – dissolving – of her corporeality, making her good soul more apparent. Suffering has purified Trilby.

Trilby's problem, initially, is that her body keeps dragging down, degrading, her soul; her body is an obstacle that keeps getting her into trouble. "More often than not . . . lovely female shapes are terrible complicators of the difficulties and dangers of this earthly life," the narrator warns, "especially for their owner" (32). Thus, the destruction of her body saves Trilby from her erotic desires. When her body wastes away, her soul grows stronger. In fact, Du Maurier suggests that Trilby is her soul, while her body is just something that she "owns," a possession that is not integral to her self. Du Maurier's representation of Trilby is thus in line with the nineteenth-century doctors who considered "illness to be a natural state for women because of what was believed to be their innate weakness."[26] As the conduct books and beauty manuals that I discussed in the first chapter indicate, strength, or "robustness," was not widely viewed as positive among women, whose heightened spirituality was ideally reflected in slender bodies and lack of appetite. *Trilby*'s "real woman," Alice, the woman with whom Little Billee should have fallen in love, has a "dear, weak, delicate shape" (163), and it is this shape that Trilby takes on through her illness.

Bram Dijkstra has contextualized *Trilby* within the widespread nineteenth-century cult of invalidism, in which "A healthy woman . . . was likely to be an 'unnatural' woman . . . To be ill was actually thought to be a sign of delicacy and breeding."[27] Comparing Trilby's consumptive look to saintliness, Dijkstra argues that, once she gets sick, "Trilby is free to become the true sexless, high-Victorian feminine ideal: the woman who, in her very physical helplessness, makes no further overt erotic demands upon the male."[28] All three men now feel "pure brotherly love" (244) for her (though Little Billee's obsession returns after her death), and even Mrs. Bagot can recognize the truth of Trilby's humble declaration that: "I'm not at all the dangerous or designing person you thought" (246).

Trilby is, of course, not anorexic. She, like Caroline, *loses* the ability to eat: "She lost weight daily; she seemed to be wasting and fading away from sheer general atrophy" (241). Trilby is certainly not rebelling against Svengali or anyone else in her refusal to eat, and she is not actively pursuing the goal of thinness. However, she is nevertheless figurative of the logic of anorexia. Describing her body, one contemporary anorexic woman prays: "Please dear God, help me, help me . . . I want to get out of my body, I want to get out."[29] Like the anorexic woman, who desires to "get out" of her body and imagines her body as an obstacle to her true (non-body) self, Du Maurier indicates quite clearly that Trilby must renounce her body to become a "true woman." The renunciation of body is explicitly carried out through food refusal, whether voluntary or not. Not eating, in *Trilby*, equals virtue, sexual self-control, purity, and femininity. Eating may be acceptable for the French grisette, but not for the good, honest English girl.

Meanwhile, as Trilby grows thin, Svengali gets heavy. After touring Europe with Trilby, his once slender body is now "stout and quite splendid in appearance" (188). Svengali draws strength, symbolized by fat, from Lucy, much like the vampires in *Dracula* and *Carmilla* who grow strong on others' blood. Du Maurier punishes him, as Stoker and Le Fanu punish their villains, with death. Of course, the gender politics of the texts are different, since in *Trilby*, the only "vampire" is male. However, as a Jew, and therefore an outsider, Svengali threatens social boundaries and national borders in ways that are similar to the New Woman's threats to male social and political hegemony. Moreover, anti-Semitic constructions of the Jew in the nineteenth century regularly feminized the Jewish man, drawing a clear connection between the imperfectly developed minds of women and Jews. Both the Jew and the aggressive woman must either be demonized and destroyed, as in Lucy's and Svengali's cases, or their threat dissipated, as in the case of Trilby. In each case, excessive consumption or disruptive consumption, whether literal or figural, is ceased, at least temporarily, and the unruly body put in its place.

CHAPTER 5

Christina Rossetti's sacred hunger

We must not look at goblin men,
We must not buy their fruits:
Who knows upon what soil they fed
Their hungry thirsty roots?
("Goblin Market" lines 442–45)[1]

Representations of fasting and starvation in the texts that I have discussed so far are largely located in the secular realm. Though Brontë, for example, connects gluttony to Catholicism, Lucy's starvation in *Dracula* is never located within a religious paradigm, nor is little Nell's wasting away an explicitly religious undertaking. Religious fasting did, however, enjoy a revival in the nineteenth century, both as part of the Oxford Movement in the Church of England, and in dissenting churches. Spiritual fasting and "material" fasting share some clear commonalities: food restriction within a religious context, like anorexia nervosa, constitutes a means of mortifying the body, and it posits, as does anorexia, a fundamental conflict between the desires of the body and the soul. By denying the body's needs and wishes, fasting becomes a means of purifying and cleansing both body and soul. However, the woman fasting at Lent undertakes a different practice than the woman restricting her food intake in order to fit into a particular dress size; there is clearly a slippage between these two behaviors, despite their similarities. How, then, does one approach religious fasting and connect it, if at all, to secular fasting? The work of Christina Rossetti opens up a fruitful discussion of these questions, as images of feasts and fasts recur frequently in her work, almost exclusively within the context of religious faith.

The repression of worldliness, particularly appetite, is a theme that runs throughout Rossetti's work, from her best-known poem, "Goblin Market," to her children's story *Speaking Likenesses*, to the devotional prose that she published with the Society for Promoting Christian Knowledge. Through grotesque depictions of eating, Rossetti, in all of these works, depicts appetite as a marker of sensuality and sin, a sign of humanity's fallen nature. The validation of corporeal hunger in "Goblin Market," in particular, has opened up a critical discussion about whether Rossetti patterned the poem upon an anorexic paradigm. After all, the denial of hunger and physicality praised in the poem seems to mirror the anorexic's attempt to transcend appetite and the needs of the body through fasting: some critics have even suggested that Rossetti may have been anorexic herself. Yet, although Rossetti's poetry initially suggests a tantalizing reading of anorexia nervosa, an explication of "Goblin Market" alongside Rossetti's other work reveals that its images of feasting and fasting are inextricably, and primarily, rooted in Christian fasting rituals, and thereby situate Rossetti within the Anglo-Catholic movement and within the tradition of medieval women saints and mystics, whose worship often included the control of food intake.[2] There is not only one type of hunger present in Rossetti's work. Instead, evocations of hunger in her poetry and prose frequently signal a very positive spiritual hunger for God, particularly Christ. The meaning of hunger, for Rossetti, therefore depends upon its placement within the spiritual or secular realms. Secular appetite strengthens the body but corrupts the soul, whereas secular hunger signifies the self-denial that brings one face to face with Christ. At the same time, however, Rossetti's religious fasting, signifying the denial of the body, fits snugly alongside secular cultural ideologies about the repression of sexual desire. Sacred and secular ideologies thus reinforce each other in her work.

RELIGIOUS FASTING AND ANOREXIA NERVOSA

As part of a larger effort to reform the Church of England by turning back to the beliefs and rituals of the medieval Church, Tractarians like Rossetti's charismatic minister William Dodsworth advocated frequent fasting to humble the flesh and to aid prayer. E. B. Pusey, for instance, cites the fasting of the apostles and early Christians to support an increased attention to church-sponsored fasting. "Regular and stated Fasts," he writes, "formed a part of the Discipline by which, during almost the whole period since the Christian Church has been founded, all her real sons . . . have subdued the flesh to the spirit, and brought both body and mind into a willing obedience to the Law of God."[3] In "Tract 18," Pusey alludes to and adopts the fourth homily in the Second Book of Homilies, "Of Good Works; And First of Fasting," one of the Church of England's cornerstone texts on fasting, which lays out three reasons for fasting:

"The first is, to chastise the flesh, that it be not too wanton, but tamed and brought in subjection to the spirit"; "The second, that the spirit may be more earnest and fervent in prayers"; "The third, that our fast be a testimony and witness with us before God of our humble submission to his high majesty."[4] Healthy Anglo-Catholics were expected to honor ritual church fasts in the liturgical calendar of the Book of Common Prayer; before Easter, Pusey once asked worshipers to go without food for three days.[5] Isaac Williams, whom Rossetti admired, speaks of "thorough repentance, – daily humbling, daily loving, daily praying, *daily fasting*, self-judging, self-correcting, self-renouncing, self-hating repentance" as "the jewel of great price."[6] Williams and other Tractarians contextualized fasting practices within other forms of self-discipline and ritual, including prayer, church attendance, obedience to the moral laws of the Church, and the fulfillment of sacraments such as the Eucharist. As Williams's quotation indicates, fasting was considered part of a wider emphasis on personal repentance as experienced through the repudiation of the self's desires; historian Peter Nockles discerns a consistent "quest for holiness through self-denial and mortification of bodily and worldly appetites" in the Oxford movement's rhetoric.[7] A strong ascetic strain, of which fasting is an indication, thus runs throughout its theology.

We know that Rossetti fasted from her brother William Rossetti's description of her "perpetual church-going and communions, her prayers and fasts."[8] William discloses that Rossetti's fasting was closely linked with her religious faith, a connection reinforced by her much-overlooked devotional prose, particularly *The Face of the Deep* and *Time Flies: A Reading Diary*. In *The Face of the Deep*, her exegesis of the Book of Revelation, Rossetti writes that:

The balances suggest scarcity short of literal nullity: hunger, but not necessarily starvation. Scarcity imposes frugality, exactness . . . No waste, latitude, margin; no self-pampering can be tolerated, but only a sustained self-denial: self must be stinted, selfishness starved, to give to him that needeth. And as the poor never cease out of the land and are in various degrees standing representatives of famine, this self-stinting seems after all to be the rule and standard of right living; not a desperate, exceptional resource, but a regular, continual, plain duty.[9]

In this passage, Rossetti links eating with self-indulgence, "self-pampering," that must be metaphorically starved by starving the body on a "regular," perhaps even daily, basis. Although she qualifies the word starvation slightly with the phrase "not *necessarily*," she also implies that, in some cases, starvation is an admirable way to repress desire and vice.

Rossetti's language evokes the contours of the thin figure, the body with no "waste" or "margin," the body trimmed down to its most basic and "exact" form. The body thus becomes the vehicle through which the devout express both personal penitence and sympathy for the suffering of the poor. Her rhetoric echoes Pusey's claim that "we may use food as medicine for the daily decays of nature, not for luxury; we may cut off self-indulgence, not 'fare sumptuously every day,' but feed the poor of Christ."[10] People must eat because the body requires food, but they should eat only as much as their health demands, not merely for pleasure. Implicit in these arguments is the idea that the body is somehow corrupt, or "selfish," and that the refusal to "indulge" it nourishes the soul. Fasting, again, constitutes part of a more general self-denial.

As she suggests in *The Face of the Deep*, Rossetti, like Pusey, associates appetite with fallen human nature, an idea developed at greater length in *Time Flies: A Reading Diary*, through Rossetti's remarkable description of an anemone:

A sensual Christian resembles a sea anemone. In the nobler element, air, it exists as a sluggish unbeautiful excrescence. In the lower element, water, it grows, blows and thrives. The food it assimilates is derived not from the height, but from the depth. It possesses neither eyes nor ears, but a multitude of feelers. It squats on a tenacious base, gulps all acquisitions into a capacious chasm, and harmonises with the weeds it dwells amongst. But what will become of it in a world where there shall be no more sea?[11]

The anemone's repulsiveness, for Rossetti, derives from a life oriented completely around the act of consumption. Like the sensual Christian, who satisfies his or her physical rather than spiritual cravings, the anemone reaches for food from the "depth," or material world. Worst of all, it can do nothing but consume. Bereft of eyes and ears, the organs associated with the "higher" senses of sight and sound, it possesses only a "multitude of feelers" and a grotesque, "capacious" mouth with which it sucks in nourishment. As Rossetti's anemone illustrates, consumption epitomizes sensuality and the temporal life of the body. However, Rossetti's ominous final question suggests that worldly success fore-shadows punishment, if not eternal damnation, at the Second Coming. Fasting, on the other hand, brings "us into communion with one another, into the Communion of Saints: and . . . fellowship with Christ."[12]

Considering Rossetti's negative depiction of eating in much of her work, it is not surprising that several critics, most notably Paula Marantz Cohen and Deborah Ann Thompson, have read "Goblin Market" within the context of anorexia nervosa. Besides the repression of hunger and sexuality that Rossetti so clearly praises in the poem, the doubling of Lizzie and Laurie indicates an anorexic paradigm because the disease is characterized by the two extremes of starvation and the obsessive desire to eat, which the anorexic attempts to repress and deny. Lizzie thus epitomizes the laudable refusal to eat, whereas Laura, by devouring huge amounts of food, stands for the desire to binge. Like the anorexic, who takes pride in her ability to fast, Rossetti gives moral meaning to abstention: the virtuous woman resists eating, while the sinful woman indulges her appetites. Laura becomes a "good" girl only when she is cured of the contamination of goblin fruit and renounces feasting forever.

Cohen has even speculated that Rossetti was herself anorexic, citing as evidence her adolescent breakdown:

Christina Rossetti probably developed anorexia in her teens and continued to suffer from the illness in some form ever afterward. Though we do not know what she weighed during her adolescence (only that she was quite slim), we do know that between the ages of twelve and sixteen her health and her personality underwent a radical change: she became withdrawn, overly sensitive, overly polite and exacting in religious matters, and began to suffer from the undiagnosed illnesses which would plague her throughout her lifetime.[13]

Rossetti did, as Cohen contends, undergo some sort of emotional and physical crisis in 1845 at the age of fourteen which Rossetti herself described as "neuralgia."[14] From a cheerful, energetic, talkative child, she emerged from her breakdown by all accounts over-scrupulous, reserved and extremely preoccupied with self-control. Her brother William recalled that her "temperament and character, naturally warm and free, became 'a fountain sealed.' "[15] The timing of Rossetti's breakdown, which probably took place around the time of her first menstruation, provides further evidence of anorexia.[16] Rossetti certainly felt profound ambivalence if not hatred towards the flesh. Many years later, she wrote to one of her nieces about an occasion on which, "being rebuked by my dear Mother for some fault, I seized upon a pair of scissors, and ripped up my arm to vent my wrath."[17] Here, Rossetti turns her anger inward, focusing on her flesh as the source of evil and "fault." However, none of this biographical evidence proves that Rossetti suffered from anorexia rather than depression or some other form of mental illness. On the contrary, Rossetti's letters cast doubt on the idea that she was anorexic; not only does she rarely mention food, but, when she does, she reveals no anxiety about her appetite. In an 1850 letter to her brother William, five years after the breakdown that Cohen identifies as anorexia, she notes that: "Before leaving Brighton we took tea with Mrs. Sortain, on which occasion we did not get enough to eat."[18] To Amelia Barnard Heimann she writes, in 1873, that: "I should like you to picture our day to yourself. We breakfast at 10 nominally (please accept all hours as nominal), and dine at 8; between which meals a bit of bread and butter is very acceptable as luncheon, but I don't think Gabriel takes a morsel."[19] Here, Rossetti implies that she and her mother regularly eat three meals a day, and that Gabriel's refusal to eat is noteworthy. Although such evidence of Rossetti's eating patterns is purely anecdotal, it suggests that her diet, while not substantial, does not unequivocally indicate the diet of an anorexic woman. More importantly, her letters do not demonstrate that Rossetti evinced a daily preoccupation with food in a manner consistent with anorexia nervosa.

Perhaps most importantly, Cohen does not sufficiently address Rossetti's deep religiosity, using it as proof of anorexia rather than (as is likely) the other way around, that Rossetti fasted *because* of her religious faith. The religious impetus behind Rossetti's fasting precludes definitively diagnosing her with anorexia nervosa, especially since there is no indication in Rossetti's biography that religious fasting drastically affected her health as anorexia nervosa would have. Women who wish to deny the secular have historically done so by limiting their food intake, since food is one aspect of their lives that they traditionally control. Rossetti was part of a long line of women and men who fasted as a means of renouncing worldliness in general and sexuality in particular. Religious fasting and anorexia nervosa are both defined by self-inflicted starvation despite a feeling of hunger and despite the presence of food; nevertheless, they should not be conflated into one pathology. Food refusal has many causes: saints who fasted in the Middle Ages, for instance, cannot conclusively be interpreted as anorexic because they fasted for entirely different reasons than anorexic women do today; their behavior was similar but their motivation (and thus the diagnosis) was not. In their comprehensive history of fasting, Walter Vandereycken and Ron Van Deth write that: "There is no trace of saints 'dieting' from a fear of becoming fat . . . Fasting saints were not obsessed by the exterior, outward appearance. By contrast, they strove for an inner, spiritual fusion with Christ's sufferings. It was not a cult of slenderness but a religious–mystical cult that dominated their [lives]."[20] Or, as Caroline Walker Bynum writes, "substituting one's own suffering through illness and starvation for the guilt and destitution of others is not 'symptom' – it is theology."[21] Victims of anorexia nervosa, on the other hand, are obsessively concerned with weight and appearance. Susan Bordo relates anorexia "to the pursuit of an idealized physical weight or shape; it becomes a project in service of 'body' rather than 'soul.'"[22] Anorexics, in other words, starve themselves to be thin, not to deny the secular; there is generally no significant religious component to their fasting. Rossetti's fasting, on the other hand, is always tied to a larger system of theology. There is no association in *Speaking Likenesses* or "Goblin Market," for instance, between starvation and the quest for a slim figure.

There are, of course, oppositions to this argument that are worth considering and integrating into an understanding of Rossetti's work. One could contend, for instance, that the Victorians merely conceptualized fasting differently than did people living in the medieval period, but that both behaviors represent the same asceticism and general hatred of the flesh. Rudolph Bell, who has detailed the fasting behaviors of Italian saints from 1200 to the present day, argues that anorexia became a behavioral pattern of female piety in the Middle Ages and Renaissance, and that many fasting saints, such as Clare of Assisi and Catherine of Siena, were in fact anorexic. Specifically, Bell claims that "[n]early half of the forty-two Italian women who lived and died in the thirteenth century and came to be recognized as saints exhibited an anorexic behavior pattern."[23] For these women, Bell contends, "[f]ood is food, not an incorporated phallic symbol, but it is no less sexual for being food. It sustains the body, corrupts life on earth, and thereby kills the soul, life everlasting."[24] Since fasting saints and women suffering from anorexia nervosa both control their food intake in an effort to discipline the body and maintain a sense of personal autonomy, nineteenth- and twentieth-century anorexia nervosa could be merely a secularized and medicalized version of overtly religious fasting and therefore related to what Foucault calls the "discursive explosion of the eighteenth and nineteenth centuries."[25] "The Middle Ages," Foucault explains, "had organized around the theme of the flesh and the practice of penance a discourse that was markedly unitary. In the course of recent centuries, this relative uniformity was broken apart, scattered, and multiplied in an explosion of distinct discursivities which took form in demography, biology, medicine, psychiatry, psychology, ethics, pedagogy, and political criticism."[26] Following Foucault, one can argue that contemporary therapists have "created" a new disease from an old one by discussing the same fasting behavior within a psychological rather than theological discourse.

Such an explanation is all the more plausible considering the increasing professionalization of medicine in the nineteenth century, a movement codified in such events as the first publication of the *Medical Directory* of practitioners in 1845 and the creation of a medical register, which officially differentiated between physicians with and without "registerable qualifications," in 1858.[27] Consequently, religious and medical authorities carried on public contests about how to interpret the behavior of girls who refused to eat. In several well-documented cases, priests or ministers argued that fasting girls were possessed by the Holy Spirit, while medical authorities dismissed the girls as either hysterics or frauds. The debate essentially centered around who would determine and interpret fasting behavior, and, more and more frequently throughout the century, physicians won. Three cases illustrate this conflict. From 1807 to 1814, a working-class woman named Ann Moore claimed to eat no food, explaining and justifying her behavior within the framework of religious piety. In *An Account of the Extraordinary Abstinence of Ann Moor* [*sic*] (1811), one of her supporters claims that her "extraordinary affliction" of being unable to eat had brought her to a "state of true repentance" and that Moore considered her inability to eat "a judgment for her sins."[28] Moore was later unmasked as a fraud after it was discovered that her daughter had been secretly feeding her, a blow to the interpretation of food refusal as a miraculous occurrence sent from God. In the most celebrated and frequently cited case, "fasting girl" Sarah Jacob (briefly discussed in chapter 1) was championed as a sort of miracle by her parents, vicar, and much of the public, while medical authorities, most notably Robert Fowler, insisted that she suffered from hysteria. Fowler's arguments were particularly compelling after Sarah's death from starvation, when he wrote that "[t]here must be something unnatural in the mental training of those individuals who, in this nineteenth century, announce themselves as patrons of the miraculous and abnormal! Who are they? They certainly are not our great students of Nature – the devotees of *facts!*"[29] Finally, in 1870, the physician Henry Barber described the case of an eleven-year-old fasting girl named Eleanor Addison who claimed that during a trance-like state "she had been in heaven, and had angels about her ... and she was so happy in their company that she desired to return to them"; consequently, she stopped eating and lay in bed with "a happy ecstatic expression."[30] Barber consulted other doctors about the case, treating the girl with warm olive oil and hot-water bottles, "nourishing the body by absorption, and driving the blood from the head."[31] As the girl recovered, he noted that "[h]undreds of people had crowded to see the child from the first . . . and as every one had long concluded she must die, this strange treatment of mine was looked upon as a cruel and unwarrantable interference"; the girl eventually regained strength and began to eat.[32] Jacob's and Addison's cases provide a nice illustration of the gradual shift from understanding fasting as anorexia mirabilis ("holy" anorexia) to understanding it as a medical condition, first hysteria and eventually anorexia nervosa, thereby suggesting a certain amount of slippage between the two kinds of fasting. Although I am not claiming that any of these three patients were actually anorexic (Addison, in particular, does not generally conform to descriptions of the disease), the significance of their cases is that physicians were disputing public perception that fasting was a holy state and were treating it instead as an illness that required intervention. In so doing, medical men were laying claim to the ability and prerogative to define pathological behavior, if necessary by supplanting religious authority. Food refusal was, gradually, medicalized and understood, in Fowler's language, not as something "miraculous," but as a series of "facts" that could be understood by science.

Despite these intriguing arguments, however, merely lumping together behaviors with clearly different etiologies is ultimately facile and prevents us from clearly understanding either phenomenon. The boundaries between anorexia nervosa and religious fasting do overlap, and, unless we can conceive of a religious tradition wholly isolated from its wider social context, we must assume mutual interaction between theology and secular ideology. Victorian proscriptions about female appetite undoubtedly reinforced the value of religious fasting, and some Victorian women may have used religious reasons consciously or subconsciously to justify food refusal because of a disgust with the fat on their bodies. Christina Rossetti, for instance, was certainly influenced both by her intense religious beliefs and by the larger secular culture in which she lived. Acknowledging non-religious fasting in *The Face of the Deep*, she writes that: "An eminent physician once told me that there are people who would benefit in health by fasting: a secondary motive, yet surely not an unlawful one. To perform a duty from a motive which is not wrong, may prove a step towards performing it from the motive which is right."[33] Here, Rossetti distinguishes between secular and sacred fasting while praising them both and drawing attention to the similarities between acts of food refusal. It would, of course, be reductive to *conflate* the behavior of medieval saints with the behavior of women in modern or contemporary England and America, or to compare the fasting of Mother Theresa with the fasting of the singer Karen Carpenter or an adolescent girl today. These behaviors are markedly different both with regard to their methods and goals. Similarly, Christina Rossetti's devoutness, along with her clear distinction between "right" and secondary motives for fasting, problematizes any reductive diagnosis of Rossetti as an anorexic. Nevertheless, religious fasting and anorexia nervosa can be viewed as related phenomena. The intensity with which Rossetti's work focuses upon the inherent rottenness of the flesh, including sexual desire, suggests her intense discomfort with sexual feelings and with the body in general, and thus her religious fasting can be interpreted as fitting hand in glove with secular proscriptions against female sexual desire.

It is important to note, also, that religious fasting is usually part of a wider mortification of the flesh that might also include giving up favorite activities and pleasures or even punishing the flesh through self-flagellation and other means. "It is only modern historians," Bynum points out, "who have given food-rejection its startling and privileged place in medieval women's piety."[34] Bynum's argument holds true for Victorian fasters as well. In January 1866, the year that he converted to the Roman Catholic church, Gerard Manley Hopkins wrote the following Lenten program in his diary:

For Lent. No pudding on Sundays. No tea except if to keep me awake and then without sugar. Meat only once a day. No verses in Passion Week or on Fridays. No lunch or meat on Fridays. Not to sit in armchair except can work in no other way. Ash Wednesday and Good Friday bread and water.[35]

Hopkins's fasting is only one of several behaviors with which he tested and proved his faith in Christ, and food only one enjoyment, along with poetry and a comfortable chair, that he forced himself to sacrifice. In the notebooks in which he minutely recorded his daily sins and scruples, Hopkins lists over-indulgence in food along with such varied behaviors as not working hard enough, arguing with others, making fun of his parents, and looking at men. On March 31, 1865, for example, he lists: "Intemperance in food-biscuits," "Wine twice a day," and "Intemperance in food at Addis' dessert" along with "Wasting much of morning in quad," "No reading done or anything," and "Wicked thoughts have occurred and not been at once driven away," among many others.[36] Differentiating himself from the anorexic woman, the control of food intake was not the primary, all-encompassing behavior of Hopkins's life; nor was it for Christina Rossetti. Perhaps most importantly, neither Hopkins nor Rossetti connect fasting with body fat. Rather, fasting was subsumed in their larger religious exercises and beliefs. As Diane D'Amico has recently argued, "[f]or Rossetti, controlling bodily and worldly appetites was an important stage in the quest for holiness; it was not an end in itself."[37] Furthermore, although the vast majority of anorexics are women, religious fasting has never been an exclusively female undertaking. Like Hooker and the other early divines to whom they turned for precedent, nineteenth-century proponents of religious fasting, such as Pusey, Dodsworth, and Williams, understood it as an endeavor undertaken both by men and by women as a means of mortifying the flesh.

Tennyson's "The Holy Grail," from *Idylls of the King* (1869), highlights the slippery distinctions between secular and sacred fasting. In the poem, a nun does penance for Camelot's adulterous sins: "she pray'd and fasted, till the sun / Shone, and the wind blow, thro' her, and I thought / She might have risen and floated when I saw her" (lines 98–100).[38] The nun's fasting renders her incorporeal, merely a walking spirit whose fasting brings her a glimpse of the Grail. Her spirit-body recalls heroines like Dickens's Agnes, whose incorporeality transforms them into exaggerated figures of femininity. Tennyson's representation of the saintly religious woman thus shares traits with the representation of the virtuous secular women, indicating the interstices between accounts of sacred and secular hunger. Tennyson also genders the activity of fasting as female, even while he indicates that it can be honorably undertaken by both men and women. On the one hand, Percivale follows the nun's example and "myself fasted and pray'd / Always, and many among us many a week / Fasted and pray'd even to the uttermost, / Expectant of the wonder that would be" (lines 130–133). By including Percivale and the other knights' fasting, Tennyson suggests that the denial of the body is an act that brings both men and women closer to God. On the other hand, Percivale and Galahad are the least rugged, stereotypically masculine of Arthur's knights, Galahad a mere "bright boy-knight" (line 156). The act of denying the body through food refusal is therefore gendered as female even when undertaken by a male, but it is not the provenance merely of female religious faith.

Tennyson's medievalism provides a nice segue to Rossetti's work, because understanding Rossetti's work within the medieval tradition of fasting saints allows the reader to acknowledge the role of fasting in Rossetti's life without grouping her with the victims of anorexia, whose fasting is secular and, in most cases, far more physically dangerous. Rossetti not only belonged to a religious movement that looked back to the authority of the pre-Reformation Church for spiritual guidance, but she studied saints and martyrs on her own, writing two collections of saints' lives, *Called to be Saints* and *Time Flies*. As Bynum explores in *Holy Feast and Holy Fast*, food played a crucial role in the lives of many medieval female saints and mystics. On the one hand, the early and medieval Churches emphasized fasting as a way to imitate Christ's sufferings and to mortify the body. On the other hand, Christians actually consumed the body and blood of God during communion, so that fasting was part of a wider set of behaviors involving food. Unlike anorexia nervosa, which attempts (but inevitably fails) to wholly annihilate the appetite, religious fasting offers recourse to a positive, sanctioned form of consumption, the Eucharist. Bynum writes that "[i]n the sermon and song, theology and story, of the high Middle Ages . . . the food on the altar was the God who became man; it was bleeding and broken flesh . . . To eat God, therefore, was to become suffering flesh with his suffering flesh; it was to imitate the cross."[39] This consumption of God was sometimes accompanied, particularly for women, by sensual pleasure, including "visions" of music, sweet smells, and delicious tastes in the mouth. Mary of Oignies, for instance, experienced God during communion as the taste of honey while Alice of Schaerbeke drank sweet liquid from the breasts of Christ.[40] Not only did "women quite unself-consciously [think] of God as food," but "the biographers who repeated their comments persistently used extended food metaphors to elaborate the significance of women's practices. James repeatedly described Mary's ecstasies as inebriation, as hunger and fullness . . . Thomas of Cantimpre spoke of Margaret of Ypres as accepting, chewing, and savoring God."[41] Food was thus the literal and metaphorical means through which many medieval women expressed religious worship and through which their faith was conceptualized by others. Although Rossetti's cultural context was, of course, very different than that of medieval women, her fasting can best be understood within a similar theological context.

SACRED AND SECULAR APPETITE

Cecil Lang, while defining the term "pre-Raphaelite," contends that "[p]re-Raphaelitism . . . strives, impossibly, to accept and reject [philosophical dualism] simultaneously: Matter and spirit are not quite different and not quite identical, they are 'the same and not the same.' Pre-Raphaelite fantasy affirms the dichotomy, Pre-Raphaelite particularity repudiates it."[42] Lang's claim is especially applicable to a reading of "Goblin Market," for, while Rossetti on the one hand conflates the spiritual and the secular realms by using similar language to describe the two (language that contemporary readers usually identify as erotic), "Goblin Market" does not reject a dualistic world view; instead, Rossetti ultimately separates matter from spirit, consistently distinguishing between sacred and secular, spirit and flesh. In "The World," for instance, the "soft, exceeding fair" (1) world metamorphoses at night into a beast "Loathsome and foul with hideous leprosy" (3), its true nature revealed. What appears beautiful is hideous, both corrupt and corrupting. Revealing a similar dualism, "Goblin Market" juxtaposes sinful consumption with a virtuous renunciation of appetite in order to teach its readers a moral lesson about the world: despite superficial similarities, bringing similar imagery to bear on different kinds of consumption does not collapse the essential moral differences between them.

The dualism implicit in "Goblin Market" stems from the poem's allegorical narrative structure. Though "Goblin Market" is not a strict allegory, it does adhere to the general structure of allegory. First, Lizzie and Laura are not fully realized "realistic" characters according to conventional literary definitions of realism; rather, they personify conflicting tendencies and are, as many critics have noted, really two halves of one whole self: "Cheek to cheek and breast to breast / Locked together in one nest" (197–198). Second, allegory, in which particulars lead to a second, more general universal meaning, allows for a dualistic epistemology and is therefore a natural vehicle for didactic literature such as religious tracts and children's lessons, two genres in which "Goblin Market" can arguably be situated. "Goblin Market" is, of course, an extremely complicated poem, and one that allows for a multiplicity of readings, as the number of essays on the poem suggests. Calling the poem an allegory, moreover, does not mean that the critic must or can ferret out *one* true meaning. On the contrary, as post-structuralist critics have argued, "[a]llegory bases itself frankly on the disruption of signifier and signified and therefore renounces the illusions of semantic unity and directness promoted by such modes as symbolism."[43] In Rossetti's poem, in particular, several allegories – about sexuality, about the economic market – coexist, and particular images fit into different allegorical readings. Such an understanding of allegory is still predicated, however, on a present relationship between signifier and signified, even if that relationship is a complicated one. Like the medieval allegories or the enormously popular work of John Bunyan, "Goblin Market" *does* subscribe to a fundamental dualism of body/spirit that must inform any sustained reading of "Goblin Market," a dualism that is particularly important for a reading of consumption images in the poem. Both anorexia nervosa and religious fasting, after all, operate on a dualistic axis, in which appetite is associated with the body, which is then disassociated from the mind or spirit. Just as allegory posits a particular as a sign for the universal, the ancient split between flesh and mind implies that the body (and its behavior) is emblematic of the spirit. It makes sense, then, that a text concerned with consumption would structure itself as allegory.

Any interpretation of "Goblin Market" hinges on the meaning of Rossetti's goblin fruit. The tantalizing fruits which open the poem – "Plump unpecked cherries" (7), "Bloom-down-cheeked peaches" (9), and "Wild free-born cranberries" (11) – clearly refer to Lizzie and Laura's state of sexual *naïveté*. However, fruit is also a common biblical symbol, with which Rossetti was familiar both from her own reading of the Bible and from Tractarian preachers such as Pusey and Dodsworth, who frequently employed fruit as emblems of spirituality in their sermons. In John Keble's enormously popular *The Christian Year*, which Rossetti read, underlined, and illustrated in her own hand, Keble regularly uses fruit imagery to symbolize worldliness and Godliness.[44] In "Eleventh Sunday After Trinity," for example, he employs them to warm sinners that: "in His wrath shall God uproot / The trees He set, for lack of fruit" (lines 32–33). Here, fruit signifies Christian faith, the opposite of Rossetti's dangerous, worldly goblin fruit. In some cases, also, a particular fruit has widely divergent symbolic meanings: for example, figs, one of the goblin fruits that Laura devours, traditionally symbolize both the female sex and the state of Israel. While the goblin figs that Laura eats are lusciously physical, in other of her poems, Rossetti draws upon the fig's sacred meaning; in "Ash Wednesday," for instance, the narrator describes herself as "figtree fruit-unbearing" (17). The language with which Rossetti describes disease-ridden goblin fruit is in many cases the same language that she uses elsewhere to describe fruit emblematic of Christian faith. Simply as an example, Rossetti's focus on the fruits' sweetness, deceptively "Sweet to tongue" (30), recalls the love of Christ in one of her devotional poems as "[m]uch sweeter . . . than honey to my mouth" ("Love of Christ Which Passeth Knowledge" 11), an image drawn from the scroll in the Book of Revelation, "sweet as honey in my mouth" (Revelation 10: 10). The phrase "Sweeter than honey from the rock" (129) in "Goblin Market" has similar biblical resonances, referring specifically to Psalm 81: 16, which reads: "And with honey out of the rock should I have satisfied thee."[45] Rossetti thus indicates that the act of consumption and the desire to consume are not *in themselves* sinful, complicating an analysis of the poem that simply reads eating as evil:

what matters, instead, is the *object* of consumption.[46] One can experience pleasure either through the sensual consumption of delicious fruits or through the consumption of God, but Rossetti clearly gives preference to the former because secular hunger corrupts while incorporeal hunger heals.

Along with leading Tractarians, Rossetti seems to have believed in the Real Presence of Christ at the celebration of the Eucharist. Although Tractarians did not accept the Roman Catholic doctrine of transubstantiation (in which bread and wine physically become body and blood), proponents of the Real Presence claimed that after the bread and wine are consecrated, Christ is present either in the actual elements of bread and wine or in the recipient him or herself, so that bread and wine "became [body and blood] in virtue, power, and effect."[47] Communion, then, is not merely symbolic or commemorative of the Last Supper. In Rossetti's devotional exegesis of Revelation, for instance, Rossetti writes that: "Christ is our Tree of Life, whereof even now we eat and drink in the Sacrament of His most Blessed Body and Blood."[48] The conception of the Eucharist as a sacred meal in which Christ is consumed is central to images of consumption in "Goblin Market," in which the eating of goblin fruit becomes an inverted communion. The goblins, for instance, "weave a crown / Of tendrils, leaves and rough nuts brown" (99–100) in a Dionysian mockery of Christ's crown of thorns, asking Lizzie to "take a seat with us, / Honour and eat with us . . . Our feast is but beginning" (368–371). This feast, however, destroys the soul rather than bringing it out of the death of sin, leaving Laura "dwindling . . . knocking at Death's door" (320–321). Laura's illness stems from her transgressive act of eating; alluding to the Edenic tree of life (and to Rossetti's conception of Christ as tree of life in *The Face of the Deep*), Rossetti notes that Laura's "tree of life dropped from the root" (260). Like the sterile goblin seed that she carefully but hopelessly tends, Laura is unable to yield spiritual fruit because of her sinful act of secular, and implicitly sexual, consumption. Nonetheless, eating also *redeems* Laura after she feasts off her sister's body. When the goblins attack Lizzie, she turns into nourishment for her sister, "a fruit-crowned orange-tree / White with blossoms honey sweet" (415–416). Again, Rossetti turns to images of honey, contrasting poisonous goblin honey to the sanctified honey of the Eucharist: because of Lizzie's sacrifice, goblin fruit has been transformed, has taken on a different meaning. No longer is fruit merely fruit, with all of its connotations of sin; it has, like the bread and wine of the Eucharist, been mystically transformed and Lizzie has become Eucharist, both Christ and food. She therefore commands Laura to: "Hug me, kiss me, suck my juices . . . Eat me, drink me, love me" (468, 471) in language simultaneously erotic and spiritual.

This conflation of sexual and sacred imagery appears repeatedly in Rossetti's religious poetry. In "The Martyr," a young woman, "Quickened with a fire / Of sublime desire" (31–32), is burned at the stake: "her breath came thickly," Rossetti writes, "With the longing to see God coming pantingly" (44–45). After death, she is ecstatically taken up into heaven, "Satisfied with hopeful rest, and replete with God" (54). In other poems, Christ is figured as a lover who can "control / And charm hearts till they grieve" ("A Bruised Reed Shall He Not Break" 11–12). Such a conflation of secular and spiritual language stems, as Antony Harrison has noted, from the courtly love poetry of Petrarch and Dante, for whom "the secular – especially the erotic – and the religious interpenetrate, often becoming metaphors for one another."[49] Rossetti's coupling of eros and agape is also an extension of Tractarian rhetoric, which took much of its inspiration from medieval discourse; Pusey, for instance, writes that the penitent must be "*quickened* by God's Holy Spirit."[50] However, the union of sexual and religious language in Rossetti's work should not be mistaken for the relativity of all pleasure. Rossetti consistently privileges the pleasure that one receives from religious faith over worldly pleasures; unlike delight derived from earthly fruit, time does not diminish spiritual joy. Using erotic language to describe religious faith both makes the spiritual experience more immediate – actually physical – and, within the context of faith, sanctifies the erotic. Ecstasy from goblin fruit eventually kills, but Eucharistic ecstasy heals when Laura is cured through Lizzie's sacrifice. Rossetti's focus on the pleasures of lawful consumption complicate a reading of the poem within the anorexic paradigm, because anorexia nervosa denies sensual pleasure altogether; it evokes a vocabulary only of sensory deprivation. Rossetti's asceticism, on the other hand, substitutes one vocabulary of pleasure for another, positing both pleasure after death and a glimpse of that pleasure on earth through Christian living.

Sylvia Bailey Shurbutt represents many contemporary Rossetti scholars in her desire to read "Goblin Market" as a revisionary response to patriarchy, claiming that: "When Laura/Eve succumbs to the goblin fruit, she is affirming her sexuality, her creativity, and her right to be an intellectual being."[51] Rossetti, Shurbutt contends, "presents women themselves narrating to their children their story, creating their own myth."[52] The metaphors of consumption in "Goblin Market," however, support a less subversive interpretation of the poem, and one truer to Rossetti's work as a whole. If Laura is sickened by fruit which represents sensual knowledge, or "poison in the blood" (554), and cured by that which represents spiritual knowledge, then Rossetti necessarily privileges the latter fruit to the exclusion of the former. Laura not only renounces goblin fruit, but teaches her children to avoid "[t]he wicked, quaint fruit-merchant men" (554–555) as well. Their "mother-hearts beset with fears" (546), Lizzie and Laura therefore pass on to their children the same system of beliefs with which they grew up, not a radical new myth. By the end of the poem, the sisters have been absorbed into the domestic, female space of the home; their husbands, though not directly involved in the narrative, are still an ideological constraint in the poem. "Goblin Market" does not end with matriarchal community but with an evocation of separate spheres, and with female creative power circumscribed.

Although Rossetti believed in a woman's creative and intellectual abilities, she did not, despite the sensuality of much of her poetry, affirm women's sexuality. Nor was Rossetti open to *all* intellectual knowledge, seeing some as dangerously worldly. In *The Face of the Deep* she argues that: "It becomes a matter of conscience what poems and novels to read, and how much of the current news of the day . . . Whilst studying the devil I must take heed that my study become not devilish by reason of sympathy."[53] Any works of art that tempt one into sinful thoughts or behavior must be avoided, Rossetti claims, because intellect ranks less important than godliness. Thus, while contemporary readers might view positively Laura's experience of sensual pleasure, or Lizzie's curiosity when she "for the first time in her life / Began to listen and look" (227–228), the poem itself does not. Lizzie's choice to "listen and look" is heroically brave and Christlike, but remember that Lizzie "stood, / In *deadly peril* to do her good" (557–558; my emphasis). "Goblin Market" extols Lizzie's actions because she undertakes them for the greater good of turning her sister from goblin temptation, not because the act of looking is in itself praiseworthy. In general, Rossetti favored a sort of holy circumspection, in which people avoid temptation that they cannot resist. She claims that "Eve's temptation and fall suggest the suitableness and safety of much . . . ignorance, and the wholesomeness of studying what is open without prying into what is secret."[54] Although Eve, like Laura, is redeemed in Rossetti's teleology, both women teach us not to reach for "secret" knowledge that might endanger our chances of salvation.

The denial of sensuality in "Goblin Market" is brought into clearer focus when the poem is considered next to an earlier poem of Rossetti's entitled "The Dead City," which explores many of the same issues of consumption and sin as the later poem, and which can be read as an earlier draft of "Goblin Market." Rossetti wrote "The Dead City" when she was seventeen and published it in *Verses*, a collection of poetry privately printed by her grandfather Gabriel Polidori in 1847. While "The Dead City" is not the same poem as "Goblin Market," and while Rossetti's aim was surely not identical in both poems, the similarities between the two nevertheless encourage the reader to read "Goblin Market" in light of the earlier poem.

"The Dead City" opens in a forest, through which the narrator "rambled . . . With a careless hardihood / Heeding not the tangled way" (1–3). As heedless as Laura at the opening of "Goblin Market," the narrator travels through a lush landscape in which "Streamlets bubbled all around / On the green and fertile ground, / Thro' the rushes and the grass, / Like a sheet of liquid glass" (16–19). However, this seemingly benign landscape, like that of the "brookside rushes" (33) in "Goblin Market," gradually shifts as the narrator stumbles upon a deserted city, "a heap of ruins old" and "scene most desolate" (84, 85). Though the city is "splendid" (91) and ostentatious, it is curiously silent and deserted. Eventually, the narrator stumbles upon a tent that contains the remains of a magnificent feast:

> In a green emerald basket were
> Sun-red apples, streaked, and fair;
> Here the nectarine and peach
> And ripe plum lay, and on each
> The bloom rested every where.
>
> Grapes were hanging overhead,
> Purple, pale, and ruby-red;
> And in panniers all around
> Yellow melons shone, fresh found,
> With the dew upon them spread.
>
> And the apricot and pear
> And the pulpy fig were there;
> Cherries and dark mulberries,
> Bunchy currants, strawberries,
> And the lemon wan and fair.
>
> (181–195)

Here, Rossetti experiments with the list that she perfects in the more sophisticated "Goblin Market." Despite the sometimes clumsy cadences and rhymes of the earlier poem, the imagery in both narratives is strikingly similar, suggesting that "The Dead City" marks Rossetti's first attempt to write the poem that eventually became "Goblin Market." The fruit in "The Dead City" is significant first of all for its sheer bulk, the lack of moderation with which the tables have been laden. As in "Goblin Market," Rossetti describes the fruit with intensely physical imagery – "pulpy," "bunchy," "juicy" – and many of the fruits appear in both poems: apples, cherries, peaches, melons, grapes, pears, currants and figs. In both poems, consumption of fruit leads to death, for in the tent the narrator discovers that the inhabitants of the city, including young children, have been turned to stone. Rossetti describes the languorous, supine positions of the stone guests in detail: a mother who lazily "lay, and smiled" (246), an old man who "slept, worn out / With the revelry and rout" (251–252) and a "strong man [who] sat and gazed / On a girl" (253–254). One young woman, "the ringlets of her hair / Round her slender fingers twined" (237–238), apparently awaits a sexual encounter, for "she blushed as she reclined, / Knowing that her love was there" (239–240). The allusions to blushing, to the "Flushing cheek and kindling eye" (214) of the stone guests, suggest their indulgence of sexual desire.

Like Jeannie, who "dwindled and grew grey" (156) after eating goblin fruit, the revelers have been transformed into stone as punishment for their "luxury and pride" (163). However, their sins are more general than the simple sexual indulgence which Rossetti indicates. Blaming the downfall of the magical city on its "warm voluptuous state" (175) and corresponding neglect of daily work, Rossetti details the banquet's "warm delicious rest; / With its couches softly sinking, / And its glow, not made for thinking, / But for careless joy at best" (207–210). Like Laura, who stops doing her domestic chores after eating the goblin fruit, the "careless" and unthinking banqueters have neglected their daily work in favor of the pleasures of flesh, including the "delicious" pleasure of doing nothing. Wondering who will pick the city's bountiful crops, the narrator notes that: "Vines were climbing everywhere / Full of purple grapes and fair: / And far off I saw the corn / With its heavy head down borne" (146–150). "The Dead City" validates action over sloth and gluttony, recalling the Victorian and Protestant ethics that define work inside or outside the home as each person's Christian and civic duty. One must work for and prepare food, as Lizzie and Laura do at the beginning and end of "Goblin Market"; consumption alone (as portrayed in the middle portion of "Goblin Market") leads to decline and even to death.

Rossetti describes labor with the biblically resonant language of vines and wine presses: "Who shall strip the bending vine? / Who shall tread the press for wine? / Who shall bring the harvest in" (151–153) the narrator

wonders. The banqueters have failed to distinguish between their corporeal appetite and the more important hunger for Christian faith, here
symbolized by Eucharistic wine. Rossetti implies that "good" hunger –
hunger for union with Christ – requires energy; she uses verbs like "strip"
and "tread" to distinguish sacred hunger from the indolent, secular
hunger of the stone guests. Faith, in Rossetti's theology, takes energy
and commitment that cannot be mustered by people solely concerned
with the enjoyments of this world.

Like "Goblin Market," "The Dead City" posits a distinction between
two kinds of consumption, an opposition that appears in several poems
in *Goblin Market and Other Poems*. In "The World," for instance, the "Ripe
fruits, sweet flowers, and full satiety" (6) of the secular world disguise
"A very monster void of love and prayer" (8): fullness is replaced by
emptiness, and eating by the threat of being eaten. "A Peal of Bells"
presents a similar dynamic of hunger and, because it is infrequently
reprinted, I will quote it in its entirety:

> Strike the bells wantonly,
>> Tinkle tinkle well
> Bring me wine, bring me flowers,
>> Ring the silver bell.
> All my lamps burn scented oil,
>> Hung on laden orange trees,
> Whose shadowed foliage is the foil
>> To golden lamps and oranges.
> Heap my golden plates with fruit,
>> Golden fruit, fresh-plucked and ripe;
>> Strike the bells and breathe the pipe;
> Shut out showers from summer hours–
> Silence that complaining lute–
>> Shut out thinking, shut out pain,
>> From hours that cannot come again.
>
> Strike the bells solemnly,
>> Ding dong deep:
> My friend is passing to his bed,
>> Fast asleep;
> There's plaited linen round his head,
>> While foremost go his feet–
> His feet that cannot carry him.
> My feast's a show, my lights are dim;
>> Be still, your music is not sweet,–
> There is no music more for him:
>> His lights are out, his feast is done;

His bowl that sparkled to the brim
Is drained, is broken, cannot hold;
    My blood is chill, my blood is cold;
    His death is full, and mine begun.

The "wanton" banquet of "A Peal of Bells" evokes the feasts of "Goblin
Market" and "The Dead City" and, like Laura, the narrator revels in her
greedy, unrestrained consumption. "Heap my golden plates with fruit, /
Golden fruit, fresh-plucked and ripe," she commands, aggressively
seeking her own pleasure rather than waiting to be seduced by a
troop of goblin men. Like the fruit that she demands, the narrator is
"fresh-plucked and ripe," a sexually experienced woman allied both
with appetite and with Dionysian, pagan rites. Indulgence in appetite is
a substitute for "thinking" and "pain," much as it substitutes for work
and responsibility in "Goblin Market" and "The Dead City."

The poem takes a dramatic turn in the second stanza, in which Rossetti
unveils the beauty of the first stanza as merely a ghastly "show" (23).
The sensual heat of the first stanza, evoked by images of burning lamps,
summer, oranges and gold, abruptly freezes in the second stanza with
the narrator's lament that "My blood is chill, my blood is cold" (29).
The heaped plates and goblets of wine give way to decay and death,
and a friend's corpse is carried to his bed, the tinkling of bells replaced
with a solemn funeral dirge. In death, starvation succeeds feasting: a
"drained" and "broken" bowl displaces the golden plates piled with
fruit. Fullness with worldly pleasures implies an inevitable emaciation
of the soul; one cannot enjoy to surfeit the pleasures of this world and
expect to have a full plate after death. Now that "His death is full," the
man's "feast is done," suggesting that he himself has been consumed
by death as a result of his sensual consumption during life. Alternately,
suffering and metaphorical starvation during life bring a happy fullness
in death. In "A Better Resurrection," for example, the speaker laments
that "My life is like a broken bowl, / A broken bowl that cannot hold /
One drop of water for my soul" (17–19). At death, however, the persona
hopes to be remolded by Christ and transformed into "A royal cup for
Him my King: / O Jesus, drink of me" (23–24). The empty bowl is thus
replaced by the full cup. "A Better Resurrection" inverts "A Peal of Bells":
for the faithful, death brings union with Christ, in which one is both
filled by Christ as a cup is filled with wine and provides sustenance
for Christ. Happiness after death, significantly, is figured in terms of
appetite.

Finally, worldly appetite is even more explicitly linked to death in "My Dream," one of Rossetti's most curious and appealing verses. The poem describes an enormous crocodile who turns violently upon his fellow crocodiles:

> An execrable appetite arose,
> He battened on them, crunched, and sucked them in.
> He knew no law, he feared no binding law,
> But ground them with inexorable jaw:
> The luscious fat distilled upon his chin,
> Exuded from his nostrils and his eyes,
> While still like hungry death he fed his maw;
> Til every minor crocodile being dead
> And buried too, himself gorged to the full,
> He slept with breath oppressed and unstrung claw.
>
> (25–34)

Rossetti playfully alluded to the poem while describing her own eating habits in an 1870 letter to Amelia Barnard Heimann: "I am house-keeper here, so you may imagine with what consummate skill all things are administered. An intinerant merchant of poultry sometimes rescues us from lamb, and we have discovered a superior local sausage. Our united efforts have floored a melon, and various other items have we *crunched with inexorable jaw*, to quote from a familiar poet."[55] As Rossetti's letter indicates, eating is at the very center of "My Dream," though she coyly and characteristically refuses to hint at the message of the poem, concluding it with the lines: "What can it mean? you ask. I answer not / For meaning, but myself must echo, What" (49–50).

Though Rossetti hides her moral within a fantastic tale, the crocodile embodies what Rossetti, in "The Three Enemies," depicts as the major obstacles to Christian faith and salvation: the world, the flesh, and the devil. Because he "waxed beyond the rest / Wore kinglier girdle and a kingly crown, / While crowns and orbs and sceptres starred his breast" (15–17), the crocodile represents the world and the quest for secular power: by greedily stuffing his "punier brethren" into his mouth, he alludes especially to the destructiveness of imperial power. His enormous appetite allies him with the flesh, as does his hyperbolically phallic tail, "Broad as a rafter, potent as a flail" (22), with which he abuses the other crocodiles but which eventually "dwindled to the common size" (35). Finally, his dragon-like appearance, gleaming "compact and green with scale on scale," evokes Satan; he looks very much like the Satanic dragon of Rossetti's short story "The Lost Titian": "flaming, clawed, preposterous."[56] Appetite and the act of eating thus act as signifiers of greed and lust for power, of overweening physicality, and ultimately of Satan himself.

After his cannibalistic feast, the crocodile meets its enemy in the form of a "wingèd vessel" (38) that, in juxtaposition to the huge crocodile, is "Supreme yet weightless" (43). The boat is clearly emblematic of divine retribution, "white . . . as an avenging ghost" (41) and both omnipotent ("supreme") and incorporeal ("weightless"). Moreover, Rossetti adds that "I know not what it bore of freight or host" (40), the word "host" a reference to the consecrated wafer or bread of the Eucharist. Upon seeing the boat, the "prudent crocodile rose on its feet / And shed appropriate tears and wrung his hands" (47–48). In these final lines of the poem, Rossetti sets up important dualisms of matter versus spirit and the secular versus the spiritual. Power is linked with the spiritual and the bodiless; the crocodile, or flesh, which stands for the degraded secular realm, finally submits to a higher, nonphysical, power. The phrase "hungry death" links the two, underscoring Rossetti's idea, expressed so forcibly in "The Dead City" and "A Peal of Bells," that sensual consumption – metaphorical consumption of the world's pleasures as well as a gluttonous desire for literal, gustatory consumption – leads to spiritual and ultimately eternal death. Flesh is, moreover, deceptive, for the crocodile's tears and repentance at the end of the poem are clearly a sham. The crocodile symbolizes those appetites and desires of the flesh that the Christian must, like Lizzie, deliberately refuse.

SPEAKING LIKENESSES: ROSSETTI'S CHILDREN'S FANTASY

The negative characterization of sensual appetite that Rossetti explores in "My Dream" and the other poems in *Goblin Market and Other Poems* resurfaces twelve years later in her children's story *Speaking Likenesses*, which Rossetti described to her brother Dante Gabriel as "a Christmas trifle, would-be in the *Alice* style with an eye to the market.[57] Rossetti shares Carroll's interest in death and his use of grotesque images, though the Victorian reading public responded much less enthusiastically to her work. *Speaking Likenesses* is a violent and unsentimental tale that gave at least one contemporary reviewer an "uncomfortable feeling" and today remains largely overlooked by scholars interested in Rossetti's canonical "adult" works.[58] Despite its neglect in scholarly criticism, however, *Speaking Likenesses* provides an important contribution to discussions of appetite and the body in Rossetti's work as a whole and in the larger genre of Victorian's children's literature. As in much nineteenth-century children's literature, Rossetti emphatically praises the renunciation of both food and sexual desire, denouncing gluttony by associating it with sexuality and selfishness. *Speaking Likenesses* portrays appetite and eating as monstrous signifiers of sexual promiscuity, implicitly debasing the body that experiences hunger by figuring both male and female sexual desire as unmitigatedly abusive and predatory. Contextualized within Rossetti's devotional writing, *Speaking Likenesses* is a tale of spiritual progress in which three children's rejection of gluttony symbolizes their assumption of progressively more moral qualities: the most virtuous of the three steadfastly denies her corporeal desires in the course of the story.

Rossetti divides *Speaking Likenesses* into three stories about a "Land of Nowhere" narrated by a caustic aunt to her nieces.[59] The first story takes place at Flora's eight birthday party, at which the little girl presides as "queen of the feast" (326). Appetite immediately becomes a source of discontent as the children quarrel over who gets the biggest sugar-plums and the narrator wonders "would even finest strawberries and richest cream have been found fault with" (327–328). Flora reveals her own greediness and peevishness, "cross and miserable" because her "sugar-plums [were] almost all gone . . . her chosen tart not a nice one" (330). Frustrated with her playmates, she deserts her own party, crying, "It's my birthday, it's my birthday" (328) and, discovering a door carved in a yew tree, enters an apartment in which animated furniture greets her and strawberries and cream – doubling the strawberries and cream at her own party – serve themselves.

Sitting down, Flora "took up in a spoon one large, very large strawberry with plenty of cream; and was just putting it in her mouth when a voice called out crossly: 'You shan't, they're mine . . . it's my birthday, and everything is mine'" (333). The voice belongs to a "cross grumbling" and "ugly" girl who, "enthroned in an extra high armchair," doubles Flora's position as queen of the feast and personifies her hearty appetite. Flora's impulse to immediately consume a "very large strawberry with plenty of cream" indicates her greediness; however, she is forbidden from eating by the selfish Queen who, along with the other children at the party, "had eaten and stuffed quite greedily; Poor Flora alone had not tasted a morsel" (334). Although the reader feels sorry for Flora, "too honest a little girl to eat strawberries that were not given her" (335), her new self-restraint differentiates her from the other children in the yew tree, whose monstrosity is established by their supernatural consumption of food.

Rossetti employs the trope of gluttony to introduce sexuality into the story. When the children decide to play games, Flora realizes that they are not human: the boys are sharp and angular, covered with hooks and quills, while the girls are sticky and slippery. Rossetti's distaste for sexuality, both male and female, is apparent in the figures of these children. The boys' bodies and names are unmistakably phallic and capable of inflicting pain – Hooks, Quills, and Angles – while the two girls, Sticky and Slime, double the simpering girls at Flora's birthday party, one of whom gives Flora a "clinging kiss" (327). More disturbingly though, the girls' names allude to female genitalia and to female emissions such as menstrual blood: "One girl exuded a sticky fluid and came off on the fingers; another, rather smaller, was slimy and slipped through the hands" (335). The adjectives that Rossetti uses, "sticky" and "slimy," suggest the repulsive nature of the female sex; Rossetti does not juxtapose a redemptive female eroticism to the masculine brutality of Hooks and Quills.

Sexuality in the story is rendered even more troubling by the rape games that the children play. The first game, Hunt the Pincushion, "is simple and demands only a moderate amount of skill. Select the smallest and weakest player ... chase her round and round the room, overtaking her at short intervals, and sticking pins into her here or there as it happens" (336). The use of the female pronoun implies that the victim is always female, while "sticking pins into her" associates sexual intercourse with pain and violence. Flora, the victim of the game, is essentially raped: "Quills with every quill erect tilted against her ... Hooks who caught and slit her frock" (336). This sexual "deflowering," however, is not merely perpetrated by boys, for Sticky, Slime, and the Queen take part as well. The Queen's presence is particularly noteworthy because her role as Flora's double emphasizes Flora's own participation in the humiliating ordeal. The passage suggests that women somehow buy into their own sexual victimization, perhaps by playing "games" of flirtation and courtship. However, women are not the only victims of those games, for "Angles many times cut his own fingers with his edges" (338). Thus, Hunt the Pincushion is not solely an expression of men's sexual violence toward women; rather, it depicts the viciousness of sexual desire *in general*. The second game, Self Help, is more obviously drawn along gender lines: "The boys were players, the girls were played" (338). Once again, the game involves enacting a symbolic rape, in which "Hooks ... dragged about with him a load of attached captives, all vainly struggling to unhook themselves" (338). The name of the game, an allusion to Samuel Smiles's *Self Help*, also suggests that aggressive individualism inevitably produces victims, and, more specifically, that masculine individualism produces female victims.

The final scene in the story underscores the connections that Rossetti draws between food and sexuality. After finishing their games, the children sit down for another feast. This time, Flora refuses to eat while the others gorge down the huge meal: "she was reduced to look hungrily on while the rest of the company feasted, and while successive dainties placed themselves before her and retired untasted" (339). As in "Goblin Market," Rossetti describes the lavish food in detail: "Cold turkey, lobster salad, stewed mushrooms, raspberry tart, cream cheese, a bumper of champagne, a meringue, a strawberry ice" (339). The children who enthusiastically participate in mock-rapes eat just as enthusiastically, "stuffing without limit" (339). Gluttony, therefore, is intimately linked to rampant sexuality. Not surprisingly, the one good girl in the room, Flora, does not "take so much as a fork" (339), recalling the cultural notion that small appetites are symbolic of virtue, self-control, and femininity. Ultimately, appetite differentiates Flora from her monstrous self, the Queen. Whereas Flora refuses to eat, the Queen consumes "of sweets alone one quart of strawberry ice, three pine apples, two melons, a score of méringues, and about four dozen sticks of angelica" (339). Just as Lizzie doubles Laura, the Queen doubles Flora by representing her appetite and therefore her latent sexuality. Because the Queen organizes and supervises Hunt the Pincushion and Self Help, she, like Carroll's Queen of Hearts, is the most sexualized and aggressive child in the enchanted room. Flora also has the potential to become a gluttonous and impulsive Queen, but she renounces the possibility: at the end of the story, when the children build houses out of glass bricks and "to her utter dismay" (340) Flora finds herself walled up with the Queen, she quickly escapes, thereby rejecting her own worst impulses. Unlike Laura, who is redeemed at the end of "Goblin Market" despite her "fall" into sensual knowledge, the Queen is never redeemed. Gluttony is a sin, pure and simple. Thus, despite images that suggest a radical critique of men's sexual violence against women, the story's conservative ending reifies the conception of female sexuality as a disruptive and threatening force.

Because the second part of the *Speaking Likenesses* trilogy lacks the overt sexual dimension of the first and third parts, it is less compelling within a discussion of Rossetti's conflation of gluttony and lust. However, the story represents an important narrative bridge between the first and third stories. Based on spiritual allegories like *Pilgrim's Progress*, *Speaking Likenesses* revolves around the protagonists' renunciation of self, symbolized by their suppression of appetite. As Nina Auerbach and U. C. Knoepflmacher note: "The stories ascend as the Christian soul does, from Flora's birthday hell to Edith's purgatory...to the martyred Maggie's chilly heaven."[60] In the successive stories of the trilogy, Rossetti's heroines are increasingly able to deny their appetites and are, accordingly, increasingly less tormented.

Edith, the second story's subject, has been promised a "gipsy feast" (343) by her mother. Standing in the kitchen with the cook, Edith pesters her with questions about the forthcoming meal, asking: "What are we to have besides sandwiches and tarts" (344)? "Cold fowls, and a syllabub, and champagne, and tea coffee, and potato-lunns, and tongue, and I can't say what besides" (344), the servant responds, revealing that the feast will be sizable. Bored and restless, Edith offers to boil the kettle for tea Immediately, the narrator undercuts the goodness of her behavior. Not only does Edith demonstrate her own appetite in her eagerness to hasten the meal, but the reader has already learned that she "thought herself by no means such a very little girl, and at any rate as wise as her elder brother, sister, and nurse" (343). Now Edith slips out of the kitchen with the kettle despite the cook's warning that a fire must be lit: "'I can light the fire,' called out Edith after her, though not very anxious to make herself heard" (344). By deciding to boil the kettle despite the wishes of cook, Edith demonstrates that pride of which the narrator accused her. The matches that she carries with her are, appropriately enough, called lucifers.

Once in the woods, Edith is lured from her errand by a grapevine covered with tantalizing fruit:

How she longed for a cluster of those purple grapes which, hanging high above her head, swung to and fro with every breath of wind; now straining a tendril, now displacing a leaf, now dipping towards her but never within reach. Still, as Edith was such a very wise girl, we must not suppose that she would stand long agape after unattainable grapes: nor did she. Her business just then was to boil a kettle, and to this she bent her mind. (345)

Edith's decision not to pluck and eat the grapes can be read two ways. Whereas Flora immediately helps herself to strawberries and cream at the enchanted party, Edith suppresses her desire for the grapes and thereby displays a laudable denial of appetite that differentiates her from the other girl. Yet, grapes frequently symbolize Christian faith and the wine of the Eucharist in Rossetti's work, an interpretation underscored in *Speaking Likenesses* by the adverb "agape." Literally, "agape" simply means open-mouthed, but the word assumes metaphorical, sacred meaning as the ancient Christian agape, or love feast, a humble meal related to the Eucharist that was eaten to symbolize fraternal love and charity. The word agape is a "technical name or proper name for various forms of fraternal meals of a semi-liturgical nature . . . the Christian love feasts had as their specific and basic purpose a practical imitation of Christ's love for men by expressing and fostering fraternal love . . . the agapae were related also to the Eucharist, even when they did not include a Eucharistic banquet."[61] Historically, the agape was closely connected to the Eucharist: "the rites were similar and not mutually exclusive."[62] The agape was carefully distinguished from lavish banquets by Church fathers: Pliny the Younger specifies that it should include "common and innocent" food and, according to Tertulian, "food was eaten in moderation."[63] John Wesley (also a proponent of fasting) introduced agape feasts to London in 1738 and, according to *The Oxford Dictionary of the Christian Church*, " 'Love feasts,' as they were called, became an established feature of Methodism until the midnineteenth century."[64] They are not, then, specifically Tractarian, but rather cross-denominational.

Rossetti suggests that, because of her unrepentant selfishness and pride, Edith does not demonstrate Christian love and is therefore unprepared to partake of the sacrament. Similarly, in Rossetti's short story *Maude*, the protagonist feels unworthy to receive Communion, saying that: "I will not profane Holy Things . . . Some day I may be fit again to approach the Holy Altar, but till then I will at least refrain from dishonouring it."[65] For Rossetti, the Eucharist was a sacrament not to be taken lightly and one that neither Edith nor Maude yet deserves. The dual meaning of the grape scene demonstrates the instability of signs of eating in Rossetti's work: while secular, physical hunger must be repressed, spiritual hunger is virtuous.

Unable to light the fire after carelessly dropping most of her matches, Edith finds herself surrounded by the animals of the wood, creatures who function as more benign versions of the Queen in their role as "speaking likenesses." Just as Edith lazily watched the cook working despite that woman's complaint that "attendance is just what I should not have liked" (344), these animals observe and annoy Edith, offering only useless advice. Two hedgehogs sit and watch but do nothing; "why they came and why they stayed never appeared from first to last" (348). The pigeons present the impractical recommendation that she fly away, to which Edith, Alice-like, retorts: "I wish you'd advise something sensible, instead of telling me to fly without wings" (348). Edith does not realize that her attempt to boil the kettle is very much like flying without wings:

she does not possess the skills necessary to light a fire and has, moreover, forgotten to fill the kettle with water. The narrator's aside: "Remember, girls, never put an empty kettle on the fire, or you and it will rue the consequences" (348), is Rossetti's comment on the destructive power of pride. By the time the nurse arrives at the scene and summarily dismisses Edith, she is weeping with frustration.

If the story of Flora in the yew tree is hellish, Edith's adventure is purgatorial in its lack of closure and deferral of pleasure. Undercutting narrative expectation, the luscious meal that Edith anticipates never takes place within the confines of the story, and it is uncertain, by the end, whether Edith will ever enjoy her gipsy feast. Her punishment has already been anticipated by the narrator who, in the preface to the story, prods her nieces to charity sewing with the admonition, "no help no story" (343). Without labor, there is no reward, and without self-abnegation, no delight. As far as the story reveals, though, Edith's only punishment for her willfulness is a miserable afternoon in the forest, certainly a less cruel punishment than that accorded to the little glutton, Flora. However, Edith must still learn self-denial, or how to serve others selflessly rather than selfishly. The final figure of the trilogy, Maggie, combines Edith's meritorious repression of appetite with the dutifulness that she lacks.

The third part of the *Speaking Likenesses* trilogy is perhaps the most important for an understanding of Rossetti's moral message. While describing the dolls for sale in Old Dame Margaret's shop at the opening of the tale, the narrator notes: "as they say in the Arabian nights, 'each was more beautiful than the other'" (351). Just as the dolls grow more and more beautiful as they progress, Rossetti's third story is the most "beautiful" of the three because it delivers her message of Christian redemption. Dame Margaret, who runs a gift shop full of toys and sweets, is distinguished by her "plain clothes and her plain table" (351). The fact that she always finds money to help out a poor neighbor reinforces the predominant Victorian correspondence of a light diet with a virtuous soul. On Christmas Eve, Margaret's orphan granddaughter Maggie offers to deliver a basket to the doctor's house, and to do so she must travel, like Red Riding-Hood, through the woods. As soon as she enters the forest, she encounters a group of playing and dancing children, and though "the thermometer marked half-a-dozen degrees of frost; [and] every pond and puddle far and near was coated with thick sheet ice" (352), the children dance so wildly that their "cheeks were flushed, their hair streamed right out like comets' tails" (354). Rossetti here reintroduces the "monstrous children" (354) that Flora meets in the first tale; now, in winter, their heat makes them all the more hellish, the girl's "pink cotton velvet" (354) party dress grotesquely out of place in a frozen forest. Their excessive heat, symbolized by their flushed cheeks, recalls the disturbing sexuality with which the children have already been associated. The children are Maggie's first temptation, for she longs to play with them, but, remembering her promise to hurry home, she leaves them (and their sexuality) behind.[66] Her first renunciation sets the tone for the rest of the tale.

After leaving the children, Maggie grows hungry and peeks at the tempting chocolate in her basket. Just as she debates whether or not to take a piece, she meets what Auerbach and Knoepflmacher have already identified as the "speaking likeness" of her hunger, a boy whose face "exhibited only one feature, and that was a wide mouth."[67] His huge mouth makes the boy a trope of walking appetite as Rossetti again emphasizes the connection between gluttony and lust; while the boy snatches at the chocolate in Maggie's basket, he prepares to devour her in a metaphorical rape: "for the two stood all alone together in the forest, and the wide mouth was full of teeth and tusks, and began to grind them" (356). Unlike Flora, however, Maggie stands up for herself, refuses to give him the chocolate, and runs away. She renounces her own appetite and, consequently, the aggressive sexuality symbolized by the Mouth-boy: to abstain from food, Rossetti implies, is to resist one's carnality.

Maggie illustrates Rossetti's belief that one should avoid even looking upon sin. As she writes in her explication of Revelation, *The Face of the Deep*: "Cover and turn away the eye lest it should behold it, stop the ear lest it should admit it; for the blessed pure in heart who shall see God, copy their Lord the Holy one who is of purer eyes than to behold evil."[68] While Flora participates (however unwillingly) in her introduction to sexual knowledge, Maggie demonstrates her moral courage by fleeing the very sight/site of sin. Moreover, when Maggie "spoke so resolutely and seemed altogether so determined" (356), the boy merely slinks off into the wood, indicating that women's renunciation of appetite is empowering, that virtue is stronger than sin.

Maggie's third renunciation, of sleep, leads her to her destination, the doctor's house. Now, however, the world of privilege renounces Maggie, for she is answered at the door only with a brief thank you and left "shut out" of the house (358). Cold and hungry, Maggie turns back toward her home. Clearly, the secular world offers nothing to a poor orphan. Heaven, however, recognizes her goodness, and in exchange for a glimpse of the doctor's Christmas tree, "the sky before her flashed with glittering gold, and flushed from horizon to zenith with a rosy glow; for the northern lights came out, and lit up each cloud as if it held lightning, and each hill as if it smouldered ready to burst into a volcano. Every oak-tree seemed turned to coral, and the road itself to a pavement of dusky carnelian" (359). The northern lights represent both a divine Christmas tree and the Star of Bethlehem; in addition, they offer the reader a glimpse of the apocalypse: the images of a volcano about to explode and of lightning hidden in seemingly benign clouds evoke the many instances of lightning and fire in Revelation, including the mountain of fire thrown into the sea (Revelation 8: 8). Moreover, carnelian is the sixth of twelve stones that decorate the walls of the New Jerusalem, toward which Maggie metaphorically travels on that cold winter night.[69] After successfully resisting temptation, Rossetti's heroine receives divine assurance that she will someday be welcomed into the community of the blessed.

Once again, Rossetti places images of consumption at the center of her moral lesson. At Dame Margaret's house, Maggie enjoys a frugal but satisfying meal of tea and toast, the only instance of eating in *Speaking Likenesses* not linked with discord and greed. The story ultimately posits that renunciation of the world's pleasures is the true measure of a Christian and that, by implication, one is not a devout Christian without sacrifice. Of the three children, only Maggie completely resists her appetite and dutifully follows instructions, sacrificing her own pleasure because she "promised Granny to make haste" (354). Renunciation of self, in Rossetti's theology, is a Christian duty carried out in large part by the renunciation of one's physical appetites; as Rossetti claims in *Time Flies: A Reading Diary*, "abstinence from food, stands for all self-mortification."[70] At the same time, however, Maggie's dinner, with its allusion to the agape feast, suggests that the Christian enjoys an alternative and positive spiritual satiety through faith.[71]

Unlike corporeal appetite, which Rossetti's heroines resist, spiritual hunger brings with it the promise of blissful fulfillment through union with Christ. As in "Goblin Market," in which the Eucharistic joining of Lizzie and Laura represents a moment of redemptive consumption, many of Rossetti's devotional poems use images of eating to symbolize the ideal relationship between God and self. Most frequently, God, often in the person of Christ, is the object of the narrator's hunger or thirst. In "As the Sparks fly Upwards," for instance, Rossetti asks God to "bid my will go free / Till I too taste thy hidden Sweetness" (6–7). Recalling the tempting grapes of *Speaking Likenesses*, she figures Christ as a "Vine with living Fruit, / The twelvefold fruited Tree of Life" ("I Know you not" 1–2) and yearns to "taste and see how good is God" ("Then they that feared the Lord spake often one to another" 21). Like medieval fasting women, Rossetti conceives of God as food, and like them she considers both fasting and the Eucharist empathic ways of identifying with the pain of Christ's crucifixion. Thus, she writes in "I know you not": "I thirst for Thee, full Fount and Flood, / My heart calls Thine as deep to deep: / Dost Thou forget Thy sweat and pain, / Thy provocation on the Cross? / Heart pierced for me, vouchsafe to keep / The purchase of Thy lavished Blood" (17–22). Here, Rossetti couples the desire to quench her spiritual thirst at Christ's "full Fount" with a reminder of His torture and death. Her consumption imagery fits well into the tradition of medieval women who, according to Bynum, "craved . . . not only sweetness, inebriation, joy" but "identification with the suffering of the cross."[72] Within a theological framework, then, Rossetti validates both the pain of hunger and the bliss of satiety.

Rossetti's ultimate wish, in her poetry, is for a oneness with God, a desire which, as I noted earlier, she describes in highly erotic language. She speaks, in "The heart Knoweth its own Bitterness," of being "full of Christ and Christ of me" (56), on the one hand portraying a fullness that she does not allow her body, and on the other hand depicting an interpenetration between Christ and narrator that is also an image of sexual union and pregnancy. Rossetti's image is curiously reciprocal. Not only does the narrator enter Christ as well as being entered by Him – thus blurring the gender distinction between herself and Christ – but their union satisfies them both. In mutuality with Christ, Rossetti even imagines *becoming* food, as in "The Offering of the New Law, the One Oblation once Offered":

> Yet, a tree, He feeds my root;
> Yet, a branch, He prunes for fruit;
> Yet, a sheep, these eves and morns,
> He seeks for me among the thorns.
>
> Sacrifice and Offering
> None there is that I can bring;
> None, save what is Thine alone:
> I bring Thee, Lord, but of Thine Own–
>
> Broken Body, Blood Outpoured,
> These I bring, my God, my Lord;
> Wine of Life, and Living Bread,
> With these for me Thy Board is spread.
>
> (21–32)

The narrator begins as a fruit-bearing branch and as food for the Lamb of God, but, by the end of the poem, Rossetti elides the distinction between the speaker and Christ. When the narrator offers her own "Broken Body, Blood Outpoured" in exchange for the Eucharist, she uses images of the crucified body of Christ, rendering it unclear where the narrator ends and God begins. Since the Eucharist consists of God's body and blood, moreover, one must read Rossetti's offering of her own body to Christ as a gift of food.

Rossetti never claims that self-denial comes easily; rather, she emphasizes the pain and loneliness of her spiritual quest, positing satiety in heaven as a reward for her hunger on earth. In *Speaking Likenesses*, Flora's, Edith's and Maggie's lessons in self-denial and starvation are so painful that they amount to torture, and only Maggie is rewarded at the end of the story. Rossetti's poetry is somewhat more hopeful. She writes, in "From House to Home," that: "Altho' today I fade as doth a leaf, / I languish and grow less . . . Tomorrow I shall put forth buds again / And clothe myself with fruit" (219–224). The narrator's starvation on earth eventually leads to her ripeness in heaven, in which, her roots "nourish[ed]" (222) with Christ's blood, she herself blossoms into food, at once both nourished and nourishment. A similar dynamic of secular hunger and sacred fullness informs "They Desire a Better Country," in which the narrator proclaims that: "I would not cast anew the lot once cast, / Or launch a second ship for one that sank, / Or drug with sweets the bitterness I drank, / Or break with feasting my perpetual fast" (5–8). By forsaking the sweetness of earth's pleasures, here figured as "feasting," in order to heed Christ's call to "Follow me here, rise up, and follow here" (14), Rossetti hopes to reach the New Jerusalem's "golden walls of home" (37–38). Although in this poem Rossetti does not envision the heavenly feasting that succeeds earthly fasting, the assumption that one must sacrifice earthly joy in order to attain heavenly bliss underlies the poem.

Fasting, while primarily a metaphor for general self-denial, also signifies the literal refusal of food and appetite that Rossetti struggled with both in her work and throughout her life. In only one poem does Rossetti try to view sensual appetite positively, and she is ultimately unable to do so. "Enrica" was written between "Goblin Market" and *Speaking Likenesses* and was inspired by a family friend, Enrica Filopanti:

> She came among us from the South
> And made the North her home awhile;

Our dimness brightened in her smile,
Our tongue grew sweeter in her mouth.

We chilled beside her liberal glow,
She dwarfed us by her ampler scale,
Her full-blown blossom made us pale,
She summer-like and we like snow.

We Englishwomen, trim, correct,
All minted in the selfsame mould,
Warm-hearted but of semblance cold,
All-courteous out of self-respect.

. . .

But if she found us like our sea,
Of aspect colourless and chill,
Rock-girt; like it she found us still
Deep at our deepest, strong and free.

(1–24)

Here Rossetti finds beauty in a fleshly woman, turning from the depictions of death in *Goblin Market and Other Poems* to images such as "full-blown blossom" and "summer-like." Fullness does not emblematize decay, but welcome warmth against "snow" and "cold." Rossetti even uses an image of consumption – "Our tongue grew sweeter in her mouth" – in a purely positive and secular way. Contrast these images with those in "A Triad," in which images of fullness verge on the grotesque, as the wife "Grew gross" and "droned in sweetness like a fattened bee" (14). Ultimately, however, Rossetti finds her own self-denial a source of strength, for "trim" "colourless and chill" Englishwomen are "Deep at our deepest, strong and free." Although Rossetti describes Enrica with affectionate language, her voluptuousness and "ampler scale" are alien to Rossetti's aesthetic of self-denial. The poem emphasizes Enrica's otherness; she is an importation from Italy who eventually returns to her own home. Rossetti remains rooted in England, gaining her inner strength and identity from self-control and renunciation. Importantly, Rossetti perceives the large, beautiful, and ostensibly hungry female body positively only within a non-religious poem; in her religious poetry, fleshliness is never interpreted so benignly.

Despite Rossetti's validation of food refusal for religious and non-religious reasons, she did not view all repression as beneficial, as one of her most famous lyrics, "In an Artist's Studio," indicates. In this poem, Rossetti employs starvation images to symbolize the slow destruction of an artist's model by the painter for whom she acts as muse; the characters in the poem are presumably based upon Elizabeth Siddal and Dante Gabriel Rossetti. Rossetti describes the painter as a sort of vampire who "feeds upon her face by day and night" (9) while the woman grows increasingly "wan with waiting" (12). The word "wan," which connotes paleness, is so closely associated with ill health and fatigue that the word, when combined with Rossetti's extraordinary image of the painter "feed[ing]" upon her face, suggests the model's thinness as well. And, of course, Elizabeth Siddal was famously thin and pale herself. In this case, the model's gradual wasting way, which her comparison to the moon (11) underscores, is represented as purely unhealthy, pathetic, and ultimately tragic. Despite the denial of sexual desire and appetite that Rossetti espouses in her poetry and prose, from "The Convent Threshold" to *The Face of the Deep*, she was personally aware of the painfulness of that struggle, and she indicates, in "In an Artist's Studio," that the context in which one does not eat is of central importance. Fasting for Christ is one thing; starving oneself in depression and misery is another. Again, Rossetti simultaneously suggests both the similarities between sacred and secular food refusal and the ultimate distinctions between them.

Conclusion: the politics of thinness

I began this book by expressing the hope that exploring anorexia nervosa as a semiotic system or cultural paradigm might help our understanding of why women today succumb to the disease and, more generally, to patterns of disorderly eating. I would like to end by speculating about the kind of political work that literary and cultural criticism can accomplish in the effort to curtail anorexia nervosa both as pathology and as cultural ideology. While I focused on the Victorian period in the introduction, I would like, briefly, to turn to contemporary culture, and end, as I began, with an anecdote.

Recently, I asked students in a course entitled "The Body in Literature and Culture" to complete the following phrase: "My body is." Their answers did not, unfortunately, surprise me: "an animal – something to fight against"; "contrary to the mind, full of urges and instincts"; "at war with me"; "breeder, sexual, animal"; "something that commits treason against myself." Perhaps most honest and sad: "I hate to see my body, especially naked." I asked students to read their own comments alongside Plato's *Phaedo*, in which Plato writes that "we shall be closest to knowledge if we refrain as much as possible from association with the body or join with it more than we must, if we are not infected with its nature but purify ourselves from it until the god himself frees us. In this way we shall escape the contamination of the body's folly."[1] My students, most of them for the first time, realized that their own hatred of the flesh has roots not merely in contemporary media images of women – although these, too, are oppressively monotonous and inarguably harmful to women's self esteem – but in a patriarchal tradition that has hated the body, especially the female body, for over a thousand years. My students, immediately after reading Plato, connected the language of disease that he employs to a larger pathologizing of the female body and to the "logic" of anorexia. Why, I asked my largely Baptist students, isn't Christ fat? Is there some model of the body that might offer us a way out of the body/soul dualism that lies at the philosophical heart of anorexia nervosa?

At the most general level, such discussions of the many causes of anorexia and its terrible toll on women help make women aware of the relationships of their bodies and to food: consciousness raising allows us to examine our own assumptions and behavior about eating, and hopefully to change unhealthy behaviors and ways of thinking. Second, unlike a disease such as breast cancer, which strikes women of different races and classes indiscriminately, anorexia nervosa has been largely restricted to middle- and upper-class women (though this may be changing). Because it is determined to a large extent by a woman's environment, interrogating and subsequently changing that environment should influence the disease's appearance and virulence. Those of us teaching in high schools, colleges, and universities have a particularly good opportunity to discuss eating disorders as a normative obsession, and to make young women aware that today's body type has not always been and does not have to be the norm.

The claim that the female body has been culturally constructed is commonplace among cultural critics, but we often overlook its obvious political implications. Women suffer from anorexia in part because of the way that female bodies are reproduced in the media. The fashion industry's role in the perpetuation of body images is particularly irresponsible. Not only do magazines like *Vogue* and *Bazaar* use a very small group of models in their fashion layouts (the same models who appear over and over again in advertisements in those same magazines), but these models are far taller and slimmer than the average woman: they are so thin that, in some photographs, their ribs and chest cavities are eerily visible through their skin. Naomi Wolf claims that models currently weigh an average of 23 percent less than the average American woman; the model Kirsty Hume, merely as an example, is five feet eleven inches tall but weighs less than 120 pounds.[2] The evidence that fashion magazines and advertisements showcase and glamorize the thin body and erase the non-thin body is available in almost any women's magazine, and is so obvious that it needs no more elaboration here.

Although women readers consistently complain about such exclusive images of female beauty, images that rarely take into account physiological or racial diversity, fashion editors and designers predictably respond that models are images of ideal beauty rather than representative of most women, and that fashion is therefore immune from political criticism. Again and again, writers stubbornly and tiresomely argue that

presenting only thin women in fashion magazines has absolutely no impact on the prevalence of eating disorders. In a *Vogue* article entitled
"The Body Myth," Rebecca Johnson simplifies the complex problem of
a culture of anorexia by arguing that fashion models such as Kate Moss
and Shalom Harlow are not to blame for an individual woman's eating
disorder but that, quoting an anonymous anorexic girl: "Mostly, I blame
myself."[3] Fat, according to Johnson, is akin to an unwelcome house guest
who comes to visit but never really belongs:

Clothes hang better on thin women. When fat settles in, it renders the body
formless, amorphous, like a landscape blanketed in snow. In athletes and very
thin people, the endoskeleton, the ligature, and the striae of muscle become
visible, reminding us of what a wondrous piece of machinery the human body is.[4]

Johnson naturalizes thinness, redefining fat as alien to the body, something that "settles in" but never becomes part of the essential body. The
"real" body consists of bones and muscles: fat, somehow, is external and
renders the body "formless" rather than merely differently formed. By
assuming that muscle and bone are more a part of the body than fat, by
stripping the body down to its most fundamental components (though
of course this in itself is arguable), Johnson erases the infinite number of
shapes and sizes that a woman's body can take. Gone are differences in
breast size, buttocks, thighs, and bellies, replaced by a single, universal
anatomical design.

Finally, and perhaps most jarringly, Johnson conceives of the body
as ultimately non-human, merely "a wondrous piece of machinery." By
turning the body into a robotic machine – epitomized, again inexplicably,
by the athlete and "very thin" person – Johnson denies both a human
body's subjectivity and its ability to experience sensual pleasure. The
prototype of the machine emphasizes speed, exactness, and regularity,
qualities associated with the thin body and with the disciplined body.
These are the traits valued, not coincidentally, by the anorexic girl.

Johnson ignores substantial evidence that implicates standards of
beauty in the development of disordered eating and eating disorders, con-
descendingly dismissing such work as "simpleminded pop psychology."[5]
Summarizing recent psychological research on body image and eating
disorders, James Rosen reports that:

Certainly a background factor for the development of body-image concerns in
women with eating disorders is the prevailing ideal of thinness as a marker of
beauty in women. Were it not for this, there would be no epidemic of eating
disorders . . . exemplars of female beauty (e.g., models and beauty contestants)

have become thinner over the last couple of decades – to the point that the ideal physique is below the actuarian norm. This change has been accompanied by an apparent increase in the prevalence of eating disorders and more reports of subclinical eating and body-image disturbances among women. In non-Western cultures where plumpness is valued, or at least not devalued . . . eating disorders are rare.[6]

Anorexia nervosa is a multidimensional illness and images of slenderness in the media are certainly not the *sole* reason for its development in women; other reasons, such as the need for control and achievement, are directly involved in most women's eating disorders. However, our culture's obsession with slenderness has clearly contributed to the surge in eating disorders and disorderly eating, and are thus enmeshed with other productive factors. Were it not for such a cultural beauty imperative, girls would not be as prone to channel their anxiety and aggression into the areas of weight loss and "fitness." Without acknowledging its implicit contradiction of her argument that images of beauty do not impact on the development of anorexia, Johnson describes a photograph of a model pinned to a bulletin board at a clinic for anorexic women, next to which a patient has written: "I wish I could look like her."[7] Johnson's bizarre conclusion: anorexic women admire, rather than resent, models; therefore, the fashion industry, in her analysis, remains wholly blameless: if anything, it is a positive presence.

Responses to "The Body Myth" were divided between those readers who took issue with the article and those who applauded Johnson's argument. For example, two women wrote to thank Johnson for the article, theorizing that: "Even in the earliest art forms, the master craftsmen sought figures that embodied extremes of beauty to suit their visions. Today . . . the subject has evolved into the slender, angelic supermodel. These women are inspiring, ethereal muses."[8] A model, according to these letter writers, epitomizes an abstract, artistic ideal, the ideal body "angelic" and "ethereal," an incorporeal image on the page. Such rhetoric is as Victorian as a Dickens novel.

Of course, *Vogue* is only one small node of power in a web of power relations that includes other magazines, the movie and television industries, the $300 billion-a-year diet industry, the publishing industry (which thrives on diet and exercise books, not on cultural criticism), and the fitness industry.[9] Power, Foucault explains, is "a chain or a system . . . the name that one attributes to a complex strategical situation in a particular society."[10] Lest I be misconstrued as suggesting that *Vogue*, Kate Moss, Jenny Craig, and Gold's Gym somehow conspire to keep women buying fashion magazines and gym memberships, I would add that intent is not at issue; rather, result is. These different entities reinforce each other by perpetuating the idea that women, and, increasingly, men, need to be thin in order to be healthy, beautiful, and happy, claims that can obviously be disputed.

Although we as a culture consider ourselves enlightened and tolerant, our attitudes toward the body are still fundamentally "Victorian." Contemporary discourse emphasizes and praises discipline over the body to the same extent – if not more so – than does Victorian discourse. Foucault points out the prominence, in the nineteenth century, of the "the theme of the 'flesh' that must be mastered," a theme echoed in today's obsessive rhetoric about diet, exercise, and fat grams.[11] Jenny Craig claims that "[n]othing looks as good as thin feels," and the slogan for L'eggs pantyhose might just as easily be an advertisement for a Victorian corset: "you'll have waist to thigh control." A recent Jantzen ad reads: "If I ruled the world passion would outweigh reason. Shopping would be the national pastime. Red would mean go. And thighs would be forever thin." Open any fashion magazine and these examples can easily be multiplied. The recent trend of retro-Dior style dresses and corsets highlights how little we have changed from a century ago: like the Victorian woman and like the anorexic woman, we view the body as something to be controlled and disciplined, subjugated to the will and the gaze. Leslie Heywood writes that "[a]norexics enact with their bodies the process that Western logic inscribes . . . the horror of the female flesh that is often the unconscious of discourse."[12] Though our preferred body type has changed since the Victorian era, the rhetoric surrounding the body has not.

In Jeremy Bentham's panopticon prison, an individual is kept in a state of self-discipline merely by the threat of being constantly watched by an invisible observer: just as the panopticon itself "induces in the inmate a state of conscious and permanent visibility that assures the automatic functioning of power," Foucault argues that panopticism as political power "had to be given the instrument of permanent, exhaustive, omnipresent surveillance, capable of making all visible, as long as it could itself remain invisible."[13] As Sandra Bartky has explored, women are symbolically imprisoned in the Panopticon, their bodies under "exhaustive, omnipresent surveillance" by others and by themselves, the woman concerned with her appearance, "a self-policing subject, a self committed to a relentless self-surveillance . . . a form of obedience to patriarchy."[14] The mirror has become a panoptic device that keeps women constantly disciplined, always aware of the shapes of their bodies in comparison with the ideal bodies on billboards and in television commercials. In an issue of *New Woman* magazine, Jane Reilly advises women to "Stand in front of a mirror naked . . . and really look at your body. You'll either be a. grossed out or b. pleased by your new muscles."[15] Is there no other, healthier response for women? Or does the non-muscular body naturally lead to feeling "grossed out?" The mirror, as Reilly implies, enables a woman to assess her own body and symbolizes the wider, judgmental gaze of society. The popular diet program Weight Watchers even exploits the fear of being seen as a marketing tool: who, exactly, watches your weight? You do. According to one study, 40 percent of 2,000 girls surveyed in Michigan considered themselves overweight; in another survey, "nearly 30,000 women stated . . . that they'd rather lose weight than achieve any other goal – despite the fact that only 25% were overweight and another 25% were actually underweight."[16] Sadly, these numbers are not even surprising to most people, since disorderly eating has become such "normal," thoroughly understandable behavior in our thinness-obsessed culture.

Recently, a proliferation of what are called "pro-anorexia" sites and chat rooms have appeared on the internet. These sites, which are designed, maintained, and frequented by women who struggle with eating disorders or disorderly eating, are designed to support women in their quest to lose enormous amounts of weight and be thin; they have names like "Sexy, Slim, and Starving," "Wafer Thin," "Paper Weight Perfection," and "I Love You to the Bone."[17] Rather than aiming to change self-destructive eating patterns, these sites offer reinforcement for those behaviors. One chat room, for instance, advertises itself: "For people who are/want to be anorexic."[18] Many of the sites include photo galleries of thin women, mostly models, as inspiration, or so-called "triggers" for food refusal, with labels like "Pictures to Envy" or "So thin and so pretty."[19] The sites also offer tips on how to lose weight, how to hide one's food refusal from one's family or physicians, how to get by without eating in public, and general encouragement for disorderly eating. Four messages posted in a chat room called "Only Popular with Anorexia" illustrate the general tone of the sites:

i feel i wont live till im skinny, im not skinny yet, but im starting to live . . . ill always diet and restrict even if i do get thin, though, if i ever get fat, put weight on, i don't know what i wd do, id break down inseide. [*sic*][20]

i don't want to be fat . . . i'd rather be dead!! and u have to ask urself [*sic*], "would i rather die overweight or beautifully thin??"[21]

i plan on doing exactly what I want with my body regardless. and if that means starving it to death then so be it. at least i can go down knowing i had the self discipline which is so obviously lacking in our society of fat-asses![22]

I don't know what i want other than to be thin . . . I feel like a failed anorexic . . . I'm sorry to ramble on but i don't know what I want other than thinness.[23]

Studies have strongly indicated that eating disorders are "catching": girls learn the behaviors from other girls and are reinforced in their food refusal or binging and purging by each other.[24] These sites, therefore, which offer anonymous and invisible "support groups" for anorexia are potentially very dangerous. Because of the unstructured format of these chat rooms, potentially life-threatening information – such as recommending 700–800 calories a day diets or suggesting that anorexia nervosa can be safely managed – is passed on to others in the form of advice and encouragement. Most crucially, the sites normalize obsessive thoughts and behavior surrounding food. What is appealing about these sites for women with eating disorders is that they assure women that their desire to be thin is healthy and admirable and that they provide a circle of understanding, caring friends who empathize with the pain and exhilaration of self-starvation. However, it is important that feminists respond to them as an extreme example of where this culture's obsession with thinness is leading girls and women, and that girls be offered other avenues for empowerment, achievement, and self-esteem than their body size.

In the 1880s, girls wrote letters to the *Girl's Own Paper* complaining about being fat; in 2001, girls have mastered internet technology to express these same fears, now greatly amplified. The nascent Victorian culture of anorexia has ballooned into today's epidemic of disorderly eating. We should therefore stop smugly congratulating ourselves on how far we have advanced beyond those repressed Victorians. Although women today have shed the corset, they have internalized the corset as the need for "self-control" and have zeroed in on body shape in a way that would have baffled most nineteenth-century men and women. Any reader comparing mainstream Victorian women's magazines and today's fashion magazines would immediately notice how much more emphasis we place on achieving the flawless body today. Moreover, the big-busted, thin-hipped hybrid body that has become today's ideal is no more "natural" or "realistic" a body type than the wasp-waisted, hourglass figure of the mid nineteenth century, or the S-curve of the turn of the century. We have merely replaced one set of beauty standards with another, more rigid and unforgiving one. Women's obsession with our bodies props up the diet, exercise, fashion, cosmetics, and publishing industries: as Terry Poulton has documented, as long as we worry, they stay in business.[25] However, in many ways, our representations of the female body share qualities with those of the Victorians: as in the nineteenth century, self-control and self-discipline are viewed as cornerstone virtues and are, still, symbolized by the slender body. The slender body is still a class marker. Women still hesitate to eat in public. Overweight people are still ruthlessly mocked (the Jenny Jones show has made a staple out of "She's too fat to dress like that!" shows) and overtly discriminated against.

Florence Nightingale complained about the effort that women of her century had to put into the dinner table, arguing that women could more productively put their energies elsewhere. Today, however, the energy that women put into *not* eating could be channeled into productive change for women. Today, for every one Caroline Helstone starving in her room, there are many more starving in our classrooms.

Notes

INTRODUCTION

1. S. Ashwell, *A Practical Treatise on the Diseases Peculiar to Women* (Philadelphia, PA: Lea & Blanchard, 1845), pp. 47–48.
2. S. Gmelch, *Gender on Campus: Issues for College Women* (New Brunswick, NJ: Rutgers University Press, 1998), p. 151.
3. For these and other physicians who discussed eating disorders, see W. Vandereycken and R. Van Deth, *From Fasting Saints to Anorexic Girls: The History of Self-Starvation* (London: Athlone Press, 1994), pp. 143–161.
4. Ashwell, *Practical Treatise*, p. 23.
5. T. Laycock, *A Treatise on the Nervous Diseases of Women* (London: Longman, Orme, Brown, Green, and Longmans, 1840) p. 73.
6. There is some disagreement in the medical community about the distinction between anorexia nervosa and bulimia. Joan Jacobs Brumberg explains that, in 1985, bulimia was given "independent disease status; according to the newest categorization, anorexia nervosa and bulimia are separate but related disorders" (J. Brumberg, *Fasting Girls: The History of Anorexia Nervosa* [New York: Plume, 1989], p. 12); however, "there is increasing support for subtyping anorexic patients into those who are pure dieters ('restrictive anorectics') and those who incorporate bingeing and purging ('bulimic anorectics')" (Brumberg, *Fasting Girls*, p. 12). Morag MacSween argues that "the binge as an ever-present threat to anorexic control is a central feature of anorexia" (M. Macsween, *Anorexic Bodies: A Feminist and Sociological Perspective on Anorexia Nervosa* [London: Routledge, 1993], p. 230); many anorexics binge now and then, and some women pass back and forth from restrictive anorexia to bulimia. My own work proceeds on the premise that anorexia nervosa and bulimia are closely related, often-overlapping diseases.
7. See I. Loudon, "Chlorosis, Anemia, and Anorexia Nervosa," *British Medical Journal* 281 (1980), 1669–1675, for a detailed discussion of the connections between chlorosis and anorexia nervosa. Others who have examined the links between chlorosis and anorexia nervosa include Brumberg, "Fasting Girls"; Vandereycken and Van Deth, "From Fasting Saints."
8. W. Parry-Jones, "Archival Exploration of Anorexia Nervosa," *Journal of Psychiatric Research* 19 (1985), 98.

9. Ibid.

10. D. McNeill, "An Extraordinary Fasting Case," *British Medical Journal* (1879), 938. For sample Victorian case histories, see also J. Adam, "A Case of Melancholia Presenting Some Exceptional Features, Prolonged Refusal of Food, and Forced Alimentation," *British Medical Journal* (18 February 1888), 348–349; H. Barbes, "Cases of Long-Continued Abstinence From Food," *British Medical Journal* (28 May 1870), 544–545; and J. Ogle "Clinical lecture on a Case of Hysteria," *British Medical Journal* (16 July 1879), 57–60.

11. S. Bordo, *Unbearable Weight: Feminism, Western Culture, and the Body* (Berkeley: University of California Press, 1993), p. 141.

12. L. Heywood, *Dedication to Hunger* (Berkeley: University of California Press, 1996), p. xvii.

13. Heywood links the pathology of anorexia nervosa with the modernist aesthetic, labeling as "anorexic logic" "that set of assumptions . . . that values mind over body, thin over fat, white over black, masculine over feminine" (*Dedication to Hunger*, p. xii). My work moves backwards from Heywood to examine the ways in which anorexia developed before the modernist period, but I am indebted to her work for the helpful phrase "anorexic logic."

14. Although I use the word "culture" throughout the book, I acknowledge that the monolithic entity that the word implies does not exist and that, as Raymond Williams writes, "Culture is one of the two or three most complicated words in the English language" (R. Williams, *Keywords: A Vocabulary of Culture and Society* [New York: Oxford University Press, 1983], p. 87). Quoting Williams again, I conceptualize culture as "the independent noun . . . which indicates a particular way of life, whether of a people, a period, a group, or humanity in general" (*Keywords*, p. 90) as applied to the Victorians from the lower middle to upper classes. Moreover, under the word culture I include both material production (corsets and other systems of clothing) and symbolic systems (literature) on the assumption that an exchange exists between a culture's literary and extra-literary expressions.

15. I am indebted, for my method, to M. M. Bakhtin (*The Dialogic Imagination*, ed. M. Holquist [Austin: University of Texas Press, 1981]), who emphasizes the need to examine every specific word in its particular ideological environment.

16. *Diagnostic and Statistical Manual of Mental Disorders: DSM IV* (Washington, D.C.: American Psychiatric Association, 1994), pp. 544–545 (hereafter *DSM*).

17. W. Gull, "Anorexia Nervosa," *Transactions of the Clinical Society of London* 7 (1874), 22. All further references to Gull will be cited parenthetically in the text.

18. C. Lasègue, "On Hysterical Anorexia," *The Medical Times and Gazette* (1873), p. 265. All further references to Lasègue will be cited parenthetically in the text.

19. See Brumberg's discussion, especially her chapter "Emergence of the Modern Disease" (*Fasting Girls*, pp. 101–125).

20. There is some disagreement in the clinical literature about what kinds of families predispose girls to become anorexics. Hsu points out that formal studies about the kinds of families that "produce" anorexics is just beginning; nevertheless, anorexia does tend to run in families, and the anorexic girl's family is more likely to be disturbed in some manner than the non-anorexic girl's. Anorexia may be, in part, a learned behavior or coping mechanism. See L. K. G. Hsu, *Eating Disorders* (New York: Guilford Press, 1990), p. 39 for a very helpful discussion of the family's role in anorexia nervosa.

21. M. Macsween, *Anorexic Bodies: A Feminist and Sociological Perspective on Anorexia Nervosa* (London: Routledge, 1993), p. 40.

22. Some good analyses of anorexia nervosa are: Brumberg, *Fasting Girls*; Macsween, *Anorexic Bodies*; and B. Turner, *Regulating Bodies: Essays in Medical Sociology* (London: Routledge, 1992). Bruch's and Crisp's foundational works on anorexia nervosa are also invaluable.

23. A. Fallon, "Culture in the Mirror: Sociocultural Determinants of Body Image," in *Body Images: Development, Deviance and Change*, ed. Thomas Cash and Thomas Pruzinsky (New York: Guilford Press, 1990), p. 102.

24. Hsu, *Eating Disorders*, p. 102.

25. Hsu's book provides the most comprehensive discussion of various theories and clinical studies of anorexia nervosa. He explains that many women who exhibit the fasting behavior of anorexia nervosa can not clinically be diagnosed as anorexic because they have not lost enough weight; however, since a fat phobia is found both in anorexic and non-anorexic populations, the two groups are not discontinuous. Thus, Hsu argues, "the emphasis on slimness, a sociocultural phenomenon prevalent among upper-class females of the West, may be a major precipitant for the onset of an eating disorder" (*Eating Disorders*, p. 81). Among the many studies that support a cultural dimension to the development of eating disorders, one study of Hispanic females "found a significant correlation between a subject's eating attitudes as measured by the Eating Attitudes Test and the level of her acculturation to American culture" (*Eating Disorders*, p. 80).

26. Quoted in T. Poulton, *No Fat Chicks: How Big Business Profits by Making Women Hate Their Bodies – and How to Fight Back* (Secaucus, NJ: Birch Lane Press, 1997), p. 96.

27. Perhaps the most well-known survey to demonstrate that dieting has become a normative obsession is the 1984 *Glamour* magazine survey in which 75% of women surveyed considered themselves overweight, even though only 25% of them actually *were* overweight, according to the Metropolitan Life Insurance Company's weight tables. Of the respondents who were actually underweight, 45% still considered themselves fat (R. Seid, *Never Too Thin: Why Women are at War with Their Bodies* [New York: Prentice Hall, 1989], p. 27).

28. Bordo, *Unbearable Weight*, p. 50.

29. Plato, "Phaedo," in *Five Dialogues*, ed. G. M. A. Grube (Indianapolis: Hackett Publishing, 1981), p. 103.
30. Ibid.
31. A. Glenny, *Ravenous Identity: Eating and Eating Distress in the Life and Work of Virginia Woolf* (New York: St. Martin's Press, 1999), p. 3.
32. Heywood, *Dedication to Hunger*, p. 28.
33. I use the words "loose" and "jiggly" because they are words that women often use in describing their own or other women's bodies. According to James Rosen, anorexic women tend to be very invested in their physical appearance; for example, they are likely to believe that people judge them primarily on their appearance rather than on other qualities. In addition, they are often very concerned about being "feminine." For example, Rosen quotes one anorexic as claiming that: "Because I'm big, I'm not feminine" (J. Rosen, "Body-Image Disturbances in Eating Disorders," in *Body Images: Development, Deviance, and Change*, ed. Thomas Cash and Thomas Pruzinsky [New York: Guilford Press, 1990], p. 195). Rosen writes that "there is no consistent evidence that eating disorder groups are less or more feminine in traditional sex-role orientation (e.g., being passive, dependent, or concerned with social approval). However, they do appear to endorse fewer masculine traits, which might reflect their lower self-esteem or sense of autonomy" ("Body Image Disturbance," p. 200). Of course, the woman who believes that her appearance is of primary importance in the way that she is perceived, and who believes that being "overweight" is a liability, is not merely paranoid; these are normative and reasonable responses in a culture obsessed with thinness.
34. H. Michie, *The Flesh Made Word: Female Figures and Women's Bodies* (Oxford University Press, 1987), p. 17.
35. E. Gaskell, *Ruth* (Oxford, 1983), pp. 116, 388.
36. Bordo, *Unbearable Weight*, p. 189.
37. E. Farrar, *The Young Lady's Friend* (Boston: American Stationers' Company, 1837), pp. 362–363.
38. Rosen, "Body-Image Disturbances," p. 190.
39. Seid, *Never Too Thin*, p. 3.
40. S. Ellis, *The Daughters of England* (London: Fisher, Son & Co., n.d., *c.* 1841), p. 183.
41. M. Santé, *The Corset Defended* (London: T. E. Carler, 1865), p. 13.
42. *The Art of Beautifying the Face and Figure* (London: G. Vickers, 1858), pp. 11, 15.
43. T. C. Allbutt, *On Visceral Neuroses* (London: J. & A. Churchill, 1884), p. 55.
44. Ibid., p. 53. Emphasis mine.
45. T. Veblen, *The Theory of the Leisure Class* (New York: Macmillan, 1899), pp. 148–149.
46. Ibid., p. 146.
47. A. Trollope, *Can You Forgive Her?* (Oxford University Press, 1982), p. 297.

48. Brumberg, *Fasting Girls*, p. 187.
49. E. Gaskell, *Cranford* (London: Penguin, 1977), p. 42.
50. Ibid., p. 115.
51. E. Gaskell, *Wives and Daughters* (London: Penguin, 1986), p. 162.
52. Ibid., p. 131.
53. Brumberg, *Fasting Girls*, p. 136.
54. I. Beeton, *Mrs. Beeton's Book of Household Management* (London: Chancellor Press, 1982), p. 1331.
55. Brumberg, *Fasting Girls*, p. 139.
56. Gull, "Anorexia Nervosa," 27; Ogle, "Clinical Lecture," pp. 57, 59.
57. F. Nightingale, *Cassandra* (Old Wesbury: Feminist Press, 1979), p. 30. All other references will be cited parenthetically in the text.
58. Vandereycken and Van Deth, *From Fasting Saints*, p. 202.
59. K. Chernin, *The Obsession: Reflections on the Tyranny of Slenderness* (New York: Harper & Row, 1981), p. 101; Orbach, quoted in M. Robertson, *Starving in the Silences: An Exploration of Anorexia Nervosa* (New York University Press, 1992), p. 49.
60. Heywood, *Dedication to Hunger*, p. 56.
61. I have taken the term "beauty myth" from Naomi Wolf's book of the same title. Wolf's chapter "Hunger" discusses anorexia nervosa today.
62. Brumberg, *Fasting Girls*, p. 4
63. Naomi Wolf, for instance, writes that Victorian women desired a "silken layer" of fat (N. Wolf, *The Beauty Myth* [New York: Doubleday, 1991], p. 192).
64. P. Vertinsky, *The Eternally Wounded Woman: Women, Doctors, and Exercise in the Late Nineteenth Century* (Urbana: University of Illinois Press, 1994), p. 9.
65. An example of a contemporary scholar diagnosing a Victorian woman with anorexia nervosa can be seen in Peter Dally's biography of Elizabeth Barrett Browning, in which he argues that the poet engaged in anorexic behavior when "it was advantageous to her" (P. Dally, *Elizabeth Barrett Browning: A Psychological Portrait* [London: Macmillan, 1989], p. 28). Although Barrett Browning lost large amounts of weight and was an extremely picky eater, it is impossible to definitively "diagnose" her, as Dally claims to do. Dally generalizes about anorexia nervosa and suggests, erroneously, that an anorexic woman can turn her disease on and off.
66. J. Butler, *Gender Trouble* (New York: Routledge, 1999), pp. 186, 179.
67. M. Foucault, *The History of Sexuality*, trans. Robert Hurley (New York: Vintage, 1990), p. 93.
68. Ibid., p. 94.
69. S. Bartky, "Foucault, Femininity, and the Modernization of Patriarchal Power," in *The Politics of Women's Bodies*, ed. Rose Weitz (New York: Oxford University Press, 1998), p. 37.
70. Ibid., p. 38.

I WAISTED WOMEN: READING VICTORIAN SLENDERNESS

1. Ellis, *Daughters of England*, p. 223 and S. Orbach, *Fat is a Feminist Issue II* (New York: Berkley Books, 1982), p. 27.
2. Brumberg, *Fasting Girls*, p. 31.
3. P. McEachern, *Deprivation and Power: The Emergence of Anorexia Nervosa in Nineteenth-Century French Literature* (Westport, CT: Greenwood Press, 1998), p. 75.
4. See P. Byrde, *Nineteenth Century Fashion* (London: B. T. Batsford Limited, 1992); C. W. Cunnington, *English Women's Clothing of the Nineteenth Century* (London: Faber & Faber, 1937); Varda Foster, *A Visual History of Costume: The Nineteenth Century* (London: B. T. Batsford, 1984); Alison Lurie, *Don't Tell the Grown-Ups: Why Kids Love the Books They Do* (New York: Avon, 1990); and Andrew Marwick, *Beauty in History: Society, Politics and Personal Appearance c. 1500 to the Present* (Gloucester: Thames and Hudson, 1988) for general discussions of Victorian clothing and its ideological implications. I write, of course, of the woman with enough leisure and resources to pursue fashion and beauty, recognizing that not all women had the financial resources to concern themselves with fashion and that not all women were interested in those pursuits or were able to pursue them.
5. H. Roberts, "The Exquisite Slave: The Role of Clothes in the Making of the Victorian Woman," *Signs* 3 (1977), p. 555.
6. Byrde, *Nineteenth Century Fashion*, p. 88.
7. *The Science of Dress* (London: Groombridge & Sons, 1856), p. 16.
8. Mrs. A. Walker, *Female Beauty, as Preserved and Improved by Regimen, Cleanliness, and Dress* (London: Thomas Hurst, 1837), pp. 149–150.
9. H. Maudsley, "Sex in Mind and in Education," in *Desire and Imagination: Classic Essays in Sexuality*, ed. Regina Barreca (New York: Meridian, 1995), p. 194.
10. Ibid., p. 207.
11. For a discussion of Maudsley's key contributions to Victorian psychiatry, see E. Showalter, *The Female Malady: Women, Madness, and English Culture 1830–1980* (New York: Pantheon Books, 1985), pp. 112–126.
12. Mrs. H. Haweis, *The Art of Beauty* (London: Chatto and Windus, 1878), p. 4.
13. V. Steele, *Fashion and Eroticism* (Oxford University Press, 1985), p. 108.
14. McEachern, *Deprivation and Power*, p. 113.
15. Foucault, *History of Sexuality*, p. 92.
16. Cunnington, *English Women's Clothing*, p. 251.
17. Ibid.
18. Steele, *Fashion and Eroticism*, p. 109.
19. F. M. Steele and E. L. Steele Adams, *Beauty of Form and Grace of Vesture* (New York: Dodd, Mead and Company, 1892), p. 100.
20. Ibid., pp. 180, 121.
21. Mrs. H. Haweis, *Art of Beauty*, p. 49.
22. C. Finch, "'Hooked and Buttoned Together': Victorian Underwear and Representations of the Female Body," *Victorian Studies* 34 (1991), 341.

23. A. Hollander, *Seeing Through Clothes* (New York: Viking, 1978), p. 98.
24. Many contemporary commentators favorably juxtaposed the stylish figure to the comparably curvaceous nudes of antiquity. Fanny Douglas, for instance, writes that "[t]he opponents of the corset and the waist are a little too fond of pointing to the Venus de Milo as proof of how beautiful a waist-less woman can be . . . Had Venus been compelled . . . to drape herself, we have little doubt she would have worn stays to give her clothes the shape they lack" (F. Douglas, *The Gentlewoman's Guide to Dress* [London: Henry & Co., *c.* 1894], pp. 123–124).
25. *Science of Dress*, p. 7.
26. Finch, "Hooked and Buttoned Together," p. 343. For more information on the history of the Victorian corset, see Nora Waugh, *Corsets and Crinolines* (New York: Theatre Arts Books, 1994).
27. Santé, *Corset Defended*, p. 91; A. Cooley, *The Toilet in Ancient and Modern Times.* 1866. (New York: Burt Franklin, 1970), p. 352.
28. Bryan Turner, in a similar argument about the characteristics shared by corsets and anorexia nervosa, notes that corsets may actually have interrupted menstrual flow by pressing down upon the uterus so that both the tight lacer and the victim of anorexia nervosa "deny sexuality and thereby . . . retain a childlike innocence by avoiding menstruation" (Turner, *Regulating Bodies*, p. 199). The problem with Turner's argument is that, as I discuss later, the corset sexualized the body; it certainly did not make a woman's body look like the body of a little girl. So, although the corset's possible cessation of menstruation links it to anorexia in its effects, it is difficult to argue that corsets made a woman *appear* less sexual.
29. M. Foucault, *Discipline and Punish*, trans. Alan Sheridan (New York: Vintage, 1995), p. 138.
30. G. Drinka, *The Birth of Neurosis* (New York: Simon and Schuster, 1984), p. 39.
31. Young Lady Herself, "Letter," *Englishwoman's Domestic Magazine* (1867), p. 333; W. B. Lord, *The Corset and the Crinoline* (London: Ward, Lock, and Tyler, 1868), p. 144.
32. *Art of Dress, or Guide to the Toilette* (London: Charles Tilt, 1834), p. 39.
33. *Health for the Million* (London: W. Kent & Co., 1858), p. 234.
34. *Etiquette of the Toilette-Table: A Manual of Utility, Elegance, and Personal Comfort by an Officer's Widow* (Glasgow: W. R. M'Phun, 1859), 85.
35. I have distilled this figure from a number of sources. Madame de la Santé cites the figure of 17 to 19 inches (Santé, *Corset Defended*, p. 193), but she was a proponent of corset-wearing and thus obviously biased in favor of a small waist. In 1866, Arnold J. Cooley writes that "most women do not permit themselves to exceed twenty-four inches round the waist, whilst tens of thousands lace themselves down to twenty-two inches, and many deluded victims of fashion and vanity to twenty-one and even to twenty-inches" (Cooley, *The Toilet in Ancient and Modern Times*, p. 352). Looking back at the Victorian era from the twentieth century, C. Willett Cunnington claims that,

in the 1860s, the fashionable waist was from 17 to 21 inches (Cunnington, *English Women's Clothing*, p. 251). Finally, Valerie Steele's research into actual corsets suggests that the average corset waist was larger than the "ideal" (as one would expect), 23 inches from 1856 to 1881 and 22 inches from 1881 to 1900 (Steele, *Fashion and Eroticism*, p. 163). The measurements that Steele cites are, of course, still very small.

36. Lord, *Corset and the Crinoline*, p. 156.
37. H. Roberts, "Reply to David Kunzle's 'Dress Reform as Antifeminism: A Response to Helene E. Roberts's 'The Exquisite Slave,''" *Signs* 3 (1977), 519.
38. Santé, *Corset Defended*, p. 12.
39. Anonymous, "Letter," *Englishwoman's Domestic Magazine* (1867), p. 502.
40. A Young Baronet, "Letter," *Englishwoman's Domestic Magazine* (1867), p. 558.
41. Steele, *Fashion and Eroticism*, p. 178.
42. Farrar, *Young Lady's Friend*, p. 198.
43. D. Kunzle, *Fashion and Fetishism: A Social History of the Corset, Tight Lacing and Other Forms of Body Sculpture in the West* (Totowa, NJ: Rowman and Littlefield, 1982), p. 574.
44. Ibid., p. 571.
45. Ibid., p. 577.
46. Hollander, *Seeing Through Clothes*, p. 213.
47. Santé, *Corset Defended*, p. 14.
48. Lord, *Corset and the Crinoline*, p. 157.
49. "Torture in the Nineteenth Century: Fashion in Tight Lacing," *Ladies' Treasury* 6 (1864), 11.
50. Nora, "Letter," *The Englishwoman's Domestic Magazine* (1867), 278.
51. Editors, *Ladies' Treasury* 6 (1864), p. 204.
52. E. Langland, *Nobody's Angels: Middle-Class Women and Domestic Ideology in Victorian Culture* (Ithaca, NY: Cornell University Press, 1995), p. 71.
53. *Etiquette for Ladies, Being a Manual of Minor Social Ethics and Customary Observances* (London: Knight & Son, 1857), pp. 8–9.
54. Vertinsky, *Eternally Wounded Woman*, p. 16.
55. *Health for the Million*, p. 75.
56. Gaskell, *Ruth*, p. 132.
57. Ibid.
58. H. G. Clarke, *The English Maiden: Her Moral and Domestic Duties* (London: Henry Green Clarke, 1841), pp. 94, 96. The word "delicacy" has a fascinating etymology. According to the *OED*, its original meaning is "Addiction to pleasure or sensual delights, voluptuousness," a meaning that grew obsolete by the mid eighteenth century in favor of its opposite definition, "Avoidance of what is immodest."
59. Allbutt, *On Visceral Neuroses*, p. 53.
60. G. Beard, *Eating and Drinking: A Popular Manual of Food and Diet in Health and Disease* (New York: Putnam & Sons, 1871), p. 104.

61. B. Dijkstra, *Idols of Perversity: Fantasies of Feminine Evil in Fin-de-Siècle Culture* (New York: Oxford University Press, 1986), p. 26. Several critics have discussed the nineteenth-century cult of invalidism. Anorexia can thus be tied to the glamorization of lassitude and consumption that Susan Sontag explores in *Illness as Metaphor*. She writes that: "The tubercular look had to be considered attractive once it came to be considered a mark of distinction, of breeding... What was once the fashion for aristocratic femmes fatales and aspiring young artists became, eventually, the province of fashion as such. Twentieth-century women's fashions (with their cult of thinness) are the last stronghold of the metaphors associated with the romanticizing of TB in the late eighteenth and early nineteenth centuries" (S. Sontag, *Illness as Metaphor; and AIDS and its Metaphors* [New York: Doubleday, 1990], p. 29). There is a thread of fashionable weakness, therefore, running throughout the whole century.

62. A. Walker, *Beauty in Women Analyzed and Classified* (Glasgow, 1892), p. 190.

63. The painter George Frederick Watts writes that the waist denotes "ideas of delicacy, lightness" (Steele, *Fashion and Eroticism*, p. 108).

64. Quoted in R. Fowler, *A Complete History of the Case of the Welsh Fasting Girl* (London: Henry Renshaw, 1871), p. 28.

65. Mrs. A. Walker, *Female Beauty*, p. 330.

66. Ibid., p. 315.

67. Ibid., p. 330.

68. Although fat symbolized desire and appetite for the Victorians, it also symbolized woman's procreative capacity and therefore her essential purpose in life. In this context, fat could be viewed as an extremely positive sign of a woman's assumption of her proper role; Mrs. Peggotty's ample form, for instance, underscores her maternal love for David Copperfield, while David's mother, with her slight body, is more child than mother, beautiful as love object, but ineffectual as caretaker of her son. In *Beauty in Women*, the physiognomist Alexander Walker considers the full-figured "nutritive beauty" the most beautiful type of woman because her rounded body signifies her submissiveness and maternal instincts: "To this class belong all the more feminine, soft, and passively voluptuous women" (*Beauty in Women*, p. 204). Victorians did not all agree on the desirablility of slenderness in women.

69. Brumberg, *Fasting Girls*, p. 182.

70. Mrs. A. Walker, *Female Beauty*, pp. 60, 63.

71. C. de l'Isère, *A Treatise on the Diseases and Special Hygiene of Females*, trans. Charles D. Meigs (Philadelphia, PA: Lea & Blanchard, 1845), p. 554 and Drinka, *Birth of Neurosis*, p. 39.

72. *The Etiquette of Courtship and Marriage: with a complete guide to the forms of a wedding* (London: David Bogue, 1851), p. 140.

73. *Ladies' Treasury* (1858), p. 142.

74. Ibid.

75. See Mary Poovey, *Uneven Developments* (University of Chicago Press, 1988); Carroll Smith Rosenberg, *Disorderly Conduct* (New York: Oxford University Press, 1985); and, more recently, Jill Matus *Unstable Bodies: Victorian Representations of Sexuality and Maternity* (Manchester University Press, 1995).
76. S. Shuttleworth, *Charlotte Brontë and Victorian Psychology* (Cambridge University Press, 1996), p. 92.
77. Farrar, *Young Lady's Friend*, pp. 346, 369.
78. A. Vrettos, *Somatic Fictions: Imagining Illness in Victorian Culture* (Stanford University Press, 1995), p. 2.
79. A. Mazur, "U.S. Trends in Feminine Beauty and Overadaptation," *The Journal of Sex Research* 22 (1986), p. 299.
80. Quoted in Drinka, *Birth of Neurosis*, p. 200.
81. See Langland, *Nobody's Angels*, and Andrew St. George, *The Descent of Manners: Etiquette, Rules and the Victorians* (London: Chalto & Windus, 1993).
82. *The Young Lady's Book* (London: Henry. G. Bohn, 1859), p. 28; Clarke, *English Maiden*, p. 162.
83. *How to Woo; How to Win; and How to Get Married* (Glasgow: W. R. M'Phun, 1856), p. 51.
84. *Etiquette for Ladies*, p. 10.
85. E. Thornwell, *A Lady's Guide to Perfect Gentility* (New York: Derby and Jackson, 1857), p. 110.
86. Gaskell, *Wives and Daughters*, p. 368.

2 APPETITE IN VICTORIAN CHILDREN'S LITERATURE

1. P. Hunt, *Criticism, Theory, and Children's Literature* (Oxford: Basil Blackwell, 1991), p. 19.
2. J. Briggs, "Women Writers and Writing for Children: From Sarah Fielding to E. Nesbit," in *Children and Their Books: A Celebration of the Work of Iona and Peter Opie*, ed. Gillian Avery and Julia Briggs (Oxford: Clarendon Press, 1982), p. 241.
3. D. Gorham, *The Victorian Girl and the Feminine Ideal* (Bloomington: Indiana University Press, 1982), p. 7.
4. D. Tolman and E. Debold, "Conflicts of Body and Image: Female Adolescents, Desire, and the No-Body Body," in *Feminist Perspectives on Eating Disorders*, ed. Patricia Fallon, Melanie A. Katzman, and Susan C. Wooley (New York: Guilford Press, 1994), pp. 308–309.
5. S. Mitchell, "Girls' Culture: At Work," in *The Girl's Own: Cultural Histories of the Anglo-American Girl, 1830–1915*, ed. Claudia Nelson and Lynne Vallone (Athens: University of Georgia Press, 1994), p. 247.
6. *Girls' Own Paper*, vols. 1–8, 1880–1887. Volume and page numbers are cited parenthetically in the text.
7. *The Girl's Birthday Book* (London: Houlston and Wright, 1860), p. 315.
8. *Child Land: Picture-Pages for the Little Ones* (London: S. W. Partridge & Co., 1873), p. 18.

9. *The Snow* (Wellington: F. Houlston & Son, 1825), p. 16.
10. *Girl's Birthday Book*, p. 346.
11. *The Illustrated Girls' Own Story-Book* (London: Ward & Lock, 1861), pp. 230, 234.
12. Ibid., p. 230.
13. C. Gilman, *The Little Wreath* (New York: Blakeman and Mason, 1864), pp. 161–162.
14. *The Stain Upon the Hand* (Philadelphia: American Sunday-School Union, 1859), pp. 11, 13–14.
15. Ibid., p. 31.
16. "Limby Lumpy," in *The Oxford Book of Children's Stories*, ed. Jan Mark (Oxford University Press, 1994), p. 59.
17. Ibid., p. 62.
18. A. and J. Taylor, *Original Poems for Infant Minds and Rhymes for the Nursery* (New York: Garland, 1976), p. 50.
19. L'Isère, *Treatise on the Diseases*, p. 543.
20. Seid, *Never Too Thin*, p. 78. See also Gorham and Brumberg.
21. One of the earliest apologists for Ruskin's gender ideology is D. Sonstroem, "Millett Versus Ruskin: A Defense of Ruskin's 'Of Queen's Gardens,'" *Victorian Studies* 20 (1977), 283–297. Also see D. Birch, "The Ethics of the Dust: Ruskin's Authorities," *Prose Studies* 12 (1989); E. Helsinger, *Ruskin and the Art of the Beholder* (Cambridge, MA: Harvard University Press, 1982); and S. Weltman, *Ruskin's Mythic Queen: Gender Subversion in Victorian Culture* (Athens: Ohio University Press, 1998) in the works cited chapter.
22. J. Ruskin, *Of Queens' Gardens, Sesame and Lilies* (Chicago: Belford, Clarke, & Co., 1890), p. 95. All other references to *Of Queens' Gardens* will be cited parenthetically in the text.
23. J. Ruskin, *The Ethics of the Dust* (Philadelphia: Henry Altemus Company, n.d.), p. 21. All other references to *The Ethics of the Dust* will be cited parenthetically in the text.
24. Undated letter. J. Ruskin, *Letters, The Complete Works of John Ruskin*, ed. E. T. Cook and Alexander Wedderburn vol. 36. (London: George Allen, 1905), p. lxx. Ruskin first proposed marriage to La Touche in 1866, the publication date of *Ethics* (although it actually appeared in December 1865).
25. Ruskin, letter to John James Ruskin, 31 August 1863. J. Ruskin, *The Winnington Letters*, ed. Van Akin Burd (London: George Allen & Unwin, 1969), p. 422.
26. I refer to *Of Queens' Gardens*, in which part of women's duty is to "assist . . . in the beautiful adornment of the state" (95).
27. S. Weltman, *Ruskin's Mythic Queen: Gender Subversion in Victorian Culture* (Athens: Ohio University Press, 1998), p. 133.
28. Compare the house-Moth to Ruskin's other description of "vampire crystals eating out the hearts of others" (Ruskin, *Ethics of the Dust*, p. 197), related to the "fat crystals eating up thin ones, like great capitalists and little laborers" (ibid.). Gluttony symbolizes greed and exploitation.

29. John Ruskin, letter to John James Ruskin, 22 March 1861. Ruskin, *Winnington Letters*, p. 284. Ruskin's letter to his father corresponds to his statement in *Ethics* that "Dancing is the first of girls' virtues" (Ruskin, *Winnington Letters*, p. 134).

30. Ruskin, *Winnington Letters*, p. 21.

31. John Ruskin, letter to Kate Greenaway, 5 July 1883. R. Engen, *Kate Greenaway: A Biography* (London: MacDonald, 1981), pp. 93–94.

32. Ibid., p. 118.

33. J. Kincaid, *Child-Loving: The Erotic Child and Victorian Culture* (New York: Routledge, 1992), p. 223.

34. J. Ruskin, "Fairy Land," *Art of England: Complete Lectures Given in Oxford* (Sunnyside: George Allen, 1884), p. 140.

35. C. Mavor, "Dream Rushes: Lewis Carroll's Photographs of the Little Girl," in *The Girl's Own: Cultural Histories of the Anglo-American Girl, 1830–1915*, ed. Claudia Nelson and Lynne Vallone (Athens: University of Georgia Press, 1994), p. 170.

36. John Ruskin, letter to Kate Greenaway, 1 May 1889. M. H. Spielmann and G. S. Layard, *Kate Greenaway* (London: Adam and Charles Black, 1905), p. 175. There is no collection of Kate Greenaway's letters currently in print; all letters are quoted from Spielmann and Layard, unless otherwise noted, and will be cited parenthetically in the text.

37. Greenaway's illustrated *The Pied Piper* was originally published in 1888. It has been reprinted in its entirety in the *Kate Greenaway Treasury*, the most complete Kate Greenaway collection that has been published. K. Greenaway, *The Kate Greenaway Treasury*, ed. Edward Ernest and Patricia Lowe (Cleveland: The World Publishing Company, 1967), p. 298.

38. Ibid.

39. Kincaid, *Child-Loving*, p. 55.

40. J. Berger, *Ways of Seeing* (London: Penguin, 1980), pp. 52, 55.

41. John Ruskin, letter to Kate Greenaway, 2 December 1883. Engen, *Kate Greenaway*, p. 103.

42. M. Warner, "John Everett Millais's 'Autumn Leaves': A Picture Full of Beauty and Without Subject," *Pre-Raphaelite Papers*, ed. Leslie Parris (London: Tate Gallery, 1984), p. 137.

43. Dijkstra, *Idols of Perversity*, p. 185, 190.

44. A. Morrison, *A Child of the Jago* (London: J. M. Dent, 1996), p. 145.

45. E. Hopkins, *The Early Training of Girls and Boys* (London: Hatchards, 1882), p. 44.

46. Taylor and Taylor, *Original Poems*, pp. 69–70.

47. The one significant exception to my conclusions is a four-page children's story, entitled "The Naughty Little Girl Who Went To See Her Grandmama," which Greenaway wrote and illustrated for a friend. The little girl in the story does things like upset a beehive, chase a butterfly, and steal gooseberries. Spielmann and Layard reprint the story in their biography.

48. Engen, *Kate Greenaway*, p. 102. It is important to note that Greenaway drew very few poor children; even the country laborers that she sometimes painted are never ragged or impoverished: her world is one in which the real troubles of childhood are almost completely erased. As Ruskin writes of Greenaway's drawings, "There are no railroads . . . to carry the children away with, are there? no tunnel or pit mouths to swallow them up, no league-long viaducts – no blinkered iron bridges? There are only winding brooks, wooden footbridges, and grassy hills without any holes cut into them" (Ruskin, "Fairyland," p. 152). Spielmann and Layard write, of her illustrations for Ruskin's *Fors Clavigera*, about a "fascinating babe in rags – the rags and babe as clean and sweet as are all the rags and babes in K. G.'s child-Utopia" (*Kate Greenaway*, p. 120). Greenaway is a much different painter than Blake, whose work she greatly admired, in her refusal to show the suffering of children. Blake's illustrations, so similar to Greenaway's in terms of costume, emphasize the pain and loneliness of poor and abandoned children like the chimney-sweeper.

49. Engen, *Kate Greenaway*, p. 39.

50. Ibid., p. 101.

51. Ibid., p. 118.

52. L. Carroll, *Alice's Adventures in Wonderland and Through the Looking Glass* (New York: Signet, 1960). All citations to *Alice's Adventures in Wonderland* and *Through the Looking Glass* will be cited parenthetically in the text.

53. *The Illustrated Girls' Own Story Book*, p. 234. This story is not the same "The Little Glutton" cited earlier. Titles like "The Little Glutton" were fairly common in juvenile literature.

54. N. Auerbach, "Alice and Wonderland: A Curious Child," *Victorian Studies* 17 (1973), p. 35.

55. M. Cohen, *Lewis Carroll: A Biography* (New York: Alfred A. Knopf, 1995), p. 131.

56. Ibid., p. 133.

57. Ibid., p. 130.

58. T. Otten, "After Innocence: Alice in the Garden," in *Lewis Carroll: A Celebration*, ed. Edward Guiliano (New York: Clarkson N. Potter, 1982), p. 55.

59. Lewis Carroll, letter to Agnes Argles, 30 November 1867. L. Carroll, *The Letters of Lewis Carroll*, ed. Morton N. Cohen and Roger Lancelyn Green (New York: Oxford University Press, 1979), p. 117.

60. Lewis Carroll, letter to Agnes Hull, 2 December 1879. Carroll, *Letters*, p. 356.

61. M. Homans, *Royal Representations: Queen Victoria and British Culture, 1837–1876* (University of Chicago Press, 1998), p. 95.

62. Kincaid, *Child-Loving*, p. 278.

63. N. Armstrong, "The Occidental Alice," *Differences: A Journal of Feminist Cultural Studies* 2 (1990), 23.

64. Ibid., p. 18.
65. S. D. Collingwood, *The Life and Letters of Lewis Carroll* (New York: Century, 1899), p. 134.
66. Cohen, *Lewis Carroll*, p. 292.
67. Lewis Carroll, letter to Edith Blakemore, 27 January 1882. Carroll, *Letters*, pp. 451–452.
68. S. Prickett, *Victorian Fantasy* (Bloomington: Indiana University Press, 1979), p. 126.
69. Cohen, *Lewis Carroll*, p. 229. Emphasis mine.

3 HUNGER AND REPRESSION IN *SHIRLEY* AND *VILLETTE*

1. Charlotte Brontë, letter to George Smith, 11 March 1852. *The Brontës: Their Lives, Friendships & Correspondence in Four Volumes*, eds. T. J. Wise and J. A. Symington (Oxford: Shakespeare Head Press, 1932), vol. 3, p. 322. All future references will be cited parenthetically in the text as *Correspondence*.
2. Charlotte Brontë, letter to W. S. Williams, 13 September 1849.
3. M. Slater, *Dickens and Women* (Stanford University Press, 1983), p. 320.
4. C. Brontë, *Shirley* (Ware: Wordsworth, 1993), p. 79. All future references will be cited parenthetically in the text. Although much recent criticism has focused on disease and neurosis in *Shirley* and *Villette*, little work has been done on hunger in these novels. For disease in Brontë's work, see M. Bailin, *The Sickroom in Victorian Fiction* (Cambridge University Press, 1994); S. Shuttleworth, *Charlotte Brontë and Victorian Psychology* (Cambridge University Press, 1996); and Vrettos, *Somatic Fictions*. S. Gilbert and S. Gubar, *The Madwoman in the Attic* (New Haven, CT: Yale University Press, 1979) and D. Lashgari, "What Some Women Can't Swallow: Hunger as Protest in Charlotte Brontë's *Shirley*," in *Disorderly Eaters: Texts in Self-Empowerment*, ed. Lilian R. Furst and Peter W. Graham (University Park: Pennsylvania State University Press, 1992), pp. 141–152, examine hunger in Brontë's novels.
5. Slater, *Dickens and Women*, p. 250.
6. C. Dickens, *David Copperfield* (London: Penguin, 1985), pp. 912; 289. All future references will be cited parenthetically in the text.
7. David focuses on the beauty of Dora's body, always aware of her physical appearance and presence. She is therefore a more sexual character than Agnes, and her sexuality is linked with her inability to keep house.
8. Slater, *Dickens and Women*, p. 360.
9. G. Houston, *Consuming Fictions: Gender, Class, and Hunger in Dickens's Novels* (Carbondale: Southern Illinois University Press, 1994), p. 54.
10. C. Dickens, *The Old Curiosity Shop* (London: Penguin, 1985), p. 148. All future references will be cited parenthetically in the text.
11. This chapter was written before the publication of Laurence Lerner's fascinating *Angels and Absences: Child Deaths in the Nineteenth Century* (Nashville, TN: Vanderbilt University Press, 1997), which places Nell's death in the

context of Dickens's other child deaths and within the representations of children's death in nineteenth-century fiction and non-fiction.

12. J. Forster, *The Life of Charles Dickens* (London: C. Palmer, 1928), p. 105. Emphasis mine.

13. Charles Dickens, letter to John Forster, 3 November 1840. C. Dickens, *Letters*, ed. Madeline House and Graham Storey (Oxford: Clarendon Press, 1965), p. 144. All future references will be cited parenthetically in the text.

14. Charles Dickens, letter to John Forster, 17 [?] January 1841.

15. Charles Dickens, letter to George Cattermole, 22 [?] December 1840.

16. F. Kaplan, *Sacred Tears: Sentimentality in Victorian Literature* (Princeton University Press, 1987), p. 50.

17. Brontë, *Shirley*, p. 1.

18. Gilbert and Gubar, *The Madwoman in the Attic*, p. 391. See their discussion of *Shirley*, pp. 372–398.

19. Glenny, *Ravenous Identity*, p. 101.

20. Vrettos, *Somatic Fictions*, p. 39.

21. Ogle, "Clinical Lecture," p. 56.

22. Gilbert and Gubar, *The Madwoman in the Attic*, pp. 390–391.

23. Lashgari, "'What Some Women Can't Swallow,'" p. 141.

24. J. Barker, *The Brontës* (New York: St. Martin's Press, 1994), p. 259.

25. Bordo, *Unbearable Weight*, p. 201; M. Lawrence, *The Anorexic Experience* (London: Women's Press, 1984), p. 33.

26. Ibid., p. 49.

27. Glenny, *Ravenous Identity*, p. 5.

28. E. Gaskell, *The Life of Charlotte Brontë* (London: Penguin, 1985), p. 379.

29. Ibid., p. 268.

30. Charlotte Brontë, letter to Ellen Nussey, 23 November 1848. *The Brontës: Life and Letters*, ed. Clement Shorter, 2 vols. (London: Hodder and Stoughton, 1952), vol. 2, p. 7. All future references will be cited parenthetically in the text as *Life and Letters*.

31. Charlotte Brontë, letter to Ellen Nussey, 10 December 1848.

32. L. Gordon, *Charlotte Brontë: A Passionate Life* (London: Chatto & Windus, 1994), p. 186.

33. Ibid., p. 69.

34. K. Frank, *Chainless Soul: A Life of Emily Brontë* (Boston: Houghton Mifflin, 1992), pp. 98–99.

35. Ibid., p. 3–4.

36. Barker, *The Brontës*, p. xviii.

37. See Shuttleworth, *Charlotte Brontë and Victorian Psychology*, p. 203 for a similar discussion.

38. For analyses of the friendship between Shirley and Caroline, see J. Maynard, *Charlotte Brontë and Sexuality* (Cambridge University Press, 1984) and H. Moglen, *Charlotte Brontë: The Self Conceived* (New York: Norton, 1976).

39. Lashgari, "'What Some Women Can't Swallow,'" p. 150.

40. C. Brontë, *Villette* (London: Everyman, 1993), p. 162. All future references will be cited parenthetically in the text. For essays on the nature of Lucy's illness, see Vrettos, *Somatic Fictions* and Showalter, *Female Malady*.

41. So many critics have discussed Lucy's repression that I take it as a point of departure rather than something to be proven. See, for instance, the following: Gilbert and Gubar, *The Madwoman in the Attic*, pp. 399–440; J. Mitchell, *The Stone and the Scorpion: The Female Subject of Desire in the Novels of Charlotte Brontë, George Eliot, and Thomas Hardy* (Westport, CT: Greenwood Press, 1994), pp. 69–83; R. Goldfarb, *Sexual Repression and Victorian Literature* (Lewisburg, PA: Bucknell University Press, 1970), p. 139–157 and Maynard, *Charlotte Brontë and Sexuality*, pp. 164–217.

42. For Charlotte Brontë's use of phrenology and physiognomy, see I. Jack, "Physiognomy, Phrenology, and Characterisation in the Novels of Charlotte Brontë," *Brontë Society Transactions* 15 (1970), pp. 377–399 and G. Tyler, *Physiognomy in the European Novel: Faces and Fortunes* (Princeton University Press, 1982).

43. In *Beauty in Women*, Alexander Walker categorizes female beauty into three types, including the intellectual, or thinking, beauty: "her high and pale forehead announces the intellectuality of her character; her intensely expressive eye is full of sensibility . . . she has not the expanded bosom, the general embonpoint, or the beautiful complexion of the second ["nutritive" or fecund] species" (142). Despite this woman's attractions, Walker finds "This species of beauty . . . less proper to woman . . . It is not the intellectual system, but the vital one, which is, and ought to be most developed in woman" (222). He goes on to claim that "intellectual ladies . . . either seldom become mothers, or . . . become intellectual when they cease to be mothers" (204); the masculine characteristic of intellect cannot coexist with true femininity or female beauty. All references from A. Walker, *Beauty in Women Analyzed and Classified* (Glasgow, 1892).

44. For example, Allie Glenny writes "Something of my own sense of what anorexia is is expressed in images of a containing space: a cage, a prison, a fortress within a moat, but also a safe-house, a room of one's own" (*Ravenous Identity*, p. 1).

45. Shuttleworth, *Charlotte Brontë and Victorian Psychology*, p. 32. An excellent discussion of the repression of desire that also touches on images of food in the novel can be found in the work of Judith Mitchell, who notes that, in *Villette*, love is "portrayed as . . . food and drink" (Mitchell, *The Stone and the Scorpion*, p. 72).

46. See Brumberg, *Fasting Girls*, p. 176.

47. A. Walker, *Intermarriage. Desire and Imagination: Classic Essays in Sexuality*, ed. Regina Barreca (New York: Penguin, 1995), p. 17; L'Isère, *Treatise on the Diseases*, p. 554; Clarke, "Sex in Education: A Fair Chance for the Girls," p. 162.

48. Matus, *Unstable Bodies*, p. 139.

49. C. Brontë, *Jane Eyre* (Toronto: Bantam, 1981), p. 269.

50. Patricia McEachern's discussion of Zola's courtesan Nana demonstrates the similarities between Zola's and Brontë's symbolic use of fat. McEachern provides a translation of Zola's description of Nana: "her wide hips that rolled in a voluptuous swaying motion" (*Deprivation and Power*, p. 81). Like Cleopatra, Nana "indulges all of her appetites without restriction" (ibid., p. 81). Both Cleopatra and Nana love to eat, and, in both cases, the voluptuous body connotes sensuality.

51. According to the *OED*, the word "fatuous" derives from the Latin *fatuus*, meaning foolish or silly. The word "fat" (meaning well-fed, plump) has its roots in the Old English *fǽt*, which is related to the Old Frisian *fatt* or *feet*, and the Middle Low German *vett*. The word "fat" with the meaning of a "presumptuous, conceited dandy; a fop" came into use from the word fatuous in the mid-nineteenth century and, of course, is now archaic. This is a likely instance of literature becoming ideology, as Brontë may well have been one of the first people to use the word "fat" in this meaning, and it is clearly related to her overall denigration of corpulence.

52. In the wildly popular anti-Catholic *Awful Disclosures*, for example, Maria Monk notes the unwillingness of priests to allow nuns to read the Bible as one of the first signs of their depravity (an evil that extends to murdering nuns and infants).

53. C. Sinclair, *Beatrice* (New York: Garland, 1975), p. 78.

54. See Bernstein, *Confessional Subjects: Revelations of Gender and Power in Victorian Literature and Culture* (Chapel Hill: University of North Carolina Press, 1997).

55. The biblical Vashti, who refuses to display her beauty at the command of her husband Ahasuerus, is diametrically opposed to the exhibitionist Cleopatra: "On the seventh day, when the heart of the king was merry with wine, he commanded . . . the seven eunuchs . . . to bring Queen Vashti before the king with her royal crown, in order to show the peoples and the princes her beauty; for she was fair to behold. But Queen Vashti refused to come at the king's command conveyed by the eunuchs. At this the king was enraged, and his anger burned within him" (Esther 1: 10–12).

56. L. Ciolkowski, "Charlotte Brontë's *Villette*: Forgeries of Sex and Self," *Studies in the Novel* 26 (1994), 224.

57. Charlotte Brontë, letter to George Smith, 6 December 1852.

58. Judith Newton has discussed the ways in which Paulina is a miniature housewife in "*Villette*," in *Feminist Criticism and Social Change*. Brontë's comparison of Paulina to a spaniel may also have its roots in her belief in phrenology. The faculty of attachment was believed by phrenologists to be: "more considerable in woman than in man; many domestic animals are endowed with it, – dogs particularly; the spaniel has it very large" (Mrs. L. Miles, *Casket of Knowledge: Phrenology* [Philadelphia: Lea & Blanchard, 1835], p. 4).

59. *Etiquette of Courtship and Marriage*, p. 93.

60. Gilbert and Gubar, *The Madwoman in the Attic*, p. 404; J. Carlisle, "The Face in the Mirror: *Villette* and the Conventions of Autobiography," *Critical Essays on Charlotte Brontë*, ed. Barbara Timm Gates (Boston:

G. K. Hall & Co., 1990), 279; Silver, "The Reflecting Reader in *Villette*," p. 291.

61. K. Millett, *Sexual Politics* (New York: Touchstone, 1969), p. 141; Carlisle, "The Face in the Mirror," p. 280; Moglen, *Charlotte Brontë*, p. 205.

62. The physician Samuel Ashwell blamed "the late hours and excitement of fashionable life" (Ashwell, *Practical Treatise*, p. 3) for chlorosis, now diagnosed as a form of anemia. Ironically, Ginevra is also the healthiest character in the novel.

63. *Health for the Million*, p. 277.

64. Carlisle discusses similarities between Ginevra and Lucy. See Carlisle, "The Face in the Mirror," p. 280.

65. Matthew Arnold, letter to Mrs. Forster 14 April 1853. Gordon, *Charlotte Brontë*, p. 227.

66. Matthew Arnold, letter to Miss Wightman, 21 December 1850. Barker, *The Brontës*, p. 663.

4 VAMPIRISM AND THE ANOREXIC PARADIGM

1. Gaskell, *Cranford*, p. 75.

2. W. M. Thackeray, *The History of Pendennis* (New York and London: Harper Brothers, 1903), p. 364.

3. Kipling's poem can be found in *The New Oxford Book of Victorian Verse*, ed. Christopher Ricks (Oxford University Press, 1987), 542.

4. For more nineteenth-century vampire stories see the following books: *The Dracula Book of Great Vampire Stories*, ed. Leslie Shepard (Secaucus, NJ: Castle Books, 1979); *Vampires: Two Centuries of Great Vampire Stories*, ed. Alan Ryan (Garden City: Doubleday & Co., 1987); *The Vampyre and Other Tales of the Macabre*, ed. Robert Morrison and Chris Baldick (Oxford: Oxford University Press, 1997).

5. Dijkstra, *Idols of Perversity*, p. 351.

6. C. Senf, "Dracula: Stoker's Response to the New Woman," *Victorian Studies* 26 (1982), 62. For other feminist readings of *Dracula*, see A. Case, "Tasting the Original Apple," *Narrative* 1 (1993), 223–243 and E. Signoretti, "Repossessing the Body: Transgressive Desire in 'Carmilla' and *Dracula*," *Criticism: A Quarterly for Literature and the Arts* 38 (1996), 607–632.

7. B. Stoker, *Dracula* (New York: Bantam, 1989), pp. 62, 39. All future references will be cited parenthetically in the text.

8. See Punter's essay, in which he presents an excellent close reading of this scene and also alludes to the body/soul split.

9. Gilman, *The Little Wreath*, David Punter, "Dracula and Taboo," in *Dracula*, ed. Glennis Byron (New York: St. Martin's Press, 1999), pp. 22–27. p. 161.

10. By offering her nourishment from his breast, Dracula not only becomes a grotesque anti-mother, but he also subverts Christian iconography in which Christ offers his followers blood from his breast.

11. Though Dracula's male hunger is also grotesque, he is the only male vampire that Stoker describes, as opposed to five female vampires (including Mina, who never fully succumbs). Clearly, women are more vulnerable to vampires, and the desires that they symbolize, than men are. The only men in the text at risk of vampirism are Jonathan, at the moment when he is at his most "quiet" (39) and passive, taking the traditionally female role as he waits for the women's advances "in a languorous ecstasy" (39) and Renfield, whose insanity links him to irrational femininity. Hunger signifies an inability to resist one's desire.

12. C. Craft, "'Kiss Me with Those Red Lips': Gender and Inversion in Bram Stoker's *Dracula*," in *Dracula*, ed. Glennis Byron (New York: St. Martin's Press, 1999), p. 111. See also C. F. Bentley, "The Monster in the Bedroom: Sexual Symbolism in Bram Stoker's *Dracula*," *Literature and Psychology* 22 (1972), 30.

13. Craft, "'Kiss Me with Those Red Lips,'" p. 111.

14. C. Bentley, "The Monster in the Bedroom," p. 29.

15. J. Halberstam, "Technologies of Monstrosity: Bram Stoker's Dracula," in *Dracula*, ed. Glennis Byron, pp. 173–196.

16. C. Lombroso and W. Ferraro, *The Female Offender*, 1895 (Littleton, CO: Fred B. Rothman & Co., 1980), p. 48. All future references will be cited parenthetically in the text.

17. Signoretti, "Repossessing the Body," p. 624.

18. B. Dijkstra also notes the thinness of vampires (Dijkstra, *Idols of Perversity*, pp. 333–351).

19. S. Le Fanu, "Carmilla," *In a Glass Darkly* (Oxford University Press, 1993), p. 265. All future references will be cited parenthetically in the text.

20. Brumberg, *Fasting Girls*, 310n.

21. Carmilla may have influenced Stoker's Arabella, in *The Lair of the White Worm*, who appears to be a beautiful woman but is actually an enormous serpent.

22. Ken Gelder suggests that Laura's mother warns her daughter not about Carmilla, but about "those who would seek to kill Carmilla," and that she "becomes, in effect, identified with Carmilla" (K. Kelder, *Reading the Vampire* [London: Routledge, 1984], p. 46). Such a deconstructive reading, however, seems unconvincing considering the fact that Laura wakes up to see Carmilla, soaked with her blood, in the room.

23. See Sander Gilman, *The Jew's Body* (New York: Routledge, 1991) and Matus, *Unstable Bodies*, for discussions of the association of the East (and, of course, Africa) with hypersexuality.

24. See Gilman, *The Jew's Body*; D. Heller, "The Outcast as Villain and Victim: Jews in Dickens's *Oliver Twist* and *Our Mutual Friend*," in *Jewish Presences in English Literature*, ed. D. Cohen and D. Heller (Montreal: McGill-Queen's University Press, 1990), pp. 40–60; A. Naman, *The Jew in the Victorian Novel: Some Relationships Between Prejudice and Art* (New York: AMS Press, 1980); and M. Ragussis, *Figures of Conversion: "The Jewish Question" and English National*

Identity (Durham: Duke University Press, 1995); for histories of Jews and anti-Semitism in Victorian Britain and for representations of the Jew in Victorian literature. Heller, in particular, discusses the literary and cultural association of Jews with the devil, and her discussion of Fagin reveals many similarities between Fagin and Svengali. See also Halberstam, "Technologies of Monstrosity," who argues very persuasively that Stoker's *Dracula* draws from anti-Semitic stereotypes.

25. G. Du Maurier, *Trilby* (London: Penguin, 1994), p. 66. All future references will be cited parenthetically in the text.
26. McEachern, *Deprivation and Power*, p. 153.
27. Dijkstra, *Idols of Perversity*, p. 26–27. For other discussions of the cult of invalidism, see Bailin, *The Sickroom*, McEachern, *Deprivation and Power*, and Sontag, *Illness as Metaphor*.
28. Dijkstra, *Idols of Perversity*, p. 36.
29. Bordo, *Unbearable Weight*, p. 147.

5 CHRISTINA ROSSETTI'S SACRED HUNGER

1 All of the poetry cited in this chapter can be found in C. Rossetti, *The Complete Poems of Christina Rossetti*, ed. R. W. Crump (Baton Rouge: Louisiana State University Press, 1990). All poetry will be cited by line number parenthetically in the text.
2 An in-depth explanation of the Oxford movement is beyond the scope of this book. See, however, the following histories of the movement: Owen Chadwick, *The Spirit of the Oxford Movement* (Cambridge University Press, 1990); Raymond Chapman, *Faith and Revolt: Studies in the Literary Influence of the Oxford Movement* (London: Weidenfeld and Nicholson, 1970); and Peter Nockles, *The Oxford Movement in Context* (Cambridge University Press, 1994).
3 E. B. Pusey, "Tract XVIII: Thoughts on the Benefits of the System of Fasting Enjoined by Our Church," in *The Oxford Movement: Being a Selection From Tracts for the Times*, ed. William Hutchison (London: Walter Scott, n.d.), p. 109.
4 *Sermons, or homilies, appointed to be read in churches in the time of Queen Elizabeth of famous memory* (New York: T. & J. Swords, 1815), p. 300. The Second Book of Homilies is mentioned in the Thirty-Nine Articles. Article xxxv, "Of Homilies," reads, "The second Book of Homilies . . . doth contain a godly and wholesome Doctrine, and necessary for these times, as doth the former Book of Homilies . . . and therefore we judge them to be read in Churches by the Ministers, diligently and distinctly, that they may be understanded of the people." My thanks to Robert Ellison for helping me locate this source.
5 J. Marsh, *Christina Rossetti: A Writer's Life* (New York: Viking, 1994), p. 63.
6 I. Williams, "Sermon VIII," in *A Course of Sermons on Solemn Subjects*, ed. E. B. Pusey (Oxford: John Henry Parker, 1847), p. 130. Emphasis mine.
7 Nockles, *The Oxford Movement in Context*, p. 43.

8 W. Rossetti, *The Poetical Works of Christina Rossetti* (London: Macmillan, 1928), p. lv.

9 C. Rossetti, *The Face of the Deep: A Devotional Commentary on the Apocalypse* (London: Society for Promoting Christian Knowledge, 1895), p. 202.

10 E. B. Pusey, *Entire Absolution of the Penitent* (Oxford: John Henry Parker, 1846), p. 29.

11 C. Rossetti, *Time Flies: A Reading Diary* (London: Society for Promoting Christian Knowledge, 1885), p. 198.

12 Ibid., p. 259.

13 P. M. Cohen, "Christina Rossetti's 'Goblin Market': A Paradigm for Nineteenth-Century Anorexia Nervosa," *University of Hartford Studies in Literature* 17 (1985), 10–11.

14 C. Rossetti, *The Family Letters of Christina Georgina Rossetti*, ed. William Michael Rossetti (New York: Haskell House Publishers, 1968), p. 5n.

15 W. M. Rossetti, *The Poetical Works of Christina Rossetti*, p. lxviii.

16 Jan Marsh, *Christina Rossetti*, suggests (but cannot conclusively prove) that Rossetti's menstruation occurred for the first time in 1845.

17 Marsh, *Christina Rossetti*, p. 50.

18 Rossetti, *Family Letters*, p. 45.

19 Ibid., p. 431.

20 Vandereycken and Van Deth, *From Fasting Saints*, p. 221.

21 C. W. Bynum, *Holy Feast and Holy Fast: The Religious Significance of Food to Medieval Women* (Berkeley: University of California Press, 1987), p. 206.

22 Bordo, *Unbearable Weight*, p. 83.

23 R. Bell, *Holy Anorexia* (University of Chicago Press, 1985), p. 149.

24 Ibid., p. 115.

25 Foucault, *History of Sexuality*, p. 38.

26 Ibid., p. 33.

27 C. Lawrence, *Medicine and the Making of Modern Britain, 1700–1920* (London: Routledge, 1994), pp. 55–56.

28 *An Account of the Extraordinary Abstinence of Ann Moor, of Tutbury, Straffordshire, England Who has for more than three years, lived entirely without food*, 1st American edition from the 2nd London edition (Boston: B. True, 1811), pp. 6–7.

29 Fowler, *A Complete History of the Case of the Welsh Fasting Girl*, p. 2.

30 Barber, "Cases of Long-Continued Abstinence From Food," 544–545.

31 Ibid., p. 545.

32 Ibid.

33 Rossetti, *The Face of the Deep*, p. 203.

34 Brumberg, *Fasting Girls*, p. 45.

35 G. M. Hopkins, *The Journals and Papers of Gerard Manley Hopkins*, ed. Humphry House and Graham Storey (London: Oxford University Press, 1959), p. 72.

36 G. M. Hopkins, *The Early Poetic Manuscripts and Note-Books of Gerard Manley Hopkins in Facsimile*, ed. Normal MacKenzie (New York: Garland, 1989), p. 155.

37 D. D'Amico, *Christina Rossetti: Faith, Gender and Time* (Baton Rouge: Louisiana State University Press, 1999), p. 62.

38 A. L. Tennyson, *Idylls of the King and a Selection of Poems* (New York: Signet, 1961). All future references to the poems will be cited parenthetically by line number.

39 Bynum, *Holy Feast and Holy Fast*, p. 54.

40 Ibid., pp. 59, 116.

41 Ibid., p. 116.

42 C. Lang, "Introduction," *The Pre-Raphaelites and Their Circle* (University of Chicago Press, 1975), p. xxvii.

43 C. Van Dyke, *The Fiction of Truth: Structures of Meaning in Narrative and Dramatic Allegory* (Cornell University Press, 1985), p. 27.

44 For Rossetti and the Oxford movement, see M. Arseneau, "Incarnation and Interpretation: Christina Rossetti, the Oxford Movement, and Goblin Market," *Victorian Poetry* 31 (1993), 79–93; J. Bristow, "'No Friend like a Sister?': Christina Rossetti's Female Kin," *Victorian Poetry* 33 (1995), 257–281; and L. Schofield, "Being and Understanding: Devotional Poetry of Christina Rossetti and the Tractarians," in *The Achievement of Christina Rossetti*, ed. D. A. Kent (Ithaca, NY: Cornell University Press, 1987), pp. 301–321.

45 D'Amico, *Christina Rossetti: Faith, Gender and Time*, p. 71.

46 See D'Amico for an extended discussion. Mary Arseneau has also argued very persuasively that Laura chooses goblin fruit over Christ's fruit ("Incarnation and Interpretation").

47 Nockles, *The Oxford Movement in Context*, p. 237. Nockles provides a detailed history of the contested place of the Eucharist in Tractarian thought.

48 Rossetti, *The Face of the Deep*, p. 34.

49 A. Harrison, *Christina Rossetti in Context* (Chapel Hill: University of North Carolina Press, 1988), p. 54.

50 Pusey, *Entire Absolution of the Penitent*, p. 20.

51 S. B. Shurbutt, "Revisionist Mythmaking in Christina Rossetti's 'Goblin Market,'" *The Victorian Newsletter* 82 (1992), p. 43.

52 Ibid.

53 Rossetti, *The Face of the Deep*, pp. 76, 321.

54 Ibid., p. 310.

55 Rossetti, *Family Letters*, p. 361.

56 C. Rossetti, "The Lost Titian," *Poems and Prose*, ed. Jan Marsh (London: Everyman, 1994), p. 311. How does one reconcile Rossetti's use of the crocodile as an emblem of evil in "My Dream" with her fondness for crocodiles? Perhaps the best explanation is that which Rossetti herself sets forth in *The Face of the Deep* when describing an octopus as a "Satanic suggestion": "I had to remind myself that this vivid figure of wickedness was not in truth itself wickedness" (*The Face of the Deep*, p. 204).

57 Rossetti, *Family Letters*, p. 44. Christina Rossetti, letter to Dante Gabriel Rossetti, 4 May 1874. For the relation between *Speaking Likenesses* and *Alice*

in Wonderland, see U. Knoepflmacher, "Avenging Alice: Christina Rossetti and Lewis Carroll," *Nineteenth Century Literature* 41 (1986), 299–328.

58 Marsh, *Christina Rossetti*, p. 45. *Athenaeum* (27 December 1874).

59 C. Rossetti, *Speaking Likenesses, Forbidden Journeys: Fairy Tales and Fantasies by Victorian Women Writers*, ed. Nina Auerbach and U. C. Knoepflmacher (University of Chicago Press, 1992), p. 338. All future citations will be cited parenthetically in the text.

60 N. Auerbach and U. C. Knoepflmacher, "A Trio of Antifantasies: Speaking Likenesses," in *Forbidden Journeys: Fairy Tales and Fantasies by Victorian Women Writers*, p. 319.

61 *New Catholic Encyclopedia* (New York: McGraw-Hill, 1967), p. 193.

62 Ibid., p. 194.

63 Ibid.

64 *Oxford Dictionary of the Christian Church*, ed. F. L. Cross. 3rd edn, ed. E. A. Livingstone (Oxford University Press, 1997), p. 26.

65 C. Rossetti, "Maude," in *Poems and Prose*, ed. Jan Marsh (London: Everyman, 1994), p. 267.

66 The third part of *Speaking Likenesses* is strongly influenced by Bunyan's *Pilgrim's Progress*, in which Christian is beset by various figures of temptation on his way to the Celestial City. The sleepers whom Flora encounters in the wood, for instance, are clearly based upon Bunyan's sleepers, Simple, Sloth, and Presumption, and upon the Hill of Difficulty in which Christian falls asleep. In its depiction of hunger, *Speaking Likenesses* draws in particular on the second part of *Pilgrim's Progress*, in which Bunyan carefully distinguishes between sacred food – symbolized by Eucharistic "wine, red as blood" (329) – and worldly food, such as that served by Madam Bubble, who "loveth banqueting, and feasting mainly well" (374). As Gaius explains, "Forbidden fruit will make you sick, but not what our Lord has tolerated" (330). Rossetti's distinctions between the sacred and secular meanings of hunger are surely influenced by her own reading of Bunyan. All parenthetical citations from J. Bunyan, *The Pilgrim's Progress* (London: Penguin, 1987).

67 Auerbach and Knoepflmacher, "A Trio of Antifantasies," p. 355n.

68 Rossetti, *Face of the Deep*, p. 97.

69 See Revelation 21: 20. In *The Face of the Deep*, Rossetti calls the sixth rock "sardius" and then comments: "Sardius, a choice sort of carnelian, is found in rocks. Red it is, the more vividly red the more costly" (p. 509). Rossetti's use of the stone carnelian in *Speaking Likenesses* seems, then, to refer to the New Jerusalem. Flora's return to her grandmother's house after her journey also recollects Christian's arrival at the Celestial City in *Pilgrim's Progress*.

70 Rossetti, *Time Flies*, p. 259.

71 Maggie's desire to see a Christmas tree, and her subsequent view of a "divine" Christmas tree, is very much like the experience of the little match girl in Hans Christian Andersen's story of the same title, in which an

impoverished child sees a vision of a Christmas tree on New Year's Eve by lighting her bundle of matches. Both stories close with the heroine's reunion with her grandmother. In her biography of Rossetti, Jan Marsh notes that Rossetti was familiar with Andersen, whose stories (though not "The Little Match Girl") her friend Mary Howitt translated in 1846 as *Wonderful Stories for Children* (Marsh, *Christina Rossetti*, p. 138). Not only does the Andersen connection provide a source for *Speaking Likenesses*, but the Christianity of Andersen's story, in which the match girl is carried to heaven by the spirit of her grandmother, underscores the Christian message of *Speaking Likenesses*.

72 Bynum, *Holy Feast and Holy Fast*, p. 119.

CONCLUSION: THE POLITICS OF THINNESS

1 Plato, *Phaedo*, p. 103.
2 N. Wolf, *The Beauty Myth*, p. 184; R. Johnson, "The Body Myth," *Vogue* (September 1996), 656.
3 Johnson, "The Body Myth," p. 658.
4 Ibid., p. 656.
5 Ibid.
6 J. Rosen, "Body-Image Disturbances," p. 197.
7 Johnson, "The Body Myth," p. 657.
8 Holowatinc and Holowatinc, "Letter," *Vogue* (December 1996), 60.
9 Wolf, *The Beauty Myth*, p. 295n.
10 Foucault, *History of Sexuality*, pp. 92–93.
11 Ibid., p. 98.
12 Heywood, *Dedication to Hunger*, p. 8.
13 Foucault, *Discipline and Punish*, pp. 201, 214.
14 Bartky, "Foucault, Femininity, and the Modernization of Patriarchal Power," p. 42.
15 J. Reilly, "The Gym: Just Go Already," *New Woman* (April 1997), 90.
16 C. Tavris, *The Mismeasure of Woman* (New York: Touchstone, 1992), p. 31; Poulton, *No Fat Chicks*, p. 13.
17 For links to these sites, see emote.org/thin/.
18 clubs.yahoo.com/clubs/pronanorexic.
19 www.geocities.com/isou33.
20 ally. 22 July 2001. clubs.yahoo.com/clubs/only popular with anorexia.
21 julia. 22 July 2001. clubs.yahoo.com/clubs/onlypopularwith anorexia.
22 Gypsy wytch. 18 July 2001. clubs.yahoo.com/clubs/only popular with anorexia.
23 Solveiguk. 20 July 2001. clubs.yahoo.com/clubs/onlypopularwith anorexia.
24 Brumberg, *Fasting Girls*, 264.
25 Poulton, *No Fat Chicks*.

Bibliography

The publisher has used its best endeavors to ensure that the URLs for external websites referred to in this book are correct and active at the time of going to press. However, the publisher has no responsibility for the websites and can make no guarantee that a site will remain live or that the content is or will remain appropriate.

PRIMARY/HISTORICAL SOURCES:

An Account of the Extraordinary Abstinence of Ann Moor, of Tutbury, Straffordshire, England Who has for more than three years, lived entirely without food, 1st American edition from the 2nd London edition. Boston: B. True, 1811.

Adam, James. "A Case of Melancholia Presenting Some Exceptional Features, Prolonged Refusal of Food, and Forced Alimentation." *British Medical Journal* (18 February 1888): 348–349.

Allan, J. McGrigor. "Allan on the Differences in the Minds of Men and Women." *Journal of the Anthropological Society of London* 7 (1869): cxcv–cccix.

Allbutt, T. Clifford. *On Visceral Neuroses, Being the Gulstonian Lectures on Neuralgia of the Stomach and Allied Disorders.* London: J. & A. Churchill, 1884.

Andersen, *Hans Christian. Hans Andersen's Fairy Tales.* Trans. L. W. Kingsland. Oxford University Press, 1991.

Anonymous. "Letter." *Englishwoman's Domestic Magazine* (1867): 502.

The Art of Beautifying and Improving the Face and Figure. London: G. Vickers, 1858.

The Art of Dress, or Guide to the Toilette. London: Charles Tilt, 1834.

Ashwell, Samuel. *A Practical Treatise on the Diseases Peculiar to Women.* Philadelphia, PA: Lea and Blanchard, 1845.

Barber, Henry. "Cases of Long-Continued Abstinence From Food." *British Medical Journal* (28 May 1870): 544–545.

Beard, George M. *Eating and Drinking: A Popular Manual of Food and Diet in Health and Disease.* New York: Putnam & Sons, 1871.

Beeton, Isabella. *Mrs. Beeton's Book of Household Management.* 1861. London: Chancellor Press, 1982.

Blake, William. *Songs of Innocence and Experience. The Complete Poetry and Prose of William Blake.* Ed. David Erdman. New York: Anchor Books, 1988. 7–32.

The Book of Health and Beauty or the Toilette of Rank and Fashion. London: Joseph Thomas, 1837.

Brontë, Charlotte. *Jane Eyre*. Toronto: Bantam, 1981.

   The Professor. London: Penguin, 1989.

   Shirley. Ware: Wordsworth, 1993.

   Villette. London: Everyman, 1993.

Brontë, Emily. *Wuthering Heights*. Oxford University Press, 1995.

The Brontës: Life and Letters. 2 vols. Ed. Clement Shorter. London: Hodder and Stoughton, 1953.

The Brontës: Their Lives, Friendships & Correspondence in Four Volumes. 4 vols. Ed. Thomas James Wise and John Alexander Symington. Oxford: Shakespeare Head Press, 1932.

Browning, Robert. *The Pied Piper of Hamelin*. *The Kate Greenaway Treasury*. Ed. Edward Ernest and Patricia Lowe. Cleveland: The World Publishing Company, 1967. 256–300.

Bunyan, John. *The Pilgrim's Progress*. London: Penguin, 1987.

Caplin, Madame Roxey A. *Health & Beauty; or Corsets and Clothing*. London: Darton & Co., 1856.

Carroll, Lewis. *Alice's Adventures in Wonderland and Through the Looking Glass*. New York: Signet, 1960.

   The Letters of Lewis Carroll. Ed. Morton N. Cohen and Roger Lancelyn Green. New York: Oxford University Press, 1979.

Child-Land: Picture-Pages for the Little Ones. London: S. W. Partridge & Co., 1873.

Clarke, Edward. "Sex in Education: A Fair Chance for the Girls." In *Desire and Imagination: Classic Essays in Sexuality*. Ed. Regina Barreca. New York: Meridian, 1995. 157–187.

Clarke, Henry G. *The English Maiden: Her Moral and Domestic Duties*. London: Henry Green Clarke, 1841.

Collingwood, Stuart Dodgson. *The Life and Letters of Lewis Carroll*. New York: Century, 1899.

Cooley, Arnold. *The Toilet in Ancient and Modern Times*. 1866. New York: Burt Franklin, 1970.

Dick, Robert. *The Connexion of Health and Beauty: or, the Dependence of a pleasing face and Figure*. London: John Chapman, 1857.

Dickens, Charles. *Bleak House*. London: Everyman, 1994.

   David Copperfield. London: Penguin, 1985.

   Letters. Ed. Madeline House and Graham Storey. Oxford: Clarendon Press, 1965– .

   The Old Curiosity Shop. London: Penguin, 1985.

Dodsworth, William. Sermon IX. *A Course of Sermons on Solemn Subjects: chiefly bearing on repentance and amendment of life*. Ed. E. B. Pusey. Oxford: John Henry Parker, 1847. 143–156.

Douglas, Fanny. *The Gentlewoman's Book of Dress*. London: Henry & Co., n.d., ca. 1894.

Du Maurier, George. *Trilby*. London: Penguin, 1994.

Ellis, Sarah Stickney. *The Daughters of England*. London: Fisher, Son & Co., n.d., c. 1841.

Etiquette for Ladies, Being a Manual of Minor Social Ethics and Customary Observances. Knight & Son, 1857.

The Etiquette of Courtship and Marriage: with a complete guide to the forms of a wedding. London: David Bogue, 1851.

Etiquette of Love, Courtship and Marriage. Halifax: Milner and Sowerby, 1859.

Etiquette of the Toilette-Table: A Manual of Utility, Elegance, & Personal Comfort by an Officer's Widow. Glasgow: W. R. M'Phun, 1859.

Farrar, Eliza. *The Young Lady's Friend*. Boston, MA: American Stationers' Company, 1837.

Forster, John. *The Life of Charles Dickens*. London: C. Palmer, 1928.

Fowler, Robert. *A Complete History of the Case of the Welsh Fasting Girl*. London: Henry Renshaw, 1871.

Gaskell, Elizabeth. *Cranford*. London: Penguin, 1977.

   The Life of Charlotte Bronte. London: Penguin, 1985.

   Ruth. Oxford University Press, 1983.

   Wives and Daughters. London: Penguin, 1986.

Gilman, Carol. *The Little Wreath*. New York: Blakeman and Mason, 1864.

The Girl's Birthday Book. London: Houlston and Wright, 1860.

Girl's Own Paper. Vols. 1–8. 1880–1887.

Gordon, Julien. *Vampires: Mademoiselle Resada*. London: Ward, Lock & Bowden, 1893.

Greenaway, Kate. *Kate Greenaway's Book of Poems*. London: Grange Books, 1993.

   The Kate Greenaway Treasury. Ed. Edward Ernest and Patricia Lowe. Cleveland: The World Publishing Company, 1967.

   Under the Window. London: George Routledge & Sons, 1878.

Grimes, J. Stanley. *Phreno-Geology: The Progressive Creation of Man*. London: Edward T. Whitfield, 1851.

Gull, William Withey. "Anorexia Nervosa (Apepsia Hysterica, Anorexia Hysterica)." *Transactions of the Clinical Society of London* 7 (1874): 22–28.

Haweis, Mrs. H. R. [Mary Eliza]. *The Art of Beauty*. London: Chatto and Windus, 1878.

Health: How to Gain and how to Keep it. 1862.

Health for the Million. London: W. Kent & Co., 1858.

"Healthy Lives for Working Girls." *Girl's Own Paper* 8 (30 October 1886) 79.

Henderson, Mrs. *The Young Wife's Own Book*. Glasgow: W. R. M'Phun, 1857.

Hinton, Eliza. *Thoughts for the Heart*. London: John Haddon, 1847.

Holy Bible. Revised Standard Version. Nashville: Thomas Nelson, 1971.

Hopkins, Ellise. *On the Early Training of Girls and Boys*. London: Hatchards, 1882.

Hopkins, Gerard Manley. *The Early Poetic Manuscripts and Note-Books of Gerard Manley Hopkins in Facsimile*. Ed. Norman MacKenzie. New York: Garland, 1989.

   The Journals and Papers of Gerard Manley Hopkins. Ed. Humphry House and Graham Storey. London: Oxford University Press, 1959.

How to Woo; How to Win; and How to Get Married. Glasgow: W. R. M'Phun, 1856.

The Illustrated Girls' Own Story-Book. London: Ward & Lock, 1861.

Kipling, Rudyard. "The Vampire." In *The New Oxford Book of Victorian Verse*. Ed. Christopher Ricks. Oxford University Press, 1990. 542.

Ladies' Treasury. Vols. 1–6. 1858–1864; vol. 3 (new series) 1867.

A Lady, *How to Dress on £15 a Year As a Lady.* London: Frederick Warne, n.d., c. 1873.

Lasègue, Charles. "On Hysterical Anorexia." *The Medical Times and Gazette* (27 September 1873), 265f.

Laycock, Thomas. *A Treatise on the Nervous Diseases of Women.* London: Longman, Orme, Brown, Green, and Longmans, 1840.

Le Fanu, Joseph Sheridan. "Carmilla." *In a Glass Darkly.* Oxford University Press, 1993. 243–319.

"Limby Lumpy." *The Oxford Book of Children's Stories.* Ed. Jan Mark. Oxford University Press, 1994. 58–62.

L'Isère, Colombat de. *A Treatise on the Diseases and Special Hygiene of Females.* Trans. Charles D. Meigs. Philadelphia, PA: Lea & Blanchard, 1845.

Lombroso, Caesar and William Ferrero. *The Female Offender.* 1895. Littleton, CO: Fred B. Rothman & Co., 1980.

Lord, William Barry. *The Corset and the Crinoline.* London: Ward, Lock, and Tyler, 1868.

Maudsley, Henry. "Sex in Mind and in Education." In *Desire and Imagination: Classic Essays in Sexuality*. Ed. Regina Barreca. New York: Meridian, 1995. 188–209.

McNeill, D. "An Extraordinary Fasting Case." *British Medical Journal* (24 June 1879): 938.

Miles, Mrs. L. *Casket of Knowledge: Phrenology.* Philadelphia, PA: Lea & Blanchard, 1835.

Mitchell, S. Weir. "Fat and Blood." In *Desire and Imagination: Classic Essays in Sexuality*. Ed. Regina Barreca. New York: Meridian, 1995. 157–187.

Morrison, Arthur. *A Child of the Jago.* London: J. M. Dent, 1996.

Nightingale, Florence. *Cassandra.* Old Westbury: Feminist Press, 1979.

Nora. "Letter." *The Englishwoman's Domestic Magazine* (1867): 278.

Ogle, John. "Clinical Lecture on a Case of Hysteria." *British Medical Journal* (16 July 1879): 57–60.

Plato. "Phaedo." Trans. G. M. A. Grube. In *Five Dialogues.* Indianapolis: Hackett Publishing, 1981. 93–155.

Pusey, E. B. *Entire Absolution of the Penitent.* Oxford: John Henry Parker, 1846.

"Tract XVIII: Thoughts on the Benefits of the System of Fasting Enjoined by our Church." In *The Oxford Movement: Being a Selection From Tracts for the Times*. Ed. William G. Hutchison. London: Walter Scott, n.d. 76–110.

Rossetti, Christina. *Called to be Saints.* London: Society for Promoting Christian Knowledge, 1895.

The Complete Poems of Christina Rossetti: A Variorum Edition. 3 vols. Ed. R. W. Crump. Baton Rouge: Louisiana State University Press, 1990.

The Face of the Deep: A Devotional Commentary on the Apocalypse. London: Society for Promoting Christian Knowledge, 1892.

The Family Letters of Christina Georgina Rossetti. Ed. William Michael Rossetti. New York: Haskell House Publishers, 1968.

Goblin Market and Other Poems. London and Cambridge: Macmillan & Co., 1862.

"The Lost Titian." In *Poems and Prose*. Ed. Jan Marsh. London: Everyman, 1994. 304–313.

"Maude." In *Poems and Prose*. Ed. Jan Marsh. London: Everyman, 1994. 252–274.

Speaking Likenesses. Forbidden Journeys: Fairy Tales and Fantasies by Victorian Women Writers. Ed. Nina Auerbach and U. C. Knoepflmacher. University of Chicago Press, 1992. 325–360.

Time Flies: A Reading Diary. London: Society for Promoting Christian Knowledge, 1885.

Verses. London: G. Polidori, 1847.

Rossetti, William, "Memoir." *The Poetical Works of Christina Rossetti*. London: Macmillan, 1928. i–lxx.

Ruskin, John. *The Ethics of the Dust*. Philadelphia, PA: Henry Altemus Company, n.d.

"Fairy Land." *Art of England: Complete Lectures Given in Oxford*. Sunnyside: George Allen, 1884.

Letters. The Complete Works of John Ruskin. Ed. E. T. Cook and Alexander Wedderburn. Vols. 36 and 37. London: George Allen, 1905.

Of Queens' Gardens. Sesame and Lilies. Chicago: Belford, Clarke & Co., 1890. 72–101.

The Winnington Letters. Ed. Van Akin Burd. London: George Allen & Unwin Ltd., 1969.

Santé, Madame de la. *The Corset Defended*. London: T. E. Carler, 1865.

The Science of Dress. London: Groombridge & Sons, 1856.

Sermons, or homilies, appointed to be read in churches in the time of Queen Elizabeth of famous memory. New York: T. & J. Swords, 1815.

Sinclair, Catherine. *Beatrice*. 1852. New York: Garland, 1975.

"The Snow." Wellington: F. Houlston & Son, 1825.

Spurzheim, J. G. *Phrenology: or the Doctrine of the Mental Phenomena*. New York: Harper & Brothers Publishers, 1855.

The Stain Upon the Hand. Philadelphia: American Sunday-School Union, 1859.

Steele, Frances Mary and Elizabeth Livingston Steele Adams. *Beauty of Form and Grace of Vesture*. New York: Dodd, Mead and Company, 1892.

Stoker, Bram. *Dracula*. New York: Bantam, 1989.

Taylor, Ann and Jane Taylor. *Original Poems for Infant Minds and Rhymes for the Nursery*. New York: Garland, 1976.

Tennyson, Alfred Lord. *Idylls of the King and a Selection of Poems*. New York: Signet, 1961.

Thackeray, William Makepeace. *The History of Pendennis*. New York and London: Harper Brother, 1903.

Thornwell, Emily. *A Lady's Guide to Perfect Gentility*. New York: Derby and Jackson, 1857.

"Torture in the Nineteenth Century: Fashion in Tight Lacing." *Ladies' Treasury* 6 (1864): 11–12.

Trollope, Anthony. *Can You Forgive Her?* Oxford University Press, 1982.

Veblen, Thorstein. *The Theory of the Leisure Class*. New York: Macmillan, 1899.

Victorian Women Poets 1830–1900: An Anthology. Ed. Jennifer Breen. London: Everyman, 1994.

Walker, Alexander. *Beauty in Women Analyzed and Classified*. Glasgow, 1892.
   Intermarriage. Desire and Imagination: Classic Essays in Sexuality. Ed. Regina Barreca. New York: Penguin, 1995. 16–34.

Walker, Mrs. Alexander. *Female Beauty, as Preserved and Improved by Regimen, Cleanliness, and Dress*. London: Thomas Hurst, 1837.

Williams, Isaac. Sermon VIII. A *Course of Sermons on Solemn Subjects*. Ed. E. B. Pusey. Oxford: John Henry Parker, 1847. 123–142.

Wood-Allen, Mrs. Mary. *What a Young Girl Ought to Know*. 1897. Philadelphia, PA: John C. Winston Co., 1928.

Wood's Household Practice of Medicine, Hygiene and Surgery. Ed. F. A. Castle. London: Sampson Low & Co., 1881.

A Young Baronet. "Letter." *Englishwoman's Domestic Magazine* (1867): 558.

The Young Lady's Book. London: Henry G. Bohn, 1859.

Young Lady Herself. "Letter." *Englishwoman's Domestic Magazine* (1867): 333.

SECONDARY/CONTEMPORARY SOURCES

Ally. 22 July 2001. clubs.yahoo.com/clubs/only popular with anorexia (1 August 2001).

Anderson, Amanda. *Tainted Souls and Painted Faces: The Rhetoric of Fallenness in Victorian Culture*. Ithaca: Cornell University Press, 1993.

Armstrong, Isobel. *Victorian Poetry: Poetry, Poetics and Politics*. London: Routledge, 1993.

Armstrong, Nancy. *Desire and Domestic Fiction*. New York: Oxford University Press, 1987.
   "The Occidental Alice." *Differences: A Journal of Feminist Cultural Studies* 2 (1990): 3–40.

Arseneau, Mary. "Incarnation and Interpretation: Christina Rossetti, the Oxford Movement, and Goblin Market." *Victorian Poetry* 31 (1993): 79–93.

Auerbach, Nina. "Alice and Wonderland: A Curious Child." *Victorian Studies* 17 (1973): 31–47.
   Our Vampires, Ourselves. University of Chicago Press, 1995.

Auerbach, Nina and U. C. Knoepflmacher. "A Trio of Antifantasies: Speaking Likenesses." In *Forbidden Journeys: Fairy Tales and Fantasies by Victorian Women Writers*. University of Chicago Press, 1992. 317–323.

Bailin, Miriam. *The Sickroom in Victorian Fiction*. Cambridge University Press, 1994.

Banner, Lois W. *American Beauty*. University of Chicago Press, 1983.

Barker, Juliet. *The Brontës*. New York: St. Martin's Press, 1994.

Bartky, Sandra Lee. "Foucault, Femininity, and the Modernization of Patriarchal Power." In *The Politics of Women's Bodies*. Ed. Rose Weitz. New York: Oxford University Press, 1998. 25–45.

Barwick, Sandra. *A Century of Style*. London: George Allen & Unwin, 1984.

Battiscombe, Georgina. *Christina Rossetti: A Divided Life*. New York: Holt, Rinehart and Winston, 1981.

Bell, Rudolph. *Holy Anorexia*. University of Chicago Press, 1985.

Bentley, C. F., "The Monster in the Bedroom: Sexual Symbolism in Bram Stoker's *Dracula*," *Literature and Psychology* 22 (1972): 27–34.

Bentley, D. M. R. "The Meritricious and the Meritorious in 'Goblin Market': A Conjecture and an Analysis." *The Achievement of Christina Rossetti*. Ed. David A. Kent. Ithaca: Cornell University Press, 1987. 57–81.

Berger, John. *Ways of Seeing*. London: Penguin, 1980.

Bernstein, Susan. *Confessional Subjects: Revelations of Gender and Power in Victorian Literature and Culture*. Chapel Hill: University of North Carolina Press, 1997.

Birch, Diana. "The Ethics of the Dust: Ruskin's Authorities." *Prose Studies* 12 (1989): 147–158.

Bordo, Susan. *Unbearable Weight: Feminism, Western Culture, and the Body*. Berkeley: University of California Press, 1993.

Briggs, Julia. "Women Writers and Writing for Children: From Sarah Fielding to E. Nesbit." In *Children and Their Books: A Celebration of the Work of Iona and Peter Opie*. Ed. Gillian Avery and Julia Briggs. Oxford: Clarendon Press, 1982. 224–243.

Bristow, Joseph. "'No Friend Like a Sister?': Christina Rossetti's Female Kin." *Victorian Poetry* 33 (1995): 257–281.

Brown, Penny. *The Captured World*. New York: Harvester Wheatsheaf, 1993.

Bruch, Hilde. *The Golden Cage: The Enigma of Anorexia Nervosa*. Cambridge, MA: Harvard University Press, 1978.

Brumberg, Joan Jacobs. *Fasting Girls: The History of Anorexia Nervosa*. New York: Plume, 1989.

Burd, Van Akin. "Introduction." *The Winnington Letters*. Ed. Van Akin Burd. London: George Allen and Unwin, Ltd., 1969. 19–88.

Butler, Judith. *Gender Trouble*. New York: Routledge, 1999.

Bynum, Caroline Walker. *Holy Feast and Holy Fast: The Religious Significance of Food to Medieval Women*. Berkeley: University of California Press, 1987.

Byrde, Penelope. *Nineteenth Century Fashion*. London: B. T. Batsford Limited, 1992.

Carlisle, Jane. "The Face in the Mirror: *Villette* and the Conventions of Autobiography." *Critical Essays on Charlotte Brontë*. Ed. Barbara Timm Gates. Boston: G. K. Hall & Co., 1990. 264–286.

Carpenter, Humphrey. *Secret Gardens: The Golden Age of Children's Literature*. Boston: Houghton Mifflin Company, 1984.

Carpenter, Mary Wilson. "'Eat me, Drink me, Love me': The Consumable Body in Christina Rossetti's 'Goblin Market.'" *Victorian Poetry* 31 (1993): 415–434.

Case, Alison. "Tasting the Original Apple." *Narrative* 1 (1993): 223–43.

Cash, Thomas F. and Thomas Pruzinsky, eds. *Body Images: Development, Deviance, and Change*. New York: The Guilford Press, 1990.

Chadwick, Owen. *The Spirit of the Oxford Movement*. Cambridge University Press, 1990.

Chapman, Raymond. *Faith and Revolt: Studies in the Literary Influence of the Oxford Movement*. London: Weidenfeld and Nicolson, 1970.

Chernin, Kim. *The Obsession: Reflections on the Tyranny of Slenderness*. New York: Harper & Row, 1981.

Christ, Carol. "Imaginative Constraint, Feminine Duty, and the Form of Charlotte Brontë's Fiction." *Critical Essays on Charlotte Brontë*. Ed. Barbara Timm Gates. Boston: G. K. Hall & Co., 1990. 60–67.

Ciolkowski, Laura E. "Charlotte Brontë's *Villette*: Forgeries of Sex and Self." *Studies in the Novel* 26 (1994): 218–234.

Cohen, Morton. *Lewis Carroll: A Biography*. New York: Alfred A. Knopf, 1995.

Cohen, Paula Marantz. "Christina Rossetti's 'Goblin Market': A Paradigm for Nineteenth-Century Anorexia Nervosa." *University of Hartford Studies in Literature* 17 (1985): 1–18.

Collingwood, Stuart Dodgson. *The Life and Letters of Lewis Carroll*. London: T. Fisher Unwin, 1898.

Craft, Christopher. "'Kiss Me with Those Red Lips': Gender and Inversion in Bram Stoker's *Dracula*." In *Dracula*. Ed. Glennis Byron. New York: St. Martins Press, 1999. 93–118.

Cripps, Elizabeth. "Alice and the Reviewers." *Children's Literature* 11 (1983): 32–48.

Cunnington, C. Willett. *English Women's Clothing of the Nineteenth Century*. London: Faber & Faber, 1937.

Dally, Peter. *Elizabeth Barrett Browning: A Psychological Portrait*. London: Macmillan, 1989.

D'Amico, Diane. *Christina Rossetti: Faith, Gender and Time*. Baton Rouge: Louisiana State University Press, 1999.

Diagnostic and Statistical Manual of Mental Disorders: DSM IV. Washington, D.C.: American Psychiatric Association, 1994.

Dijkstra, Bram. *Idols of Perversity: Fantasies of Feminine Evil in Fin-de-Siècle Culture*. New York: Oxford University Press, 1986.

Drinka, George Frederick. *The Birth of Neurosis*. New York: Simon and Schuster, 1984.

Engen, Rodney. *Kate Greenaway: A Biography*. London: MacDonald, 1981.

Ewing, Elizabeth. *History of Children's Costume*. New York: Charles Scribner's Sons, 1977.

Fallon, April. "Culture in the Mirror: Sociocultural Determinants of Body Image." In *Body Images: Development, Deviance and Change*. Ed. Thomas Cash and Thomas Pruzinsky. New York: Guilford Press, 1990. 80–107.

Fallon, Patricia, Melanie Katzman, and Susan Wooley, *Feminist Perspectives on Eating Disorders*. New York: The Guilford Press, 1994.

Finch, Casey. "'Hooked and Buttoned Together': Victorian Underwear and Representations of the Female Body," *Victorian Studies* 34 (1991): 337–363.

Foster, Vanda. *A Visual History of Costume: The Nineteenth Century*. London: B. T. Batsford, 1984.

Foucault, Michel. *Discipline and Punish: The Birth of the Prison*. Trans. Alan Sheridan. New York: Vintage, 1995.

The History of Sexuality. Vol. 1. Trans. Robert Hurley. New York: Vintage. 1990.

Frank, Katherine. *A Chainless Soul: A Life of Emily Brontë*. Boston: Houghton Mifflin Company, 1992.

Freeman, Sarah. *Mutton and Oysters: The Victorians and their Food*. London: Victor Gollancz Ltd., 1989.

Furst, Lilian and Peter W. Graham, eds. *Disorderly Eaters: Texts in Self-Empowerment*. University Park: The Pennsylvania State University Press, 1992.

Gelder, Ken. *Reading the Vampire*. London: Routledge, 1984.

Gibbs-Smith, Charles H. *The Fashionable Lady in the 19th Century*. London: Her Majesty's Stationery Office, 1960.

Gilbert, Sandra and Susan, Gubar. *The Madwoman in the Attic*. New Haven, CT: Yale University Press, 1979.

Gilligan, Carol. *In a Different Voice: Psychological Theory and Women's Development*. Cambridge, MA: Harvard University Press, 1982.

Glenny, Allie. *Ravenous Identity: Eating and Eating Distress in the Life and Work of Virginia Woolf*. New York: St. Martin's Press, 1999.

Gmelch, Sharon Bohn. *Gender on Campus: Issues for College Women*. New Brunswick, NJ: Rutgers University Press, 1998.

Goldfarb, Russell M. *Sexual Repression and Victorian Literature*. Lewisburg: Bucknell University Press, 1970.

Gordon, Lyndall. *Charlotte Brontë: A Passionate Life*. London: Chatto & Windus, 1994.

Gorham, Deborah. *The Victorian Girl and the Feminine Ideal*. Bloomington: Indiana University Press, 1982.

Gypsy wytche. 18 July 2001. clubs.yahoo.com/clubs/only popular with anorexia (1 August 2001).

Halberstam, J. "Technologies of Monstrosity: Bram Stoker's Dracula." In *Dracula*. Ed. Glennis Byron. New York: St. Martin's Press, 1999. 173–196.

Harrison, Antony H. *Christina Rossetti in Context*. Chapel Hill: University of North Carolina Press, 1988.

Heller, Deborah. "The Outcast as Villain and Victim: Jews in Dickens's *Oliver Twist* and *Our Mutual Friend*," In *Jewish Presences in English Literature*. Ed. Derek Cohen and Deborah Heller. Montreal: McGill-Queen's University Press, 1990: 40–60.

Helsinger, Elizabeth. *Ruskin and the Art of the Beholder*. Cambridge, MA: Harvard University Press, 1982.

Hesse-Biber, Sharlene. *Am I Thin Enough Yet?: The Cult of Thinness and the Commercialization of Beauty*. New York: Oxford, 1996.

Heywood, Leslie. *Dedication to Hunger: The Anorexic Aesthetic in Modern Culture.* Berkeley: University of California Press, 1996.

Hickok, Kathleen. *Representations of Women: Nineteenth Century British Women's Poetry.* Westport, CT: Greenwood Press, 1984.

Hollander, Anne. *Seeing Through Clothes.* New York: Viking, 1978.

Holowatinc, Natasza and Karolina Holowatinc. Letter. *Vogue* (December 1996): 60.

Homans, Margaret. *Royal Representations: Queen Victoria and British Culture, 1837–1876.* University of Chicago Press, 1998.

Houston, Gail Turley. *Consuming Fictions: Gender, Class, and Hunger in Dickens's Novels.* Carbondale: Southern Illinois University Press, 1994.

Hsu, L. K. George. *Eating Disorders.* New York: Guilford Press, 1990.

Hunt, Peter. *Criticism, Theory, and Children's Literature.* Oxford: Basil Blackwell, 1991.

Ingham, Patricia. *Dickens, Women and Language.* New York: Harvester Wheatsheaf, 1992.

Jack, Ian. "Physiognomy, Phrenology, and Characterisation in the Novels of Charlotte Brontë." *Brontë Society Transations* 15 (1970): 377–399.

Jackson, Rosemary. *Fantasy: The Literature of Subversion.* London: Methuen, 1981.

Johnson, Rebecca. "The Body Myth." *Vogue* (September 1996): 653–658.

Jordanova, Ludmilla. *Sexual Visions: Images of Gender in Science and Medicine Between the 18th and 20th Centuries.* Madison: University of Wisconsin Press, 1989.

Julia. 22 July 2001. clubs.yahoo.com/clubs/only popular with anorexia (1 August 2001).

Kaplan, Fred. *Sacred Tears: Sentimentality in Victorian Literature.* Princeton University Press, 1987.

Kincaid, James. *Child Loving: The Erotic Child and Victorian Culture.* New York: Routledge, 1992.

Knoepflmacher, U. C. "Avenging Alice: Christina Rossetti and Lewis Carroll." *Nineteenth Century Literature* 41 (1986): 299–328.

   Ventures Into Childland: Victorians, Fairy Tales, and Femininity. University of Chicago Press, 1998.

Kunzle, David. *Fashion and Fetishism: A Social History of the Corset, Tight Lacing and other Forms of Body Sculpture in the West.* Totowa, NJ: Rowman and Littlefield, 1982.

Lang, Cecil. "Introduction." *The Pre-Raphaelites and Their Circle.* University of Chicago Press, 1975. xi–xxix.

Langland, Elizabeth. *Nobody's Angels: Middle-Class Women and Domestic Ideology in Victorian Culture.* Ithaca, NY: Cornell University Press, 1995.

Lashgari, Deirdre. "What Some Women Can't Swallow: Hunger as Protest in Charlotte Brontë's *Shirley.*" In *Disorderly Eaters: Texts in Self-Empowerment.* Ed. Lilian R. Furst and Peter W. Graham. University Park: Pennsylvania State University Press, 1992. 141–152.

Lawrence, Christopher. *Medicine in the Making of Modern Britain, 1700–1920.* London: Routledge, 1994.

Lawrence, Marilyn. *The Anorexic Experience.* London: Women's Press, 1984.

Lawson, Kate. "Reading Desire. *Villette* as 'Heretical Narrative.'" *English Studies in Canada* 7 (1991): 53–71.

Leighton, Angela. *Victorian Women Poets: Writing Against the Heart.* New York: Harvester Wheatsheaf, 1992.

Levy, Anita. *Other Women: The Writing of Class, Race, and Gender, 1832–1898.* Princeton University Press, 1991.

Loudon, Irvine. "Chlorosis, Anemia, and Anorexia Nervosa." *British Medical Journal* 281 (1980): 1669–1675.

Lundin, Anne. "Under the Window and Afternoon Tea: Twirling the Same Blade of Grass." *The Lion and the Unicorn* 17 (1993): 45–56.

Lurie, Alison. *Don't Tell the Grown-Ups: Why Kids Love the Books They Do.* New York: Avon, 1990.

Macsween, Morag. *Anorexic Bodies: A Feminist and Sociological Perspective on Anorexia Nervosa.* London: Routledge, 1993.

Marcus, Stephen. *The Other Victorians.* New York: Norton, 1985.

Marsh, Jan. *Christina Rossetti: A Writer's Life.* New York: Viking, 1994.

Marwick, Andrew. *Beauty in History: Society, Politics and Personal Appearance c. 1500 to the Present.* Gloucester: Thames and Hudson, 1988.

Mason, Michael. *The Making of Victorian Sexuality.* Oxford University Press, 1995.

Matus, Jill. *Unstable Bodies: Victorian Representation of Sexuality and Maternity.* Manchester University Press, 1995.

Mavor, Carol. "Dream Rushes: Lewis Carroll's Photographs of the Little Girl." In *The Girl's Own: Cultural Histories of the Anglo-American Girl, 1830–1915.* Ed. Claudia Nelson and Lynne Vallone. Athens, GA: University of Georgia Press, 1994. 156–193.

Maynard, John. *Charlotte Brontë and Sexuality.* Cambridge University Press, 1984.

Mazur, Allan. "U.S. Trends in Feminine Beauty and Overadaptation." *The Journal of Sex Research* 22 (1986): 281–303.

McEachern, Patricia A. *Deprivation and Power: The Emergence of Anorexia Nervosa in Nineteenth-Century French Literature.* Westport, CT: Greenwood Press, 1998.

Medvedev, P. N. and M. M. Bakhtin. *The Formal Method in Literary Scholarship.* Trans. Albert J. Wehrele. Baltimore: Johns Hopkins University Press, 1978.

Mermin, Dorothy. "Heroic Sisterhood in 'Goblin Market.'" *Victorian Poetry* 21 (1983): 107–118.

Michie, Helena. *The Flesh Made Word: Female Figures and Women's Bodies.* New York: Oxford University Press, 1987.

Millett, Kate. *Sexual Politics.* New York: Touchstone, 1969.

Mitchell, Judith. *The Stone and the Scorpion: The Female Subject of Desire in the Novels of Charlotte Brontë, George Eliot, and Thomas Hardy.* Westport, CT: Greenwood Press, 1994.

Mitchell, Sally, "Girls' Culture: At Work." In *The Girl's Own: Cultural Histories of the Anglo-American Girl, 1830–1915.* Ed. Claudia Nelson and Lynne Vallone. Athens: University of Georgia Press, 1994. 243–258.

Moglen, Helene. *Charlotte Brontë: The Self Conceived*. New York: W. W. Norton, 1976.

Morgan, Marjorie. *Manners, Morals and Class in England, 1774–1858*. London: St. Martin's, 1994.

Naman, Anne Aresty. *The Jew in the Victorian Novel: Some Relationships Between Prejudice and Art*. New York: AMS Press, 1980.

New Catholic Encyclopedia. New York: McGraw-Hill, 1967.

Newton, Judith. *"Villette."* In *Feminist Criticism and Social Change*. Ed. Judith Newton and Deborah Rosenfelt. New York: Methuen, 1985. 105–133.

Nockles, Peter. *The Oxford Movement in Context: Anglican High Churchmanship, 1760–1857*. Cambridge University Press, 1994.

Orbach, Susie. *Fat is a Feminist Issue II*. New York: Berkley Books, 1982.

Otten, Terry. "After Innocence: Alice in the Garden." In *Lewis Carroll: A Celebration*. Ed. Edward Guiliano. New York: Clarkson N. Potter, 1982. 50–61.

The Oxford Dictionary of the Christian Church. Ed. F. L. Cross. 3rd edn. Ed. E. A. Livingstone. Oxford University Press, 1997.

Parry-Jones, William L. "Archival Exploration of Anorexia Nervosa." *Journal of Psychiatric Research* 19 (1985): 95–100.

Perkins, David. *Is Literary History Possible?* Baltimore: The Johns Hopkins University Press, 1992.

Poovey, Mary. *Uneven Developments*. University of Chicago Press, 1988.

Poulton, Terry. *No Fat Chicks: How Big Business Profits by Making Women Hate Their Bodies – and How to Fight Back*. Secaucus, NJ: Birch Lane Press, 1997.

Prickett, Stephen. *Victorian Fantasy*. Bloomington: Indiana University Press, 1979.

Rackin, Donald. "Love and Death in Carroll's Alices." In *Soaring with the Dodo: Essays on Lewis Carroll's Life and Art*. Ed. Edward Guiliano and James R. Kincaid. Charlottesville: Lewis Carroll Society of North America, 1982. 26–45.

Ragussis, Michael. *Figures of Conversion: "The Jewish Question" and English National Identity*. Durham, NC: Duke University Press, 1995.

Reilly, Jane W. "The Gym: Just Go Already." *New Woman* (April 1997). 80f.

Reis, Pamela Tamarkin. "Victorian Centerfold: Another Look at Millais's *Cherry Ripe*." *Victorian Studies* 35 (1992): 201–205.

Roberts, Helene. "The Exquisite Slave: The Role of Clothes in the Making of the Victorian Woman." *Signs* 3 (1977): 554–569.

"Reply to David Kunzle's 'Dress Reform as Antifeminism: A Response to Helene E. Roberts's 'The Exquisite Slave?''" *Signs* 3 (1977): 518–519.

Robertson, Matra. *Starving in the Silences: An Exploration of Anorexia Nervosa*. New York: New York University Press, 1992.

Rosen, James. "Body-Image Disturbances in Eating Disorders." In *Body Images: Development, Deviance, and Change*. Ed. Thomas F. Cash and Thomas Pruzinsky. New York: Guilford Press, 1990. 190–214.

Rosenblum, Dolores. *Christina Rossetti: The Poetry of Endurance*. Carbondale: Southern Illinois University Press, 1986.

Russett, Cynthia. *Sexual Science: The Victorian Construction of Womanhood.* Cambridge: Harvard University Press, 1989.

St. George, Andrew. *The Descent of Manners: Etiquette, Rules and the Victorians.* London: Chatto & Windus, 1993.

Schiebinger, Londa. *The Mind Has No Sex?: Women in the Origins of Modern Science.* Cambridge: Harvard University Press, 1989.

Schofield, Linda. "Being and Understanding: Devotional Poetry of Christina Rossetti and the Tractarians." In *The Achievement of Christina Rossetti.* Ed. David A. Kent. Ithaca, NY: Cornell University Press, 1987. 301–321.

Schwartz, Hillel. *Never Satisfied: A Cultural History of Diets, Fantasies, and Fat.* New York: Doubleday, 1986.

Seid, Roberta. *Never Too Thin: Why Woman Are at War with Their Bodies.* New York: Prentice Hall, 1989.

Senf, Carol. "Dracula: Stoker's Response to the New Woman." *Victorian Studies* 26 (1982): 33–49.

Showalter, Elaine. *The Female Malady: Women, Madness, and English Culture 1830–1980.* New York: Pantheon Books, 1985.

Shurbutt, Sylvia Bailey. "Revisionist Mythmaking in Christina Rossetti's 'Goblin Market.'" *The Victorian Newsletter* 82 (1992): 40–44.

Shuttleworth, Sally. *Charlotte Brontë and Victorian Psychology.* Cambridge University Press, 1996.

——— "'The Surveillance of a Sleepless Eye': The Constitution of Neurosis in Villette." In *One Culture: Essays in Science and Literature.* Ed. George Levine and Alan Rauch. Madison: University of Wisconsin Press, 1987. 313–335.

Signorotti, Elizabeth. "Repossessing the Body: Transgressive Desire in 'Carmilla' and Dracula." *Criticism: A Quarterly for Literature and the Arts* 38 (1996): 607–632.

Silver, Brenda. "The Reflecting Reader in *Villette.*" In *Critical Essays on Charlotte Brontë.* Ed. Barbara Timm Gates. Boston: G. K. Hall, 1990. 264–286.

Slater, Michael. *Dickens and Women.* Stanford University Press, 1983.

Smith-Rosenberg, Carroll. *Disorderly Conduct: Visions of Gender in Victorian America.* New York: Oxford University Press, 1985.

Solveiguk. 20 July 2001. clubs.yahoo.com/clubs/only popular with anorexia (1 August 2001).

Sontag, Susan. *Illness as Metaphor; and AIDS and its Metaphors.* New York: Doubleday, 1990.

Spielmann, M. H. and G. S. Layard. *Kate Greenaway.* London: Adam and Charles Black, 1905.

——— "Kate Greenaway: A Biographical Sketch." In *The Kate Greenaway Treasury.* Ed. Edward Ernest and Patricia Tracy Lowe. Cleveland: World Publishing Company, 1967. 24–69.

Stanwood, P. G. "Christina Rossetti's Devotional Prose." *The Achievement of Christina Rossetti.* Ed. David A. Kent. Ithaca: Cornell University Press, 1987. 231–249.

Steele, Valerie. *Fashion and Eroticism.* Oxford University Press, 1985.

Tavris, Carol. *The Mismeasure of Woman*. New York: Touchstone, 1992.

Tennyson, G. B. *Victorian Devotional Poetry: The Tractarian Mode*. Cambridge, MA: Harvard University Press, 1981.

Thompson, Deborah Ann. "Anorexia as a Lived Trope: Christina Rossetti's 'Goblin Market.'" *Mosaic* 24 (1991): 89–106.

Tolman, Deborah and Elizabeth Debold, "Conflicts of Body and Image: Female Adolescents, Desire, and the No-Body Body." In *Feminist Perspectives on Eating Disorders*. Ed. Patricia Fallon, Melanie A. Katzman, and Susan C. Wooley. New York: The Guilford Press, 1994. 301–317.

Turner, Bryan. *Regulating Bodies: Essays in Medical Sociology*. London: Routledge, 1992.

Tyler, Graeme, *Physiognomy in the European Novel: Faces and Fortunes*. Princeton University Press, 1982.

Van Dyke, Carolynn. *The Fiction of Truth: Structures of Meaning in Narrative and Dramatic Allegory*. Ithaca, NY: Cornell University Press, 1985.

Vandereycken, Walter and Ron Van Deth. *From Fasting Saints to Anorexic Girls: The History of Self-Starvation*. London: Athlone Press, 1994.

Vertinsky, Patricia. *The Eternally Wounded Woman: Women, Doctors, and Exercise in the Late Nineteenth Century*. Urbana: University of Illinois Press, 1994.

Vrettos, Athena. *Somatic Fictions: Imagining Illness in Victorian Culture*. Stanford University Press, 1995.

Warner, Malcolm. "John Everett Millais's 'Autumn Leaves': A Picture Full of Beauty and Without Subject." In *Pre-Raphaelite Papers*. Ed. Leslie Parris. London: Tate Gallery, 1984. 126–142.

Waugh, Nora. *Corsets and Crinolines*. 1954. New York: Theatre Arts Books, 1994.

Weltman, Sharon. *Ruskin's Mythic Queen: Gender Subversion in Victorian Culture*. Athens: Ohio University Press, 1998.

Williams, Leslie. "The Look of Little Girls: John Everett Millais and the Victorian Art Market." In *The Girl's Own: Cultural Histories of the Anglo-American Girl, 1830–1915*. Ed. Claudia Nelson and Lynne Vallone. Athens: University of Georgia Press, 1994. 124–155.

Williams, Raymond. *Keywords: A Vocabulary of Culture and Society*. New York: Oxford University Press, 1983.

Wolf, Naomi. *The Beauty Myth*. New York: Doubleday, 1991.

Wullschlager, Jackie. *Inventing Wonderland*. New York: The Free Press, 1995.

Index

Allbutt, T. Clifford 12–13, 43
anorexia mirabilis, *see* fasting, religious
anorexia nervosa
  body image, and 4, 6–19, 25–26, 28,
    31, 43, 48, 53–54, 58–59, 172–178
  chlorosis, and 1–2
  class, and 6, 13–15, 172
  clinical definition of 4–6
  continuum model of 13, 15–19, 26–27,
    48–50
  cultural constructedness of 3, 7–9, 26–27,
    48, 173–174, 177–178
  development of, in Victorian period 1–3,
    9, 26–27, 43, 53–54, 58–59, 144–145
  dieting, and 6–7, 11–13, 54, 177, 181n
  discovery of 1–3
  family dynamics, and 5, 15–18, 181n
  gender norms, and 3, 6, 9–13, 15–19,
    26–27, 48–50
  personality associated with 4–5, 16, 89
  pro-anorexia movement, and 176–177
  protest, as 17–18, 90–91
  religious fasting, and 136–147
  self-control, and 5, 9–12, 36, 40,
    47–48, 52, 54–55, 58, 60, 75, 91,
    93, 175, 177
  sexuality, and 3, 5–6, 10–11; 13–14, 48, 52,
    55, 93
appetite, symbolism of 9–15, 27–28, 45–48,
    49–50, 122
Brontë, Charlotte, in work of 85–115 *passim*
Carroll, Lewis, in work of 71–79
children's authors, in work of 54–58
Dickens, in work of 82–85
Du Maurier, in work of 117, 127–135
Le Fanu, in work of 124–127
Rossetti, Christina, in work of
Stoker, in work of 118–127 *passim*
vampire literature, in 117–118
  see also eating
Aristotle 8–9, 47

Arnold, Matthew 115
Ashwell, Samuel 1–2, 196n

Barber, Henry 143–144
Bartky, Sandra 23–24, 175
Beard, Henry 43
beauty, images of, *see* anorexia nervosa and
    body image; body type, constructedness of
Beeton, Isabella 15
Bentham, Jeremy 175
body image, *see* anorexia nervosa and body
    image
body type
  constructedness of 6–7, 22–24, 35, 39, 48
  Victorian 19, 24, 25–27, 30–44, 48, 53–54,
    122–123, 133–134
Bordo, Susan 3, 8, 10, 77, 91, 142
Briquet, Pierre 1
Brontë, Charlotte 21–22, 60, 81, 136
  anorexia nervosa in work of 87–93
  Catholicism, and 106–108
  eating in work of 85–87, 95, 97, 99,
    102–104, 111, 114
  class and eating in work of 86–87,
    96–99, 111
  fat in work of 89, 98, 101, 104–106, 109,
    114–115
  hunger in works of, *see* starvation in works of
  Jane Eyre 10, 81, 105
  life of 93–94
  The Professor 95, 101, 106
  repression and/or self denial in works of 88,
    90–92, 95, 100, 101–103, 113
  sexuality in work of 89, 92, 95–96, 103–105,
    109, 110–114
  Shirley 82, 85–100, 104, 115
  slenderness/thinness in work of 87–92, 98,
    100–102, 106, 107–112
  starvation in works of 81, 87–93, 96–97,
    99–100, 101–104
  Villette 55, 92–115, 121

Brontë, Emily 93–94
Brumberg, Joan Jacobs 13–15, 19, 25, 45
bulimia 1–2, 7, 54, 107, 179n
Butler, Judith 22
Bynum, Caroline Walker 141–142, 145, 147

Carroll, Lewis 53, 78–80, 158
   *Alice in Wonderland and Through the Looking
      Glass* 71–79
   appetite, and 71–73, 77–78
   attraction to young girls 75–76, 79
   maturation, in work of 74–76, 78–79
childhood, Victorian
   and culture of anorexia 52, 53–54
   restrictions on eating in 46–47, 57–58
   sexualization of 52, 63–67, 84
children's literature, Victorian 19–20
   and culture of anorexia 52, 78
   representations of appetite and eating
      in 52, 54–59, 71–79, 120
   politics of 51–52
   sexuality in 56, 64–67
   see also names of individual authors
Chipley, William Stout 1
chlorosis 1–2, 196n
Clarke, Edward 103
Clarke, Henry 43
class 13–15, 36, 40–42, 83, 86–87, 96–99,
   111, 122–123, 127
   see also anorexia nervosa and class; clothing,
      class marker, as; corset, class symbolism
      of; slenderness, class and
clothing, Victorian 28–30
   class marker, as 31, 40–41
   gendered symbolism of 28–29, 31
conduct literature, Victorian 11–12, 21, 28–31,
   34–35, 37, 43, 45–49, 51, 112, 114–115,
   124–125
corset 31–40, 185–186
   class symbolism, and 36, 40–42
   sexuality of 37–40
culture of anorexia, definition of 27

Dickens, Charles 10, 60, 80, 82, 110, 174
   body in work of 82–85, 125
   David Copperfield 81–83
   hunger in work of, 82–84
   The Old Curiosity Shop 83–85, 89
   sexuality in work of 82, 84
dieting, *see* anorexia nervosa, dieting and; eating
Dijkstra, Bram 66–67, 117–118, 134
Dodsworth, William 137, 146, 149
dress, *see* clothing
dualism, body/soul 8–9, 17, 91, 101, 107,
   120, 128, 133–134, 148–149, 172

Du Maurier, George 20, 116–117
   anti-Semitism in work of 127, 134–135
   body in work of 117, 128–135
   eating in work of 129–130, 133
   sexuality in work of 128, 130–134
   starvation in work of 132–134
   Trilby 127–135
   vampire imagery in work of 128, 134

eating
   class marker, as 122–123
   gendered activity, as 15–16, 45–47, 49–50,
      54–57, 129–130
   restrictions placed upon 45–47, 57–58
   sexuality, and 45–46, 49–50, 56, 122
   social activity, as 9, 15–17, 55, 58, 124–125
eating disorders, *see* anorexia nervosa; bulimia;
      chlorosis
Eliot, George 10
Ellis, Sarah Stickney 12, 25
Englishwoman's Domestic Magazine 36, 38–39,
      40–41

Farrar, Eliza 11, 39, 47
"fasting girls" 44–55, 143–144
fasting, religious 4, 21, 136–138, 141–147
Ferraro, William, *see* "Lombroso, Caesar"
food, prohibitions against 14, 45–47, 49–50,
      58–59, 103
Foucault, Michel 22–23
   Discipline and Punish 36, 175
   History of Sexuality 15, 31, 142, 174–175
Fowler, Robert 143–144

Gaskell, Elizabeth
   Cranford 14, 116
   The Life of Charlotte Brontë 93
   Ruth 10, 42–43, 130
   Wives and Daughters 14, 50
gender, Victorian paradigms of 3, 9, 11–13,
      27–29, 41–50, 59, 62, 98, 114–115,
      117–118, 133–134
Girl's Own Paper 39, 52, 53–54, 79, 80,
      177
Gorham, Deborah 52
Greenaway, Kate 52, 68–71, 74
   body in work of 68–69
   friendship with John Ruskin 63–64, 70
   The Pied Piper of Hamelin 65–66
Gull, William Withey 1, 4–5, 16, 26–27, 43

Haweis, Mrs. H. R. 30, 34
Heywood, Leslie 3, 8–9, 18, 175
Hopkins, Gerard Manley 145–146
hysteria 26, 48

invalidism, cult of 12, 43–45, 133–134, 187n

Jacob, Sarah 44–45, 143

Keble, John 149
Kincaid, James 64, 66, 76, 84
Kipling, Rudyard 117

La Mode Illustreé 34, 51
Lasègue, Charles 1, 4–5, 16–17, 26–27, 43
Laycock, Thomas 2
Le Fanu, Sharidan 20
    body size in work of 124–125
    Carmilla 116, 124–127, 134
    eating in work of 124–125
    sexuality in work of 125–127
l'Isère, Colombat de 46, 58, 103
Lombroso, Caesar 121–123

Maudsley, Henry 29–30
McNeill, D. 2
Millais, John Everett 66
Milton, John 30
Mitchell, S. Weir 48, 117
Moore, Anne 143
Morrison, Arthur 67

Nightingale, Florence 17–18

Ogle, John 16, 89
Oxford Movement 21, 136, 137–138, 139,
    146–147, 149, 151, 163

Plato 8–9, 171
pro-anorexia, *see* anorexia nervosa, pro
    anorexia movement
Pusey, E. B. 137–138, 146, 149, 151

race
    anorexia nervosa and 6, 172
    representations of body, and 56, 105,
        122, 134–135
Rossetti, Christina 21–22, 60, 74, 91
    anorexia nervosa and 137, 139–142
    "As the Sparks Fly Upwards" 166
    "Ash Wednesday" 149
    "A Better Resurrection" 156
    "A Bruised Reed Shall He Not Break"
        151
    "The Dead City" 152–156, 158
    dualism in work of 148–150, 158
    eating in work of 139, 146, 149–157,
        159–161, 163, 166–168
    Eucharistic imagery in work of 150–151,
        155, 158, 162–163, 166–168

"Enrica" 168–169
fasting, religious, and 137–139, 144,
    141–142, 146–147, 166, 168, 170
The Face of the Deep 138–139, 144, 150, 152,
    165, 170
"Goblin Market" 125, 137, 139–140, 142,
    148–158, 161, 166
"The Heart Knoweth its Own
    Bitterness" 167
"I Know You Not" 166–167
"In an Artist's Studio" 169–170
life of 140–141, 157
"The Martyr" 151
"My Dream" 157–158
"The Offering of the New Law" 167–168
Oxford Movement, and 136–138
"A Peal of Bells" 155–156, 158
sexuality in work of 137, 149–151, 154–156,
    159–161, 165, 167
Speaking Likenesses 136, 142, 158–168
"Then they that feared the Lord" 167
"They Desire a Better Country" 168
Time Flies 138–139, 166
"A Triad" 169
"The World" 148, 155
Ruskin, John 52
    attraction to young girls 63–66, 70–71
    The Ethics of the Dust 59–62, 68, 71, 79
    female body, in work of 60–63
    friendship with and admiration of Kate
        Greenaway 63–66, 69–70
    innocence in work of 61, 64–65
    Of Queens' Garden 59, 60, 62;

Santé, Madame de la 36, 38, 40
Sinclair, Catherine 107
slenderness, symbolism of 4, 6–7, 11–15,
    27–28, 38–45, 48, 173
    anorexia nervosa, and *see* anorexia nervosa
        and body image
    class and 13, 40–42, 122–123, 178
    pursuit of 25–26, 28, 30–50, 53–54, 172–178
    and sexuality 38–40, 44–45, 48
Socrates 8–9
Steele, Valerie 30, 39
Stoker, Bram 20
    body size in work of 118, 121–125
    Dracula 116–125, 134, 136
    eating in work of 119–121
    sexuality in work of 118–125, 126
"supermodels" 37, 172–173

Taylor, Jane and Ann 57–58, 69
Tennyson, Alfred Lord 146–147
Thackeray, William Makepeace 116

thinness, symbolism of, *see* slenderness,
    symbolism of
Thornwell, Emily 49
tight lacing, *see* corset
Tractarian movement, *see* Oxford movement
Trollope, Anthony 13

vampires 20
    anorexic paradigm, and 116–118, 121,
        125–127
    sexuality of 117–135
    symbolism of 117–118
Van Deth, Ron 18

Vandereycken, Walter 18
Veblen, Thorstein 13

waist
    class symbolism, and 36, 40–42
    invalidism, cult of, and 44–45
    sexuality, and 38–40, 44–45
    symbolism of 18–19, 30–50
Walker, Alexander 44, 101, 103
Walker, Mrs. Alexander 29, 45–46
Williams, Isaac 138, 146

Zola, Emile 105, 121

CAMBRIDGE STUDIES IN NINETEENTH-CENTURY
LITERATURE AND CULTURE

General editor

Gillian Beer, *University of Cambridge*

Titles published

1. The Sickroom in Victorian Fiction: The Art of Being Ill
by Miriam Bailin, *Washington University*

2. Muscular Christianity: Embodying the Victorian Age
edited by Donald E. Hall, *California State University, Northridge*

3. Victorian Masculinities: Manhood and Masculine Poetics in Early
Victorian Literature and Art
by Herbert Sussman, *Northeastern University, Boston*

4. Byron and the Victorians
by Andrew Elfenbein, *University of Minnesota*

5. Literature in the Marketplace: Nineteenth-Century British
Publishing and the Circulation of Books
edited by John O. Jordan, *University of California, Santa Cruz*
and Robert L. Patten, *Rice University, Houston*

6. Victorian Photography, Painting and Poetry
by Lindsay Smith, *University of Sussex*

7. Charlotte Brontë and Victorian Psychology
by Sally Shuttleworth, *University of Sheffield*

8. The Gothic Body: Sexuality, Materialism and Degeneration
at the *Fin de Siècle*
by Kelly Hurley, *University of Colorado at Boulder*

9. Rereading Walter Pater
by William F. Shuter, *Eastern Michigan University*

10. Remaking Queen Victoria
edited by Margaret Homans, *Yale University*
and Adrienne Munich, *State University of New York, Stony Brook*

11. Disease, Desire, and the Body in Victorian Women's Popular Novels
by Pamela K. Gilbert, *University of Florida*

12. Realism, Representation, and the Arts in Nineteenth-Century
Literature
by Alison Byerly, *Middlebury College, Vermont*

13. Literary Culture and the Pacific: Nineteenth-Century Textual Encounters
by Vanessa Smith, *University of Sydney*

14. Professional Domesticity in the Victorian Novel:
Women, Work and Home
by Monica F. Cohen

15. Victorian Renovations of the Novel: Narrative Annexes
and the Boundaries of Representation
by Suzanne Keen, *Washington and Lee University, Virginia*

16. Actresses on the Victorian Stage: Feminine Performance
and the Galatea Myth
by Gail Marshall, *University of Leeds*

17. Death and the Mother from Dickens to Freud
Victorian Fiction and the Anxiety of Origin
by Carolyn Dever, *Vanderbilt University, Tennessee*

18. Ancestry and Narrative in Nineteenth-Century British Literature
Blood Relations from Edgeworth to Hardy
by Sophie Gilmartin, *Royal Holloway, University of London*

19. Dickens, Novel Reading, and the Victorian Popular Theatre
by Deborah Vlock

20. After Dickens: Reading, Adaptation and Performance
by John Glavin, *Georgetown University, Washington DC*

21. Victorian Women Writers and the Woman Question
edited by Nicola Diane Thompson, *Kingston University, London*

22. Rhythm and Will in Victorian Poetry
by Matthew Campbell, *University of Sheffield*

23. Gender, Race, and the Writing of Empire
Public Discourse and the Boer War
by Paula M. Krebs, *Wheaton College, Massachusetts*

24. Ruskin's God
by Michael Wheeler

25. Dickens and the Daughter of the House
by Hilary M. Schor, *University of Southern California*

26. Detective Fiction and the Rise of Forensic Science
by Ronald R. Thomas, *Trinity College, Hartford, Connecticut*

27. Testimony and Advocacy in Victorian Law, Literature, and Theology
by Jan-Melissa Schramm, *Trinity Hall, Cambridge*

28. Victorian Writing about Risk: Imagining a Safe England
in a Dangerous World
by Elaine Freedgood, *University of Pennsylvania*

29. Physiognomy and the Meaning of Expression
in Nineteenth-Century Culture
by Lucy Hartley, *University of Southampton*

30. The Victorian Parlour: A Cultural Study
by Thad Logan, *Rice University, Houston*

31. Aestheticism and Sexual Parody 1840–1940
by Dennis Denisoff, *Ryerson University, Toronto*

32. Literature, Technology and Magical Thinking, 1880–1920
by Pamela Thurschwell, *University College London*

33. Fairies in Nineteenth-Century Art and Literature
by Nicola Bown, *Birkbeck College, London*

34. George Eliot and the British Empire
by Nancy Henry, *The State University of New York, Binghamton*

35. Women's Poetry and Religion in Victorian England
Jewish Identity and Christian Culture
by Cynthia Scheinberg, *Mills College, California*

36. Victorian Literature and the Anorexic Body
by Anna Krugovoy Silver, *Mercer University, Georgia*